- The recent political background of NEA's successful fight for the creation of a cabinet-level Department of Education

- NEA's long standing support of the Equal Rights Amendment

Recounting this most crucial period in NEA history, West identifies the key people involved in each movement, discusses the evolution of the Association's internal structure, and evaluates the actions of members, staff, and officers in response to the challenges of the period. Tracing its growth into an important part of the educational establishment, he tells the story of an organization that deeply influences the policies shaping both the work of 2 million teachers and the education of 50 million children.

About the Author

ALLAN M. WEST served as an NEA staff member in several positions, including Associate Director of the Membership Division and as Associate, Deputy, and Acting Executive Secretary before he retired to write this book. He is the author of many scholarly and popular publications on education.

The National Education Association: The Power Base for Education

The National Education Association:
The Power Base for Education

Allan M. West

THE FREE PRESS
A Division of Macmillan Publishing Co., Inc.
NEW YORK

Collier Macmillan Publishers
LONDON

Library of Congress Catalog Card Number: 80-66130

Printed in the United States of America

printing number
1 2 3 4 5 6 7 8 9 10

Contents

v

vi   Contents

Preface

The National Education Association is a different organization from the NEA that met in Philadelphia in 1957 to celebrate its centennial. Changes in the Association have occurred as a result of converging social forces in a period of social change unprecedented in the nation. Equally important, the Association has been reshaped by the judgments and actions of its members, staff, and officers.

This volume attempts to identify and analyze some of the forces that influenced changes in the NEA and to identify the roles of groups and individuals who gave leadership to the NEA's response.

This is not a complete history of NEA. It was my purpose to write the story of the NEA in the twenty-three years from 1957 to 1980 with emphasis on the changes that have occurred. The reader who is familiar with the NEA will discover that some programs and units have received little or no mention. It is because this volume's focus is on change, and little change has occurred in some activities.

It is doubtful that those who were deeply involved in coping with the changes of the past two decades realized fully the impact those changes would have on the NEA. As John Gardner tells us, "History never looks like history when you are living through it. It always looks confusing and messy, and it always feels uncomfortable."[1]

There were times when the history of the NEA was messy and uncomfortable. But there were also times of challenge, hope, vision, and genuine excitement.

Organizations have a life of their own. They can be healthy or ailing. To remain healthy they must be constantly renewed. One of the best ways to ensure continuous renewal is to make it easy for new leadership to emerge from the ranks. The sustained infusion of newly elected leaders to policymaking bodies stimulates the reexamination of existing policies. The regeneration of an organization by fresh leaders, who do not know what is impossible, can often achieve results thought to be unattainable by their predecessors. If not given constant attention, organizations can set up protective devices to avoid the discomfort of change and become unresponsive to the needs of members. In the past two decades sweeping changes have taken place in the NEA's programs and structure, with broad participation of Association members. The organization has emerged from the effort a stronger, more cohesive, and more effective advocate for better schools for students and better conditions for teachers.

The NEA serves both the interests of its members and the general welfare of society. I consider myself fortunate to have had the experience of living and dealing with the forces of change in one of the most exciting periods in history. Obviously, I am not an unbiased observer, having served on the staff of the NEA or a state affiliate of the NEA for more than thirty years. But neither am I uncritical.

This volume is the story of an organization adapting to change as observed by an insider, one who has personally shared the pain and promise of the effort. In my twelve years as an NEA staff member I held six positions. Beginning in 1961 as associate director of the Membership Division, I became special assistant to the executive secretary (1962), assistant executive secretary for Field and Urban Services (1964), associate executive secretary (1968), deputy executive secretary (1970), and acting executive secretary (1972–1973).

Some may wonder why I undertook to write about the NEA's experiences in dealing with the forces of change in the period from 1957 to 1980. There are three reasons. Many NEA members and long-time nonmember friends of the organization do not understand fully why the NEA has changed so radically in the past twenty-three years. I hope I can shed some light on the changes and the social developments that influenced them. The NEA has aggressively influenced national public policies governing the education of fifty million children and two million teachers. The direction of this influence should be of interest to every American family. And, finally, the NEA has attempted to meet the forces of change head on and to adapt to them creatively and with sensitivity. I hope the NEA's experience may have value for other national organizations that have yet to deal with some of those same forces.

Acknowledgments

Grateful acknowledgment is given to all who contributed in any way to the preparation of this book. I regret that the limitations of space prevent me from listing the individual names of the many persons who furnished information, submitted to personal interviews, sent taped responses to my questions, or otherwise gave me helpful advice and criticism.

There are a few individuals whose special contributions must be recognized. Terry Herndon, executive director of the National Education Association, gave me free access to all files, documents, and publications requested. In addition he assigned Irma L. Kramer, special assistant to the executive director, to serve as my NEA contact. Her broad knowledge of the Association and its programs was invaluable to me throughout the effort. I am also indebted to Robert Chanin, Samuel B. Ethridge, and James H. Williams, who reviewed portions of the manuscript and made helpful suggestions.

The generous assistance of Alice Morton, NEA archivist, is acknowledged.

My wife, Ferne Page West, has been a full partner in the project, having assisted with the research and typing of all early drafts and offered valuable suggestions and criticisms.

Finally, the assistance of the editors of The Free Press is recognized for improving the quality of the manuscript and for their helpful advice throughout the effort.

The National Education Association:
The Power Base for Education

CHAPTER ONE

In the Beginning

To elevate the character and advance the interests of the profession of teaching, and to promote the cause of popular education in the United States." Daniel B. Hagar wrote these words to express the purpose of the first national teachers' organization in the United States, a century and a quarter ago. Although the emphasis and programs have changed, these words in the first charter still give general direction to the National Education Association (NEA) as it seeks through its action programs to improve the nation's schools and the conditions under which teachers work.

The original organization—the National Teachers Association—was founded in Philadelphia on August 26, 1857, by forty-three educators from a dozen states and the District of Columbia.

Two men, Daniel B. Hagar and Thomas W. Valentine, were the organizers of the Philadelphia meeting. Hagar was president of the Massachusetts Teachers Association and principal of the Normal School in Salem. Valentine, a grammar school teacher in Brooklyn, was president of the New York Teachers Association. Valentine, who first conceived the idea for a national organization, drafted the call for the Philadelphia meeting, and Hagar was chairman of a committee to write the constitution and by-laws. Both men signed the call for the meeting along with the presidents

1

of eight other state associations in New Hampshire, Vermont, Pennsylvania, Indiana, Illinois, Wisconsin, Iowa, and Missouri.

Thirteen years later, in 1870, the National Association of School Superintendents and the American Normal School Association joined with the American Teachers Association to form the National Education Association. In doing so, the two new groups became the first two departments of the NEA. Wesley described the NEA at that early period as "a kind of super holding company that coordinated the state associations by providing an annual convention where ideas, theories, and principles were discussed, leaving the practical application to the state and local organizations."[1]

The annual conventions—both national and state—became the chief forums for the discussion of school programs, practices, and educational principles. Few publications existed, and radio and television were not to be realized for many years. As a result, the conventions had great impact on the schools at a critical period in their development.

Membership dues in the Association were one dollar annually until 1875, when they were increased to two dollars.

When the Association was only five years old, Congress passed the Morrill Act. The act was supported by the NEA and provided land grants to the states for the founding of colleges to promote both liberal and practical education with emphasis on agriculture and the mechanic arts.

In the early conventions the need was often expressed for a federal agency to gather facts about education in the states as a means of making state-by-state comparisons of school progress.

The greatest accomplishment of the first decade of the teachers' organization came when President Andrew Johnson signed a bill on March 2, 1867, creating a federal Office of Education.

Women, originally barred from membership, were admitted in 1866. The Teachers Association was thus one of the first organizations to recognize and move to correct the injustices to women prevalent in that period. Prior to this action, women could, with the approval of the board of directors, become honorary members and were permitted to submit papers to be read to the convention by their male colleagues. The 1866 action admitted women to active membership on the same basis as men.[2]

The Women's Rights conventions begun in 1848 at Seneca Falls, New York, and continuing with interruptions during the Civil War, had been advocating equality for both women and Negroes. In 1859, the ninth national convention petitioned state legislatures to eliminate the word "male" from state constitutions and legislate for all citizens, and inquired, "Where, under our Declaration of Independence, does the white Saxon man get his power to deprive all women and Negroes of their inalienable rights?"[3]

In addition to the admission of women to the NEA, another "first" occurred in 1866: the Congress passed, over President Andrew Johnson's veto, a civil rights bill guaranteeing equal protection under law to the freed Negroes and giving to the federal courts the jurisdiction of cases involving such rights. Susan B. Anthony, presiding at the Eleventh National Women's Rights Convention in New York City, declared, "The Negro and woman now hold the same civil and political status, alike needing only the ballot. . . ."[4]

THE CONVENTION PERIOD: 1857—1892

Between 1857 and 1956, the NEA held ninety-four conventions at which, Wesley estimated, 19,000 speeches were delivered. This figure, he said, included only those speeches and papers that were printed or summarized in the annual volume *Addresses and Proceedings*. If all the speeches delivered at the meetings of departments and associated organizations were included, the number would exceed 100,000.[5]

Between 1866 and 1892, the Association was a convention and committee organization, and active membership never exceeded 10,000. However, the combined membership in the state affiliates was many times that number. No employed national staff existed, the Association had no permanent headquarters, and the chief emphasis of the action programs was on the improvement of instruction. W. T. Harris, St. Louis school superintendent and later U. S. commissioner of education, classified the subjects discussed at the annual conventions held between 1858 and 1890. During that period, education theory and psychology accounted for 16 percent of the subjects considered. Other topics and the frequency of their discussion were: high schools and colleges (15%), normal schools (11%), manual training and technical schools (9%), courses of study (6%), kindergartens (5%), primary grades (5%), music education (5%), moral and religious instruction (5%), philosophy of methods (4%), federal aid to education (3%), graded and ungraded schools (2%), supervision (2%), foreign education systems (2%), textbooks (2%), education of minorities (2%), and other topics (6%).[6]

While many references were made to the need for improving salaries, security, and other conditions of employment, these problems were left to the state and local affiliates. Although never specifically verbalized, the national attitude appears to have been that education was a "people-oriented" enterprise and therefore any improvement in the enterprise would benefit the individuals involved. Federal aid for schools, for example, would improve education, but it would also improve the economic condition of teachers because about three out of every four school dollars went to pay teachers' salaries.

Following the Civil War, the establishment of public high schools increased rapidly. In the thirty years from 1860 to 1890, the number of public high schools grew from 325 to 2,536. The early high schools were not established without opposition. The public obligation to provide an elementary school education had been established, but the prevailing attitude was that those families wishing further education for their children should assume full responsibility for the cost. The labor of high-school-age children was needed by the agrarian society of the period. The further education of girls was questioned. The academies, largely church-supported, viewed the public high school as a threat. The colleges feared the loss of control over courses of study and scholastic standards. The continued resistance of taxpayers slowed the movement but did not halt it. And the Kalamazoo Decision of 1874 settled the question of using tax funds for the support of public schools.

The growth of the high schools and the resolution of the social problems involved explain the inclusion of many of the convention topics selected for discussion.

The 1884 convention at Madison, Wisconsin, according to Fenner, was "a milestone in Association history. Between 5000 and 6000 educators from every state in the union and from foreign lands came together to form what was called at the time 'the grandest and most numerous assemblage of educators that ever came together on the American continent.'" The Madison Convention considered the problems of the Negro and the American Indian, and a special meeting billed as a women's evening was applauded by the female members, who comprised 54 percent of those in attendance. President Thomas W. Bicknell said the meeting was planned "as a confession and penance for past shortcomings." Exhibits of educational materials first appeared at this convention.

So popular was the Madison Convention that the Association was able to pay all expenses and transfer $3,000 to the Permanent Fund. (Two years later, when the constitution was amended, a Board of Trustees was created to manage the Association's finances—an action that was to become the center of controversy in subsequent years.) The success of the meeting was attributed largely to the planning, organization, and leadership of President Bicknell, described as "majestic, over six feet tall, straight as a ship's mast, with a full beard, a bald strip running back over the top of his head, two wisps of iron-gray hair standing out on the sides after the fashion of two horns, and with the voice of Stentor."[7]

As the Madison Convention adjourned in the summer of 1884, the Democratic Convention meeting in Chicago nominated Grover Cleveland as its presidential candidate, and the cornerstone of the base of the Statue of Liberty was laid in New York harbor.

During the Association's first thirty-five years, conventions were its most important activity. The discussions were often spirited and forthright—"so spirited and forthright . . . they led Governor Cushman K. Davis of Minnesota to observe that a reading of the proceedings . . . had convinced him that the National Education Association was not a 'mutual admiration society.' "[8] Nevertheless, the conventions served the purpose of sharing ideas and experiences in a period in which the nation's public schools were growing rapidly and developing the uniquely American education system. In the national school systems of most other nations, direction came from the central government. With state and local control, American schools were organized to serve the will of the individual communities and states. The similarity of the state school systems can be accounted for in large measure by the early influence of the national forum provided by the annual conventions of the NEA. For it was in those conventions that out of the diversity of approaches agreement was reached concerning the purposes of education and the best professional practices. By this process, rather than by proscription of a central government, was fashioned a national policy of education from the state and local experiences.

Some important changes in the formal organization of the NEA and some internal issues that arose in the convention period, deserve mention.

In 1898, the first full-time executive secretary was appointed. Dr. Irwin Shephard, president of the State Normal School at Winona, Minnesota, had been serving as a part-time secretary since 1893. On his appointment to the permanent position, he resigned his presidency of the normal school and devoted his full energies to the NEA.

It had been the practice of the Association to make the headquarters wherever the secretary happened to live. During the Shephard administration, his Winona home became the headquarters. When the work load became too great for Dr. Shephard and his stenographer and clerk, members of the Shephard family were pressed into service.

In the early 1900s, some dissatisfaction began to be felt about a number of issues: the powers of the president; the semi-independent status of the prestigious Council on Education responsible for planning the conventions and assigning studies; the control of the funds by the Board of Trustees, and the lack of opportunity for classroom teachers to participate adequately in NEA affairs although they provided most of the Association's revenue.

The occasion for these dissatisfactions to become openly expressed was the expiration in 1906 of the charter granted to the Association by the District of Columbia. It was decided to ask Congress to grant the Association a new charter.

Members argued before a congressional committee that Association money should be at the disposal of the members, rather than in the hands of a small committee.[9] The officers were reluctant to give more control to members because they feared that the convention could be controlled by members residing in cities where the conventions were held. These members could attend in greater numbers and give undue weight to their special interests.

The views of the officers prevailed, and the new charter was approved by the Congress and signed by President Theodore Roosevelt on June 30, 1906, without the reforms urged by members. But a defeat for the conservatives came four years later when the first woman was elected president of the Association and publicly charged mismanagement of the Permanent Fund by the trustees. While a thorough investigation did not sustain the charges of mismanagement, Fenner wrote that the period from 1910 to 1913 was the most "discordant of NEA history." It was charged that "squads of squabbling women had injected partisanship and questionable campaign tactics into what had hitherto been a dignified, professional procedure."[10]

This controversy marked the beginning of the decline in the influence of higher-education leaders in the NEA. The Department of Higher Education withdrew from the NEA in 1924. The withdrawal was due, in part, to the conflict and to the Association's new emphasis on the wartime economic problems of members in the elementary and high schools.[11]

The conflict over mismanagement created an interest in forming a Representative Assembly in which affiliated associations would be represented by delegates in proportion to their membership in the Association. Such an organization was achieved in 1920 after a series of defeats and postponements. The Representative Assembly was widely accepted, and 463 local associations and 44 state associations sent delegates to its first meeting in 1921.

In 1912, Secretary Shephard resigned because of failing health. He was succeeded by Durand W. Springer, a former treasurer of the Association, whose knowledge of the NEA's finances was well known and made him an acceptable candidate. Springer was a high school principal, a musician, a former commerce teacher, and a certified public accountant from Michigan.

The Department of Classroom Teachers was organized within the NEA in 1913, and that same year saw the publication of the Association's first professional journal—the *NEA Bulletin*. The *Bulletin* was the forerunner of the *NEA Journal* and *Today's Education*.

THE COMMITTEE PERIOD: 1892–1917

The influence of the NEA from the beginning was exerted through convention speeches, debates, and reports of committees. At the first meeting after the Association was founded, three committees were appointed. Their respective tasks were to recommend a course of study for high schools; to prepare an ideal program for the education of youth; and to report on school registers and annual reports. In later years, a number of committees were named to deal with important problems arising from the growth of the schools, two world wars, and the economic depression.

The Committee of Ten

The Committee of Ten was named in 1892 to recommend a program of instruction for the rapidly growing, but uncoordinated, American high schools. The high schools faced the difficult tasks of educating pupils for college entrance and of providing terminal education for those not going to college. Entrance requirements varied widely among individual higher institutions, which made the task of preparing pupils for college entrance virtually impossible. In attempting to meet local needs, high school courses of study were far from uniform.

The Committee of Ten, headed by Charles W. Eliot, president of Harvard, organized a series of committees for each of the disciplines. In its report to the Association two years later, the committee recommended a specific program, including precise time periods required for the mastery of each curriculum area.

While the report of the Committee of Ten was hailed by the commissioner of education as "the most important educational document ever published in this country," it became the center of vigorous conflict. Those who saw value in the local experimental approach to determining the proper mission of the high school charged the committee with seeing the function of the high school only as a college-preparatory institution. Nevertheless, the committee report had great influence on the developing high schools and added lively interest to the debates in the annual conventions.

Other Committees

The Committee of Ten was followed by a series of other committees, each dealing with a fundamental problem of the developing school system. Some of the subjects assigned to them for study were: the organization of school systems, teacher training, the coordination of studies in primary and grammar schools, rural education, the establishment of a national university, normal schools, salaries, tenure of office and pensions of teachers, the National Bureau of Education, library administration, the professional preparation of high school teachers, articulation of high schools and college, college entrance requirements, health problems in education, and good race relations.

Commission on Reorganization

The Commission on Reorganization of Secondary Education (1913–1921) involved the contributions of sixteen subcommittees with a total membership of over one hundred, drawn from thirty states. Two reports published in 1916 and 1918 had great influence on the American high schools. The first, "Social Studies in Secondary Education" (1916), recommended a course in problems of democracy that marked "the first time that a responsible agency had advocated the classroom study of contemporary issues as distinguished from formalized subjects."[12]

The second bulletin, "Cardinal Principles of Secondary Education" (1918), influenced the direction of American secondary education perhaps more than any other publication in this century. As time passed, it was recognized as applying to all levels of education, not exclusively to secondary education. The report was published and distributed widely by the U. S. Office of Education, and in 1927 the National Congress of Parents and Teachers adopted the seven objectives as a permanent platform for their organization. (In 1966, almost a half-century after the Seven Cardinal Principles were drafted, NEA Research sent them to a nation-wide sample of teachers. They were asked, "Is this a satisfactory list of the major objectives of education today, as you would see them?" More than 85 percent said "yes.")

Executive Secretary Springer resigned in 1917, after having administered the affairs of the Association through five years of financial uncertainty. The country was virtually united against Germany when German submarines torpedoed three U. S. ships, causing the loss of many American lives. The following month, President Woodrow Wilson, asked Congress for a declaration of war against Germany.

Teachers' average annual salaries were $640. Those not called to active duty in the national services were offered much higher salaries in industry and war-related activities. Building of schools ceased as builders turned to wartime construction projects and many schools closed for lack of qualified teachers. Others remained open with whatever persons could be persuaded to accept teaching assignments. At the same time, schools and the Association were called upon to provide many extra services related to the war effort. The active membership of the NEA was 8,446.

These were the conditions when Dr. James William Crabtree was named executive secretary in 1917. And they were among the conditions that caused the Association in 1918 to appoint a Commission on the Emergency in Education.

Commission on the Emergency in Education

The commission, under the vigorous leadership of Dr. George D, Strayer of Teachers College, Columbia University, and motivated by the desperate condition of the schools in the early months of World War I, became one of the most aggressive and effective bodies in NEA history.

The commission was appointed jointly by the NEA and the Department of Superintendents. Its work covered a two-year period, and its membership included twenty-nine able leaders of the Association.

NEA President Mary C. C. Bradford submitted to the 1918 convention the commission's progress report, which, she said, contained a complete national plan for education and represented the greatest achievement of the educational year 1917–18. The report contained a description of the school crisis; the preparation, supply, and salaries of teachers; special problems of rural schools; a program for physical health education; problems of immigrant education and adult illiteracy; compulsory continuation schools; and the need for a National Department of Education and national cooperation with the states to strengthen the public schools.

Joseph Swain, chairman of the Committee on Salaries, Tenure, and Pensions and president of Swarthmore College, made a report to the 1918 convention on the nation's responsibility for public education that gave notice of actions to come. He said:

> Education is a national matter. The man who denies that at this hour is not worth listening to. The man who denies that education is a national matter is capable of denying that our army and navy are national matters, of thinking that our states and towns and cities, left to themselves, could carry on the War . . . may the time never come when the people in this locality or that lose con-

trol over the teaching of their own children. But the child is of concern to a wider region than the place in which he is born; and the wealth of a community is no measure of the promise of its human material. Can we permit boys and girls, perhaps of rare gifts, just because they happen to have been born on the outskirts of the country, to have only the outskirts of education? Those boys and girls are the nation's highest assets. The nation must do its share toward bearing the burden of their training.

But suppose the nation cannot be made to see its duty. Then there is only one other way: the teachers, by concerted action and the application of the principle of collective bargaining, must compel the nation to wake up.[13]

The final report of the commission was presented to the 1920 convention, and Chairman Strayer announced that a bill had been prepared embodying the commission's program and recommendations. It had been introduced in Congress in the fall of 1918. Strayer reported the bill had received the unqualified endorsement of the two previous conventions. In addition, it had been endorsed by the annual meetings of the Department of Superintendents and fourteen national civic, church, and patriotic groups. The bill proposed the reorganization of the federal Office of Education, making it a Department of Education, headed by a secretary in the president's cabinet; an appropriation for reducing illiteracy; and programs for the Americanization of immigrants, physical education, teacher training, equalization of school opportunity, and partial payment of teacher's salaries.

THE LEGISLATIVE PERIOD: 1918–1957

A Legislative Commission was appointed in 1920 to secure the passage of the bill embodying the recommendations of the Commission on the Emergency in Education. Such a legislative unit has been maintained continuously since that time to work with Congress and the various federal agencies.

Although all of the recommendations of the Commission on the Emergency in Education were not achieved immediately, its efforts brought significant results. The public was aroused and made aware of school problems, teachers' salaries were increased, hundreds of new schools were constructed despite wartime restrictions, the trend to reduce school taxes was halted, programs were initiated for the Americanization of immigrants, the education profession was united, and NEA membership was increased. But a national Department of Education headed by a cabinet member became a continuing objective.

During the Springer administration, the Association headquarters were in Ann Arbor, Michigan. When Dr. Crabtree was appointed, the office was moved to Washington, D.C. The first office was located in two rooms at 1125 Fourteenth Street, Northwest, but shortly after was moved to what was known as the Battleship Building, at 1400 Massachusetts Avenue, Northwest. Here Dr. Crabtree and his staff of three occupied the lower floor as an office, and, to conserve Association resources, the Crabtree family occupied the upstairs rooms.[14]

The Association soon outgrew the small office and in 1919 purchased the four-story Guggenheim mansion at 1201 Sixteenth Street, Northwest, the site of the present Washington headquarters building. The mansion was purchased for $98,000 and was occupied by the Association in the summer of 1920. In 1980, the only visible remnant of the original mansion was the mantelpiece in the state dining room.

The Research Division was established in 1922 to provide data on the school systems of the states and related information as a basis for state and national legislation and to promote public understanding of the schools and the problems of teachers. Since the public schools are a microcosm of society, social changes impinge upon school systems and require them to adapt programs to society's changing needs. To make such adjustments, school systems have, through the years, looked to the NEA for reliable, up-to-date information. A review of the *Research Bulletins* and special studies produced by the NEA since 1922 would reveal a reasonably accurate reflection of changes in society during that period.

Second Commission on the Emergency in Education

An official Code of Ethics for the Teaching Profession was adopted by the NEA in the economic boom year 1929. As the following bust years of the Great Depression began to create new financial problems for schools, the NEA appointed a second, joint Commission on the Emergency in Education, with Dr. John K. Norton of Teachers College, Columbia University, as chairman.

The commission was sponsored jointly by the NEA and the Department of Superintendents. Its mission was to help the schools meet the adversities of the Depression. Conceiving itself as a board of strategy, it assembled data on the plight of unpaid teachers, closed schools, and curtailed school terms and attempted to counter the self-serving propaganda of conservative groups advocating reduced school taxes.

The commission urged federal support to assist school systems that depended heavily on local property tax revenue, a large portion of which was in default in many systems during the Depression years. It also organized a network of consultants in every state to carry on a campaign for support of the public schools.

The final report of the joint commission recommended the establishment of an Educational Policies Commission (EPC). The Association acted on the recommendation in 1935, creating the EPC for a five-year period. The EPC consisted of 10 nationally prominent educators and 900 consultants drawn from all sections of the country. As defined by the two sponsors, the commission's function was "to prepare, publish, and disseminate, from time to time, statements of proposed policy regarding the conduct of education in the United States, and the international relationships of American education."[15]

The Educational Policies Commission was a unique body. It had no policymaking function within the NEA. It was free to make wide-ranging surveys and to make public pronouncements based on its findings and conclusions without being inhibited by the policies of the two sponsoring associations. Because of the prestige of its members, the EPC was able to get public attention for its pronouncements. It therefore had an impact on public opinion in the nation for more than thirty years.

Among the commission's most influential studies were: "The Purposes of Education in American Democracy" (1938); "Learning the Ways of Democracy; A Case Book on Civic Education" (1940); "Education and the People's Peace" (1943); "Education for All American Youth" (1944); and "Education for All American Children" (1948).

Dr. J. W. Crabtree, who had become executive secretary under crisis conditions in the early days of World War I, retired in 1934 during the school crisis caused by the Depression. During the seventeen years of his administration NEA membership had increased from 8,466 to 160,883. On his retirement, the trustees proudly declared the NEA to be the largest professional organization in the world and credited Dr. Crabtree's services and courageous leadership for the achievement.

Willard E. Givens took office as the NEA's fourth executive secretary in 1935, within a few weeks of Franklin D. Roosevelt's issuance of the executive order establishing the Works Progress Administration (WPA). The same year, Congress passed the National Labor Relations and Social Security acts. Dr. Givens, a former superintendent of Oakland and San Diego schools, had been president of the NEA state affiliate in California—The California Teachers Association—and an active participant in NEA affairs.

Organizational Structure

In the early years of the Givens administration, progress was made in streamlining the complex governance structure of the Association.

The Washington convention of 1934 had amended the bylaws to remove the past presidents and state superintendents as ex officio members of the Representative Assembly. The next step was to amend the charter to make it possible for the elected bodies to modify Association programs and organizational structure without the necessity of securing congressional approval. This was accomplished in 1937 when Congress approved an amended charter. The charter was signed by President Roosevelt on June 14, 1937.

The following month, the bylaws were amended to eliminate past presidents from the Board of Directors. The term of office for directors was lengthened from one to three years, and provision was made for one-third of the Board to be elected each year. New qualifications were adopted for Board members, requiring them to have been active members of the local, state, and national organizations for the three years immediately preceding their nomination. The 1937 bylaw changes also enlarged the membership of the Executive Committee from five to nine, two being elected by the Representative Assembly and two elected by the Board of Directors.

While the streamlining of the NEA governance machinery was taking place, another trend was developing. Many independent organizations, with their own governance, staff, membership dues, and programs, concerned with specific facets of education, were becoming departments of the NEA. Some organizations, such as the National Association of Secondary Principals, moved their offices to Washington to become a part of the growing number of participants in the national coalition of school organizations under the NEA umbrella.

The process of accretion of departments began before the turn of the century with the affiliation of five departments—School Administrators (1870), Vocational Education (1875), Kindergarten and Primary Education (1884), Business Education (1892), and Science Teachers (1895)—and greatly accellerated in the 1930s, 1940s, and 1950s. By its centennial year (1957), the NEA had twenty-one departments with offices and staffs in the NEA's Washington headquarters building. An additional nine departments had offices in locations other than Washington, and most of them functioned with part-time staffs. Thus, the NEA became in this period a dual organization: a coalition of national independent organizations in Washington and a national organization of educators in Washington with a network of state and local affiliates. To further complicate relationships, many departments had their own state and local counterparts. To house the growing number of national affiliated organizations and normal growth of NEA programs, the Association purchased property east of the headquarters on M Street in 1937.

The bylaws were amended again in 1939 to allow those states with 20,000 NEA members a second member on the Board of Directors.

In 1942, the Association was able to burn the mortgage "on its half-million-dollar home" through membership growth and prudent administration. Membership in 1942 was 217,943.

Program Emphasis

Easily the top priority of the NEA in the period from 1918 to 1957 was federal school legislation. The headquarters were established in Washington to provide a voice for education in the Congress, the administration, and the national press, television, and radio.

Education had, from the adoption of the federal Constitution, been considered a state responsibility. The constitutions of the states recognized the responsibility and also the unique function of local boards of education as representing their local constituents, but functioning within limits fixed by the state legislatures.

As the nation grew and communications and transportation improved, it became clear that the entire nation had a stake in the quality of education being provided to American children. The first concern was for information about what was happening in the states. This need led to establishment of the federal Office of Education in 1867.

The NEA's early federal proposals, from 1870 to 1890, were for federal assistance to the states for the elimination of illiteracy.

In the early 1900s, proposals advocated vocational training to meet the demands of industrial growth. The Smith-Hughes Act of 1917 provided assistance to the states on a matching basis.

The Smith-Towner Bill in the 65th Congress (1917–1919) developed and drafted by an NEA commission, included aid for the education of illiterates, Americanization education of immigrants, federal funds for the partial payment of teachers' salaries, and establishment of a federal Office of Education, headed by a cabinet officer. The NEA commission shocked the nation with its report that more than five million foreign-born Americans could neither read nor write English. Also, the report revealed that one in four draftees ages twenty-one to thirty-one in World War I were found to have been functionally illiterate and one in three had been disqualified for service for physical disability.

After hearings, the bills were reported favorably by both the Senate and House Education Committees, but in the congestion of business in the final days of the session, no action was taken.

In the following four sessions of Congress, similar bills were introduced but not acted upon.

The Republican party platform in 1924 supported the creation of a cabinet post for a Department of Education and Relief. The NEA opposed the linking of education and relief but gave support to a cabinet-level Department of Education. When this proposal failed, the Association concluded that the NEA and the coalition of several national organizations could not carry sufficient weight with Congress to secure passage of a federal school-support bill without the support of active, articulate supporters in the states and congressional districts. Despite volumes of persuasive testimony before committees by many national organizations and dramatic factual reports of school needs and inequalities, congressmen responded to what they perceived to be the wishes of their local constituents. This experience caused the NEA leadership to begin planning for greater involvement of the state and local affiliates in the development and promotion of federal legislation.

President Hoover in 1929 appointed a National Advisory Committee on Education to study the relation of education to the federal government. The committee report two years later recommended the establishment of a Department of Education at the cabinet level, and a bill was introduced in the House of Representatives based on the committee's recommendations. However, no action was taken.

In 1933 President Roosevelt named an advisory Commission on the Emergency in Education. The NEA gave both financial and staff support to the president's commission, whose work was responsible for a number of short-range emergency programs for schools, including aid to rural schools, adult education, nursery schools, school construction, and building repairs. Aid was also provided through the National Youth Administration to needy college students, and the Reconstruction Finance Corporation was authorized to refinance school indebtedness.

Bills were introduced in the 74th (1935–1937), 75th (1937–1939), and 76th (1939–1941) sessions of Congress. None passed. Although in the 76th Congress the Senate Committee on Education and Labor reported the Harrison-Thomas-Fletcher measure favorably for action by the Senate, the chairman of the House Education Committee refused to call a meeting to consider the proposal.

A bill to equalize educational opportunities among the states was introduced in the 77th Congress (1941–1943). It included a provision for aid to school districts located in defense areas. This proposal established the need for special assistance to schools in impacted areas where the location of army bases or other federal activities was causing an influx of pupils and taxing the ability of school systems to provide facilities and instruction from local and state funds. The Congress responded by passing the Lanham Act.

Federal support bills were before Congress constantly from 1943–44 to 1957. The Senate had approved bills for school support in 1948 and 1949, but not until 1956 did a federal school-support bill reach the floor of the House for debate. In that year, the Kelly Bill HR1 was killed after a racial amendment was approved by the House. The amendment caused supporters in those states with segregated school systems to withdraw their support, and the bill was defeated.

So the NEA's first century closed without achieving either of the Association's long-term legislative goals—the creation of a separate federal Department of Education headed by a cabinet officer and general support for schools administered by the states without federal controls. These two goals were destined to await the action of the 89th Congress in 1965 and the 95th Congress of 1979.

However, the groundwork done by the NEA and its allies in its first century was vitally important. It set the stage for the achievement of a separate Department of Education and a new national policy for the financing of schools early in its second century.

Although the two longstanding goals were not reached, much valuable school legislation was enacted by Congress with NEA leadership and support in the NEA's first hundred years. Some were mentioned earlier, such as the Morrill Act of 1862, the establishment of the U. S. Office of Education in 1867, the Smith-Lever Act for Agriculture and Home Economics Education (1914), the Smith-Hughes Act for Vocational Education (1917), and the Child Labor Laws (1900–1924). Others include the abolition of loyalty oaths for teachers in the District of Columbia (1937), exclusion of teachers from the Hatch Act (1938–1942), the GI Bill of 1944 and extensions to veterans of subsequent wars, defeat of the proposed "millionaires' amendment" to limit federal taxes in peacetime to 25 percent (1944), legislation making available to schools surplus property used to train over ten million persons for wartime service (1944), bills for federal aid to impacted areas, first enacted in 1941 and renewed since that time, and the Mason Bill granting tax relief to retired teachers (1954).

Consolidation of School Districts

Economic pressures on schools and teachers and the limited ability of many state legislatures to respond gave federal school support a top priority among NEA programs in the period from 1918 to 1957. There were, however, a number of other important concerns in which the Association was engaged. For example, in 1918 there were too many small, uneconomical school districts in the nation. In some states there were more school board members than teachers because of the large number of small districts. Each time the federal school-support bill was mentioned, opponents argued that federal support to the many small, uneconomical units would retard consolidation and waste public funds.

The reduction of the number of school districts during the legislative period by the NEA, the school boards, and state governments was one of the most important movements for school improvement in the Association's first century. Between 1940 and 1957 the number of school districts was reduced from 120,000 to 55,000. The result was more effective use of public funds, and improved education for millions of children.

Unification

Dr. Crabtree, as early as 1917, recognized the need for a unified organization of the teaching profession. One of his first announced goals upon becoming executive secretary was "100 percent membership in local, state, and national associations with every teacher at work on the problems of the profession."[16]

It was not until 1944 that solid progress was made to tie the three levels of the profession together. The Representative Assembly in that year increased membership dues and adopted a five-year plan of unification and expansion. At the end of the five years, six states had acted to collect one annual membership fee that made a person a member of the local, state, and national organizations. By 1957, seven states had adopted the unified membership plan. Although seven states represented only 14 percent of the nation's fifty, it was a beginning of an important movement that would add strength to the Association by making more effective use of its resources and by improving coordination of local, state, and national programs.

Dr. Givens recognized the need for a closer tie among the NEA and its state and local affiliates. His messages to the Representative Assembly and the Board of Directors did much to secure the acceptance of the unification concept during his administration. On his retirement, others continued to press for a single organization with one annual membership dues payment.

Membership Promotion

Membership promotion in the early years of the Association required a great deal of effort, and progress was slow. The principal means of promotion were the annual conventions and Association publications. It was not until the state and local affiliates accepted the responsibility for enrollment of members in all three levels of the profession that membership began to grow rapidly. In the first fifty years, membership increased from 43 to 5,044. In the second fifty—1907 to 1957—it grew from 5,044 to 703,829. However, only six in ten members of the NEA's state affiliates also held membership in the NEA in 1957. The completion of the task of bringing the three levels of the teaching profession into one organization with a single membership dues payment remained to be achieved in the Association's second century.

Improvement of Instruction

By 1957, the NEA was the largest publisher of educational materials in the United States. Its catalog in that year included titles covering the entire breadth of the school curriculum. The content of its publications sought to keep members abreast of new developments in education, new concepts, and practical ideas for classroom use. The Association's Research Division produced factual data that supported the legislative proposals of its state affiliates. It also ground out materials for the use of local salary committees in negotiating teacher salary schedules.

The NEA in 1957 was a storehouse of information on education at every level. Walking through the nine-million-dollar NEA headquarters, one would get the impression of a large organization at work on all facets of the school program, from music and physical education to mathematics and science, and from kindergarten to higher education. At the end of its first century, the prevailing philosophy of the NEA's role was to improve education, leaving it to the state legislature and local school boards to win a fair share of school budgets for members' salaries and benefits.

However, a movement was developing within the NEA by 1957 that would bring it into direct action on the problems of members. In 1941 the National Commission for the Defense of Democracy Through Education was created. Its responsibilities were to investigate alleged cases involving the violations of teachers' rights, attacks on school systems, and improper or unfair practices involving schools or school personnel, and to work for conditions essential for effective teaching and learning.

The commission, after concluding that a case was of concern to the profession and consistent with its purposes, would make an investigation. Following the investigation, a report would be written and printed, including a complete review of the facts and the commission's findings and recommendations. After reviewing the report with the parties involved, the commission would make the reports available to the press and other media. Through this procedure, the Association was often able to assist a community or school system to resolve problems through local democratic procedures.

Through its first century, the NEA provided a forum for exchanging ideas and information on education. It published information to assist its members in the performance of their professional activities. It drafted and proposed education legislation to the Congress and the national administration and promoted the approval of such proposals. With the exception of national legislation, a majority of the NEA's efforts were to support and strengthen the professional performance of its members and its state and local affiliates. The NEA sought to advance the welfare of its members by providing resources to its affiliated state and local organizations and to schools that, in turn, would make possible economic benefits to members.

This procedure was not an indication that the NEA was not unconcerned with economic issues. It was a strategy based on the conviction that the American public was more concerned about quality schools for pupils than it was in the welfare of those who provided the service. Therefore, it was argued that urging citizens to provide good schools for children would bring better results than pressing for fair and adequate salaries for teachers.

In the lobby of the old NEA headquarters building stood an almost life-size statue of Horace Mann. Over the statue was a quotation from Horace Mann's 1859 address to the graduating class at Antioch: "Be ashamed to die until you have won some victory for humanity." This spirit, embraced by staff and officers with a religious fervor, permiated the atmosphere of the organization. They were all engaged in a noble cause and made no apology for their idealism.

The story of the NEA's first century is a story of how an organization attempted to adapt to changing social conditions in a society beset by three major wars, one major economic depression, and a number of lesser emergencies. It is a story of the building of a uniquely American school system and the articulation of the three levels of education into a unified system engaged in the noble purpose of providing equal access to all, as yet imperfect, but unmatched in its achievements by any other system in the world.

The conclusion of a century provided an opportunity for NEA to review its achievements and formulate some goals for the future. A centennial history was written. Special issues of Association publications were printed. A five-year plan of expansion was adopted. Annual dues were increased to ten dollars. A centennial convention was held in the city of the

NEA's birth. The president of the United States cut a huge birthday cake in a nationwide celebration to which similar meetings in the states were joined by closed-circuit television. Congratulations were received and prognostications ventured. None dimly perceived the scope and nature of the changes that would be required of the NEA in the first quarter of its second century.

The centennial celebration of 1957 offered only a brief respite for participants to catch their breath before entering a period of change that would transform the NEA into a very different organization to carry on the work of elevating the character and advancing the interests of the profession of teaching, and promoting the cause of education in the United States.

CHAPTER TWO

Change

Two words—"growth" and "change"—describe the first twenty-one years of the second century in the life of the National Education Association. The NEA enrolled 703,800 members in its centennial year, 1957. By 1979, membership had more than doubled, reaching 1,709,673.

The change in the character of the Association is even more dramatic than the increase in numbers. In its first hundred years, the NEA elected ninety-seven presidents; only ten were practicing classroom teachers. Forty-four were college and university presidents, including such prestigious leaders as Nicholas Murray Butler, president of Columbia University; Charles W. Eliot, of Harvard University; William M. Beardshear, of Iowa State University; Joseph Swain, of Swarthmore College; and David Starr Jordan, of Stanford University. Eight were principals. Eleven held other positions, including editors of education journals, university deans, and administrators or supervisors in state education agencies.

Classroom teachers are now firmly in control of the Association. Every president elected since 1968 has been a practicing teacher, and of the twenty presidents elected since 1957, fourteen have been teachers.

Collective Bargaining

For more than a century, the NEA has been an advocate of teachers' salaries commensurate with the importance of the service teachers perform. The Association has, with its network of fifty state affiliates, given emphasis to winning appropriations from the state legislatures and the Congress. The task of securing an equitable share of the local school district budgets for salaries of the professional school staff has been the responsibility of the local NEA affiliates. In the absence of legal authorization to engage in collective bargaining, local affiliates had for many years engaged in a variety of informal procedures as a means of participating with their employing school boards in determining salaries and conditions of employment.

In 1979, thirty-one states had collective bargaining laws covering 60 percent of the nation's teachers. The NEA has in operation a nationwide electronic data system providing backup service to its state and local affiliates and is seeking a federal law to cover those teachers not covered by a state statute and those covered by laws too weak to meet reasonable standards.

To help local teacher groups take advantage of the new opportunities and to develop new leaders, full-time staff members have been employed under a cooperative arrangement by the NEA and its state and local affiliates. By 1979, the NEA had won collective bargaining rights for more than half of its 10,000 local units.

Civil Rights

Once regarded as conservative on civil rights, the Association has, in recent years, aggressively brought both individual and class action law suits in support of integration of schools and protection of the constitutional rights of teachers, pupils, and school administrators. It had organized task forces to monitor school systems on compliance with the 1954 Supreme Court desegregation decision and has engaged aggressively in a wide variety of other activities to bring the nation's practices into harmony with our national ideals of racial equality.

Since its founding in 1857, the NEA has enrolled members without racial restrictions; however, black teachers in the "separate but equal" period were barred by law and custom from joining the white state associations affiliated with the NEA. To provide black teachers an opportunity to participate in professional affairs on a national basis, the NEA affiliated both black and white state associations in eighteen southern and border states and in the District of Columbia. In 1964 the Representative Assembly served notice that those affiliates in states with dual associations must take immediate steps to remove all restrictive membership clauses dealing with race from their constitutions and bylaws, and to present a plan to effect the complete integration of their associations by July 1, 1966. The Executive Committee was given discretionary power to act in cases of failure to comply with the provisions of the resolution. The two subsequent Representative Assemblies strengthened and clarified the resolution.

By 1970, all but two states had formed a single association open to all members without racial restrictions. In many cases, the new constitutions included built-in safeguards to assure minority members full participation in Association affairs. But this result was not achieved without the suspension of four affiliates and the expulsion of two. All were subsequently reaffiliated when they were brought into compliance. The merger of dual associations in the remaining two states was announced at the 1977 Representative Assembly.

The American Teachers Association (ATA), a national organization, was formed in 1904 to provide opportunities for black educators to attend to the special needs of their members beyond state borders. In 1927 a joint committee of the NEA and the ATA was established to improve conditions for teachers and pupils in segregated schools. In 1963 the Representative Assembly asked the joint committee to "consider whether and under what conditions it would be desirable and feasible to merge the two associations." Conditions were agreed upon, and at the 1966 Representative Assembly a ceremony was held marking the signing of a certificate of unification of the two associations.

Upon learning of the NEA's progress in merging the black and white national organizations, Congressman James Corman, a member of the National Advisory Committee on Civil Disorders, had a statement entered in the *Congressional Record*, titled, "Path of Unity Paved by National Education Association." In it, he referred to the fact that the professions in general have reflected the divisiveness that is part of our dual societies—one black and one white—and singled out the NEA as "one [group] in particular which deserves the applause of the entire nation" for setting an example for other professions to follow.[1]

Legislation and Political Action

The NEA has for many years been recognized as a spokesman for education in the Congress. However, not until 1976 did the NEA begin to openly support candidates for president and other national offices.

In the 1976 general election, the Association for the first time endorsed candidates for national offices and backed the endorsements with cash and manpower. The NEA's new role caused the *Roanoke Times* (Virginia) to publish an article titled "NEA: Once Sleeping Giant Awakes to Position of Power." Robert A. Dobkin, Associated Press labor writer, wrote:

> Once a slumbering giant, the National Education Association has awakened as a fiercely aggressive union with clout at both the bargaining table and in national politics.
>
> With 1.8 million members in nearly every community across the country, the NEA emerged as a nation-wide political force in the 1976 elections, putting together its money, manpower and political savvy to help elect its friends to Congress and the White House. "We asked for their help and they delivered," said an appreciative Hamilton Jordan, President Carter's campaign manager.[2]

In 1973, the NEA and the American Federation of State, County, and Municipal Employees (AFSCME) joined forces to form the Coalition of American Public Employees (CAPE). Its purpose: to cooperate on programs of mutual interest to improve conditions for public employees. AFSCME, the fastest-growing union within the AFL-CIO, thus joined with the nation's largest teachers' organization to create a political force with the backing of four million members. Within weeks of the coalition's birth, a bill was introduced in Congress to recognize the right of public employees to engage in collective bargaining with their public employers.

Role of Women

The Association did not admit women to active membership until 1866 nor elect a women president until 1910; yet in 1979 it was among the nation's most militant advocates of equal rights for women.

Wesley described the election of the first woman president of the NEA in these words:

> Boston, Massachusetts, July 1910. The nominating committee has just made its report. It was almost unanimously in favor of electing Z. X. Snyder of Colorado as President for the ensuing year. He had been a faithful member, held an honorable position, and deserved recognition by the Association. For more than 50 years, the report of the nominating committee had become the will of the Association. But something was different in 1910.
>
> Katherine D. Blake of New York, a member of the nominating committee, made a minority report. She proposed to substitute the name of Ella Flagg Young for Z. X. Snyder. Her motion was seconded. The president was scrupulously fair. The minority had its day and, lo, the minority became the majority and Ella Flagg Young, a woman, became the President of NEA.
>
> Frances G. Blair, Commissioner of Education in Illinois, A. E. Winship, the noted editor from Boston, and other prominent persons approved the change and greeted it as progress. James H. Baker of Colorado, James M. Greenwood of Missouri, and other prominent faithfuls were opposed to the feminine revolution. Nicholas Murray Butler, Editor of the *Educational Record*, lamented

the loss of dignity, the entry of politics, and prophesied the eventual downfall of the NEA. In fact, he withdrew to his academic tent and sulked in silence, but the NEA survived. It still survives in spite of women, or possibly because of women.[3]

Nine of the last nineteen presidents have been women.

The policy of the Association in 1957 was to take official positions only on matters directly affecting education. The Representative Assembly in 1956 approved a resolution recommending a study of the implications of the Equal Status for Women amendment to the United States Constitution. The executive secretary reported in July 1957 that the Executive Committee had considered the matter twice and voted to advise the Representative Assembly that, in its opinion, the NEA should not endorse the proposed constitutional amendment: "The amendment is not a matter which is of direct interest to the teachers as such. In areas where the Association may claim to speak for teachers, all discrimination based on sex is already opposed." The committee voted a third time to withhold support of the amendment.[4]

Contrast these actions with those taken by the 1975 Representative Assembly, which voted not to hold meetings in states that had not ratified the Equal Rights Amendment (ERA).

In that same meeting, the Assembly asked for equality of Social Security benefits for men and women. Two years later, in 1977, the Assembly voted to refuse support to candidates for public office who opposed ratification of ERA.

In 1978, the Representative Assembly took three New Business actions on the equal rights issue. It supported extension of the deadline for ratification of the amendment by the states. It reaffirmed its position to work for ratification of ERA as a major legislative priority. And it voted to notify the governors and chambers of commerce in all states that had not approved ERA that NEA would not support or promote tourism in those states until they ratified the amendment.

The 1975 Assembly also amended and strengthened a position taken in a previous resolution endorsing the use of nonsexist language, supporting the Supreme Court decisions on reproductive freedom and family planning, and advocating elimination of sexism and sex discrimination from the school curriculum.[5]

NEA Structure

Most organizations that have been in existence for more than a hundred years tend to set up safeguards against abrupt changes in policy. The NEA was no exception. Its decisionmaking machinery in 1957 included a Representative Assembly of 5,000 members; a seventy-seven member Board of Directors; an Executive Committee of eleven; a five-member Board of Trustees; a president elected for a one-year term; and a full-time executive secretary. There were also twelve vice-presidents and a treasurer.

The NEA had thirty autonomous departments in 1957, twenty-one of which occupied rent-free space in the headquarters building in Washington. Departments included: the Department of Kindergarten–Primary Education and the Association for Higher Education; the Department of Classroom Teachers and the American Association of School Administrators, and curriculum departments ranging from the National Art Education Association to the United Business Education Association.

The original idea in creating departments was that mutual benefits would be derived from cooperative relationships. Some departments' activities were carried on under joint sponsorship with the NEA. Others pursued independent programs. The combined budgets of the departments in the centennial year, 1957, were only slightly lower than the annual NEA budget.

Under the bylaws, an organization could become affiliated as a department if its purposes were consistent with those of the NEA; if it had three years of successful operation; and if it had a petition signed by 250 members and the approval of the NEA Board of Directors. The bylaws also provided that members of departments must also be NEA members. However, this was not enforced, and some organizations enrolled fewer than half of their members in the NEA.

"Unity in Diversity" was a common motto among those who saw mutual benefits in the arrangement. Cooperative publishing, mailing, purchasing, a credit union, and a common retirement system were among the more valued economic benefits that held the group together. Also, the ease of communication among several groups housed in the same building with a common lunchroom and a variety of meeting rooms facilitated cooperation on programs of general concern.

In the relatively tranquil days before collective bargaining, the rise of militance by teachers, and NEA intervention into the civil rights area, the consortium of education organizations did work effectively and with benefit to the NEA and to education at all levels.

In the early 1960s, however, tensions began to be felt. Coordinating the efforts of more than thirty separate groups while dealing with issues demanding swift action was an impossible task. At the same time, the Representative Assembly became more and more concerned about the lack of support for NEA programs and lagging NEA membership promotion by some departments. One member of a 1966 team studying the Association's structure observed that the NEA family of organizations resembled the definition once applied to a university: "a number of autonomous departments joined together by a common system of plumbing."

The NEA bylaws were amended in 1968, giving affiliates a choice of selecting from among three categories of affiliation with varying degrees of affinity to the NEA. This arrangement lasted until 1972. The current *NEA Handbook* lists five nongovernance affiliates, compared with thirty departments and other affiliates in 1957. This development, while understandable, has had a great impact on the NEA and will be discussed in greater depth in subsequent chapters.

To bring its governing documents into harmony with the NEA's new direction and to address the need for a more efficient decisionmaking structure, a Constitutional Convention was convened in 1972 to write an entirely new constitution and revise the bylaws.

CHAPTER THREE

Causes of Change

The dramatic changes in the NEA in the short span of two decades following a century of relative tranquility and steady growth were the result of events and social changes of one of the most turbulent periods in the nation's history. Equally important, they were brought about by leaders who were alert enough to perceive the impact of social changes on the organization and who cared enough to insist that the Association respond to the new needs of its members.

Among the events and social conditions that triggered the changes were: changes in the teaching staff, changes in the school districts, the failure of local and state governments to respond to school needs, the impact of the civil rights revolution, President Kennedy's Executive Order 10988, the urban crisis, the New York collective-bargaining election, and new public expectations of the public schools.

Changes in the Teaching Staff

Between 1957 and 1979 our pupil population increased from thirty-three million to forty-three million. The largest increase came in the high schools. While elementary school enrollment grew from twenty-four to twenty-five million, high school enrollments almost doubled. In 1957 high schools enrolled ten million. By 1979 they enrolled over eighteen million. The rapid rise in the high school population is significant for two reasons: (1) high school teaching attracts male teachers, and (2) it costs about one-and-a-half times as much to educate a high school pupil as it does to educate a pupil in the elementary schools.

Increased enrollments in the period 1957 to 1979 caused a corresponding increase in the number of teachers required. In those twenty-two years the size of the nation's teaching staff approximately doubled, increasing from 1.2 million to 2.2 million. Since most of the new teachers were recent college graduates, the average age of teachers declined from forty-one to thirty-eight between 1960 and 1979.

Today's teachers are better trained. In 1957, only 53 percent held bachelor's degrees and only 25 percent had master's degrees. By 1979, 99.7 percent were holders of bachelor's or higher degrees and 46 percent held at least master's degrees.

What is the significance of this younger, better-trained, more masculine teaching staff? These changes in the teaching staff, occurring as they did in the provocative climate of the early 1960s, produced a new breed of teacher. This new breed had a more aggressive spirit and demanded a voice in determining what went on in the classroom. They watched the courts and narrow-based self-interest community groups change school policy often, with little leadership exercised by divided local school boards. Recognizing the need for a countervailing force, teachers insisted that their organizations protect them from the chaos that threatened many school systems.

To understand fully the actions of teachers in the critical period of the early 1960s, they must be viewed in relation to the milieu of forces of that period. Kraft invented a name for it—"the crumbling consensus"—to describe the occurrence of a condition that, he said, "is easier to feel than to define." It appeared, he said, "at an imprecise time in the 1960s in what was a relatively well established order. Then we came up against a spirit of confrontation. Wives became more assertive in challenging husbands, children in defying parents, students in sassing teachers, and workers resisting orders from the boss."[1] He might have added that teachers refused to accept economic offers from school boards, unions failed to ratify contracts recommended by their negotiating committees, and management's recommendations to stockholders' meetings were met with resistance.

School Finance Laws and School Consolidation

One of the strongest movements in this century is the effort led by the NEA and associated organizations, the Parent-Teacher Associations, and the National School Boards Association for equal school opportunities for all children.

Early in the century, it became apparent that wide disparities existed in the quality of schooling being received. Since school support came largely from property tax revenues, schools were good in areas where land was rich or industry was concentrated. Where land was poor and little or no concentration of wealth existed, schools were poor. Also, the number of children of school age were not distributed equally among school districts. Often the poor districts made a higher tax effort to support poor schools than more favored communities that enjoyed good schools with a low or moderate sacrifice. Similar disparities existed among sections of individual states and among the states.

To remedy these inequalities, two fronts were opened up by the school organizations. The first began early in the century to secure a broader tax base by consolidating small school systems into larger, more economical units. Between 1940 and 1957, the number of school systems in the nation was reduced from 120,000 to 55,000. In 1978, there were 15,000.

This movement had a powerful effect on the schools. Larger districts could offer a wider range of opportunities to pupils, more economical-sized classes were possible, the wide disparity in taxable wealth was narrowed, and larger systems could attract a higher quality of leadership. Moreover, school consolidation was advocated by school boards and school leaders as a means of producing better education. Therefore, when it was voted by the community, the pressure was on school personnel and school boards to deliver the promised results.

So successful were the results of consolidating small districts into larger ones that little thought was given to possible losses to a system that becomes too large. Most of the research studies dealt with the inadequacies of small, uneconomical units. Only in recent years have we learned that difficulties can arise when school systems get too big.

Problems of individual teachers get lost in the bureaucracy. Small problems that go unsolved become large problems, morale drops, and classroom performance is affected. "Bigness," said Dr. John K. Norton in his report of a study of urban school problems,

> may lead to overcentralization in the control and administration of schools. The individual citizen, teacher and pupil may justly come to feel that he is ignored and without influence in effecting desirable change.
>
> In large urban systems, it is impossible for all teachers to get together in one auditorium because of the numbers involved. Also, the problems of transportation interfere with all city teacher assemblies such as are feasible in smaller cities and towns.[2]

In recent years, progressive school systems have been seeking ways to improve communications and provide opportunities for staff participation that can influence decisions. Teachers have seen collective bargaining as a promising means of participating in such school policy decisions.

Equalization of School Opportunity

A second front aimed at equalizing school opportunity was organized shortly after the movement to consolidate schools. It sought to secure state legislation that would tax all wealth in a state uniformly for school purposes and distribute revenue to local school systems according to need.

In the first half of the century, cities and urban areas were the elite school systems of the nation. Young teachers would compete for positions in city systems. If at first they failed, many would accept positions in rural and suburban areas with the ambition of returning to teach and enjoy the higher salaries and cultural opportunities of the city at a later time. City systems pioneered in winning retirement systems and other benefits not available to teachers in other areas until statewide retirement systems were established.

The NEA Research Division in 1946 published *School Finance Goals*, a bulletin that has had great influence in improving state school finance laws. It ranked each state according to the degree to which seventy-seven desirable goals were being achieved. The goals were developed by national authorities in school finance. This bulletin became an influential working guide for the constant improvement of state school finance laws.

The 1946 goals emphasized equalizing the differences between poor and rich districts, which often meant rural and urban districts. To help poor rural districts meet minimum standards, allowances for such expenses as transportation to remote schools were advocated. Distribution of at least 50 percent of state aid was recommended on an objective equalization formula, with more dollars going to poor districts than to those most favored.

The application of the equalization principle advocated by the NEA in state school finance laws did a great deal to equalize school opportunity for all children. Differences, while narrowed, still exist. However, in the past fifty years, many city and affluent school systems have felt that such equalization as exists was achieved at their expense. It must be admitted that affluent districts have lost their previously favored position and therefore feel the Association has not served them as well as it has their rural and suburban colleagues. This sense of unequal benefits, in addition to understandable traditional attitudes of self-sufficiency, accounts in large measure for the lack of strong NEA affiliates in many large cities. These attitudes and feelings constituted a substantial obstacle to the NEA in early contests with the American Federation of Teachers in bargaining elections in the early 1960s.

The method of financing schools developed by Strayer, Mort, and others has been found to be in need of revision in recent years. These plans distributed state funds to school systems on the basis of a guaranteed number of dollars per pupil or per classroom unit. But we learned in the 1960s that the education of some urban children required more dollars than others because of special needs that the school finance plans failed to recognize. They did not recognize the wide differences in school needs of the great numbers of new city residents, including many victims of rural poverty, racial discrimination, language handicaps, and emotional and physical disabilities.

The failure of governments—both city and state—to adjust their school finance plans in response to the new conditions in urban schools was an important factor in producing the chaos in urban education in the early 1960s.

Urban Problems

In the period from 1950 to 1976, the percentage of black people living in the South declined from 60 to 52 percent. The latest census figures show that the states with the largest population of blacks are New York, Illinois, and California.

Conant, in 1961, compared the schools attended by white children in suburbia with the schools attended by black children in the urban slums. In view of the resulting data and his observations during his study of the American high school, he gave this prophetic warning:

> I am convinced we are allowing social dynamite to accumulate in our large cities.
> . . .Without being an alarmist, I must say that when one considers the total situation that has been developing in the Negro city slums since World War II, one has reason to worry about the future. The building up of a mass of unemployed and frustrated Negro youth in congested areas of a city is a social phenomenon that may be compared to the piling up of inflammable material in an empty building in a city block. Potentialities for trouble—indeed, possibilities of disaster—are surely there.[3]

Another articulate voice that attempted to awaken the nation to the plight of the urban poor was that of Michael Harrington. In his book *The*

Other America (1962), he estimated there were about fifty million poor in America, including "unskilled workers, the migrant farm workers, the aged, the minorities, and all the others who live in the economic underworld of American life."

"The new poverty," said Harrington, "is constructed so as to destroy aspiration; it is a system designed to be impervious to hope. The other America does not contain the adventurous seeking a new life and land. It is populated by the failures, by those driven from the land and bewildered by the city, by old people suddenly confronted with the torments of loneliness and poverty, and by minorities facing a wall of prejudice."[4]

Harrington declared the cities incapable of dealing with the new poverty because of the white middle-class flight from the city, the decentralizing of industry, and the shrinking tax base. He might have added that the antiquated governmental machinery of too many of our cities made it difficult or impossible for them to respond to the needs of the poor. It has been said that Harrington's writings greatly impressed President Johnson and influenced him to propose to the Congress a national War on Poverty.

These serious problems of America's large cities had a great impact on city schools and the attitudes and feelings of their teachers. City teachers were frustrated in their efforts to meet pupils' needs. Specialized services were often unavailable. School systems lacked the resources to respond to the needs, and communications between teachers and decisionmakers were stifled in the bureaucratic machinery of the big-city systems.

Civil Rights

The movement by public employees for the right to participate in the development of policies that affect them has been gathering strength for many years. With the breakthrough effected by the enactment of the Wisconsin statute in 1959, followed by the Kennedy presidential order covering federal employees, the pressure was greatly accelerated. When that pressure from teacher groups was met by resistance from school boards, the civil rights movement provided the model for dealing with them. Economic pressures and the proven effectiveness of civil rights activists appealed to the younger, better-trained, and more masculine core of teachers. Many of the young male teachers were GIs who had returned from World War II, Korea, and Vietnam and qualified for teaching positions under the GI bill. These young men lacked the inhibitions of previous generations about taking the risks involved in the public demonstrations and strikes to obtain economic and social justice. When given assurance that their organizations would back them up, as the civil rights groups were doing, teachers proved that they, too, were willing to fight to improve their conditions.

Civil rights issues, including problems of compliance with the 1954 decision of the Supreme Court and related issues, will be covered in more detail in Chapter 5.

New York City

Early in 1961, the United Federation of Teachers (UFT) won the approval of the Board of Education to hold a referendum to determine whether the city's teachers wanted collective bargaining. The UFT had the backing of the Industrial Union Department of the AFL-CIO. The referendum, held in June 1961, revealed that a substantial majority of New York teachers favored collective bargaining.

The following December, a second election was held to select an organization to represent all New York City teachers in collective bargaining with the Board of Education. When the ballots were counted, the UFT had defeated the hastily assembled NEA affiliate and the independent Teachers Union by substantial majorities. The election was held following a series of confrontations between the UFT and the Board of Education, including the use of the strike.

This election in the nation's largest city and center of communications gave impetus to the collective-bargaining movement for teachers and created—as it was designed to do—an image of the strike as an invincible weapon with which teacher groups could wrest concessions from reluctant school boards. The New York City campaign had a significant effect on the attitudes of teachers toward both collective bargaining and the use of the strike as a means of enforcing teachers' demands. Although much of the activity was "stage-managed" to create that impression, the New York City strike appeared to teachers across the nation as a successful use of teachers' collective power that forced concessions from the Board of Education. It therefore had an impact on both the thinking and actions of teachers and the NEA in the developing events of the early 1960s.

Presidential Order 10988

A breakthrough of great significance for public employees occurred on January 17, 1962, when President John F. Kennedy issued Executive Order 10988. The order authorized employees of the federal government to participate in the formulation and implementation of personnel policies through organizations of their choice.

The first three sentences express the rationale for the executive order:

1. Participation of employees in the formulation and implementation of personnel policies affecting them contributes to effective conduct of public business.
2. The efficient administration of the government and the well-being of employees require that orderly and constructive relationships be maintained between employee organizations and management officials.
3. Subject to law and the paramount requirements of the public service, employee-management relations within the federal service should be improved by providing employees an opportunity for greater participation in the formulation and implementation of policies and procedures effecting the condition of their employment.

The order provided for:

1. Informal, formal, and exclusive recognition of employees' organizations, depending upon the number of members represented
2. Exclusion from recognition of any organization which asserts the right to strike, advocates the overthrow of the government, or discriminates in its membership because of race, color, creed or national origin
3. Exclusion from participation of management employees where a conflict of interest would exist
4. A procedure for recognition of employee organizations
5. The negotiation of written agreements with exclusive representatives of employees including grievance procedures
6. The head of each agency to issue, no later than July 1, 1962, appropriate policies, rules, and regulations for the implementation of the order
7. The Civil Service Commission and the Department of Labor to prepare, jointly, a set of proposed standards of conduct for employee organizations and a proposed code of fair labor practices for the federal service.

The presidential task force that produced the order included Secretary of Labor Arthur J. Goldberg, who was its chairman; John W. Macy, Jr., chairman of the Civil Service Commission; the Director of the Bureau of the Budget; the postmaster general; the secretary of defense; and the special counsel to the president. President Kennedy declared the Order will "be a source of strength to the entire Federal Civil Service." Chairman Goldberg predicted: "The voice of the organizations of federal employees will increasingly be heard in the councils of government throughout the land," and John Macy hailed the order as marking "the start of a new era in personnel management in government."[5]

Executive Order 10988 was a landmark development in employer-employee relations in the public sector, for it marked the first national effort to extend to public employees some of the benefits of formal procedures for reaching agreement with their employers long enjoyed by employees in private industry.

With the issuance of the executive order and the Standards of Conduct for Employee Organizations and the Code of Fair Labor Practices, issued on May 21, 1963, the highest level of government had recognized the right of public employees to engage in negotiations with their employing agencies. This action, taken by the federal government, established a precedent for similar actions to be taken by state governments in thirty-one states by 1980.

Other Social Forces

It is obviously impossible to identify all of the forces that influence change or to trace their effects upon a group of people or an organization. Nevertheless, I am certain that the malaise of the 1960s influenced the changes that have taken place in the NEA and made changes possible that, in a more tranquil period, would have been impossible.

Deeply divided by the Vietnam War and school desegregation and frustrated by their inability to influence situations through the system, people increasingly resorted to overt action to express their feelings and influence public policy. Having marched in a civil rights or peace demonstration to express strongly held beliefs and observing constructive results made it more acceptable to walk a picket line in behalf of better school conditions and more equitable rewards for teachers.

Living daily with the unfolding revelations of Watergate may well have influenced the way school pupils viewed those in authority in schools and government. And, at the time of this writing, the press carried reports of parents filing legal actions against teachers for the failure of their children to perform up to parental standards. Such added pressures intensify the need for teachers to press vigorously for conditions and support services that enable them to succeed.

Unification

The NEA did not come into existence until the need for a national voice for teachers and education was felt by community and state teachers' organizations.

Local organizations of teachers appeared first. Fenner says, "The Society of Associated Teachers of New York City, established in 1794, was one of the first, perhaps the very first, teachers' association in the United States."[6]

State organizations were founded in 1845 in Rhode Island and New York. By the time a national organization appeared, twenty-three of the thirty-one states then in the union had already formed state teachers' associations. The organization that later became the NEA—the National Teachers Association—was born in Philadelphia in 1857. Wesley explained the birth of the Association by saying: "Ten State Teachers' Associations met in Philadelphia in 1857 and created a parent for themselves. Slowly, one by one, the other state associations and those which were organized subsequently acknowledged the parental nature of the national association. Having been created as a parent, the National Teachers' Association proceeded to increase its offspring by the simple process of adoption."[7]

Having been created last, the national organization became the third level of a three-tiered profession, local, state, and national. From 1857 to 1975, few subjects had been discussed more than how to unify the three levels of the teaching profession.

This question remained a discussion topic until the Great Depression years of the 1930s when Pennsylvania and a handful of other state associations took action to organize a "co-inclusive" enrollment plan. This plan provided for enrolling members in the local, state, and national associations in a single transaction. In the early years, enrollment in the national organization was by direct contact through Association publications. Under this method, growth was slow and inefficient. It was not until local and state affiliates accepted the responsibility to enroll members in all three levels that membership began to grow. For many years, individual members selected which levels they would join. Since the activities of the local and state organizations were more visible than those of the NEA, national membership always lagged behind the local and state enrollments. However, as communications and transportation facilities have improved, members are much more aware of the need for a voice in national affairs.

The movement to unify the teaching profession begain in earnest in 1944 at the Pittsburgh meeting of the Representative Assembly. At that meeting, dues were increased and a plan for unification and expansion was adopted.

In a letter to Association leaders, President F. L. Schlagle and Executive Secretary Willard E. Givens declared the action of the 1944 Assembly one of the most historic—comparable to the 1857 meeting in Philadelphia, at which two organizations united to form the NEA; the 1884 meeting in Madison, at which all sections of the nation were represented for the first time; the 1910 meeting in Boston, which elected the first woman president; and the 1921 first meeting of the Representative Assembly in Des Moines.[8]

At the 1944 Pittsburgh meeting, Oregon adopted a policy of unification with a single enrollment in all three levels of the professional organization. The following year, Hawaii and Montana followed Oregon's lead.

By 1950, six states were unified, Arizona, Idaho, and Nevada joining the original three. In the decade 1950–1960, only one state voted to unify, but in the 1960s the movement caught fire with the addition of thirteen states. Twelve more were added in 1970 and 1971, bringing the total to thirty-two.

In 1972, the new constitution and bylaws provided that all states must either be unified or adopt a plan to unify before September 1, 1972. All fifty states, the Overseas Education Association, and the District of Columbia and Puerto Rico had become unified by 1975–1976.

The unification movement bound together the 10,000 local and 53 state organizations into a single united teaching profession, concluding an effort spanning more than forty years. This movement is in large part responsible for increasing NEA membership from 703,829 in 1957 to 1,709,693 in 1979; but unification goes beyond enrolling more members more efficiently. It means program coordination at all three levels—local, state, and national. This achievement has given confidence to members that the NEA now has the power to represent the interests of teachers and the American public schools in the local communities and the state and national capitals where public policies are made.

All of the foregoing social forces have influenced the NEA to change as a matter of survival. Together, they required the NEA to foresake its traditional role. It had to transform itself from a national lobby and supermarket of educational resources to an activist organization with the power to call the signals and mobilize the total power of the teaching profession in a common national effort to protect and advance the interests of both members and the schools. Naturally, this transformation altered the power relationships between the NEA and its affiliates. These problems will be dealt with in the following chapters.

CHAPTER FOUR

The Right to Bargain

Of all the changes in the NEA since 1957, the one to make the greatest impact has been collective bargaining.

To appreciate fully the pervasive nature of the changes, it is necessary to understand how professional organizations had operated prior to formal negotiations and the organizational concepts that gave direction to their programs.

From its organization in 1857, the NEA had a strong interest in improving teachers' salaries and conditions of work. The Association's efforts have taken place at all three levels of government—community, state, and national. The NEA has spearheaded the activity nationally by proposing legislation, testifying before committees, lobbying members of Congress, and working with the administration and federal agencies in the development of administrative regulations for implementing the legislation.

One of the earliest needs of education was for reliable information about education in the states. Proceedings of the early conventions repeatedly decried the lack of a central clearing house for collecting and sharing comparable data on the school systems in the states.

In 1867, ten years after its formation, the Association achieved its first legislative victory—the establishment of the federal school agency that later became the U.S. Office of Education. In 1922, recognizing the need to analyze school data, to identify national trends, and to put the data in a form for ready use by state and local affiliates, the NEA created a Research Division. The information collected and disseminated by these two agencies has provided the basis for most state school finance legislation and the resulting economic benefits to teachers and pupils.

The top priority of the NEA's state affiliates had been to win the passage of state legislation to finance adequate teachers' salaries, school operations, and facilities. State affiliates also published annual salary manuals and summaries containing a mixture of salary principles, comparative salaries among school systems in the state, and relevant economic data. They also organized leadership training programs for local leaders.

It had been the traditional function of the local community affiliates, with backing of the state and national organizations, to negotiate with their school boards to secure from the combination of local, state, and federal moneys an equitable division between salaries and other school expenses. But without legal backing, if the board listened and then said no, the teachers' only alternatives were to accept the board's offer, resign, or engage in an illegal strike. However, some state associations provided informal mediation services in impasse situations.

The generally accepted public policy concerning the right of public employees to strike was stated by Calvin Coolidge in connection with the Boston police strike: "There is no right to strike against public safety by anybody anywhere at any time." Yet no official orderly procedures existed, and no public means of dispute settlement were available. This left all teachers' organizations with no structured statutory procedures for participating in policy decisions on matters affecting their employement. Thus, illegal strikes by teachers did occur when conditions became bad enough.

In the absence of legal machinery, local teachers' associations adopted a variety of informal procedures for securing a hearing for their views before the school board. These procedures ranged from securing from the board of education a verbal agreement to meet and confer with teacher representatives, to written policies that recognized an obligation to involve teachers in decisions affecting their work.

In Norwalk, Connecticut, a group contract was achieved in 1946, following a strike by the Norwalk Teachers Association. The Connecticut Supreme Court ruled in 1951 that school boards could negotiate with teachers' organizations. Six years later, the Norwalk teachers negotiated an agreement containing an appeal procedure with the state commissioner of education serving as mediator.[1]

Until 1959, when the Wisconsin legislature passed a law covering public employees, no other state expressly authorized collective-bargaining procedures for teachers. A number of states, however, including Connecticut, expressly declared strikes by public employees to be illegal, and in some states without such laws, the courts had ruled strikes to be illegal.

Between the mid-1940s and 1960, few subjects received as much attention in the professional literature as did the issue of involving those persons who are affected by school policies in the planning and formulating of those policies. Morale studies showed that those who were actively involved identified with the purposes of the policies, understood them better, and, since they had a proprietorship interest in them, were more likely to support them. Furthermore, studies showed that such participation raised the morale of the participants and increased their satisfaction in their work.

These cooperative approaches plus a growing list of problems tended to heighten the desire of teachers for a greater voice in the determination of school policies. This was especially true in the larger, more impersonal school systems.

The relation of employer to employee in education over the years has differed from the industrial model. The professional association viewed the public—not the school superintendent—as the employer. The school superintendent, principals, and teachers were all employees of the public. All had a commmon professional responsibility to the pupils, and their cooperative efforts were required to produce good schools. Consistent with this philosophy, all held membership in the same association, and all—theoretically, at least—had an equal voice in policy determination.

Traditionally, before 1960, teachers, school administrators, boards of education, parents, and other interested citizens groups, with state teachers' associations usually serving as catalysts, developed school proposals and together lobbied them through the legislatures.

The nature of the school operation was such that about 75 percent of the operating budget went to pay the salaries of the professional staff. Therefore, if school revenues from the state legislatures could be increased, three out of four dollars so appropriated would go to the salary budget. Accordingly, state NEA affiliates have through the years given emphasis to the state legislative function. As a result, most state associations are consistently named among the most influential lobbies in their states.

As early as 1948, the NEA recognized the need for strengthening the affiliates in the large cities. Big-city teachers, who had for years felt self-sufficient, were beginning to experience problems with which they were unable to cope. And many felt the central administration was neither sympathetic to the teachers' needs nor able to respond with appropriate help. Few formal grievance procedures existed, and calls for help often went unanswered.

Teachers told the NEA Research Division that their chief complaint was their inability to teach as well as they knew how, because of conditions they were powerless to change. Some of the conditions were: too many pupils; pupils with emotional problems whom teachers were neither equipped to help nor able to refer to appropriate agencies; lack of parental support; lack of relevant instructional materials; too many distractions and nonteaching duties; and inadequate salaries and other economic benefits.

Most of these problems could not be solved by state or federal legislation. A local solution was needed. Urban teachers needed a stronger voice in the local community to get the attention of both the central school office and the community. Problems of big-city schools were not limited to those of teachers. Principals also had problems.

University of Chicago professor Donald A. Erickson gave this description of some of the problems of big-city schools to an NEA seminar on negotiation:

> Since no two schools or neighborhoods are identical, the purportedly democratic universalism of our large systems is grossly inequitable. It feeds all neighborhoods the same medicine, regardless of the afflictions. In particular, since prevailing methods are fitted to the middle class, the more we standardize the more we shortchange the poor. At least until the advent of system-wide reform, those who seek improvement in slum schools may need to fight the central office.
>
> . . . The principal usually is depicted as the vicar of the general superintendent, the school board's emissary in the local building, enforcing upon teachers the demands of top officials. I have the strong impression, on the contrary, that every effective inner-city principal I have seen has been at odds with headquarters, covertly, if not overtly. Far from prodding teachers to conform to the system, he goads the system to adapt to his community, and when he cannot change the central office, he bends, ignores, defies, or circumvents its edicts to make learning possible in his school.[2]

Erickson went on to say that teachers not fortunate enough to work in schools with such principals must accept the responsibility to seek a program specifically designed for the pupils in their particular neighborhood, rather than ask, "What is the established method?" When protected by a strong organization, it would be possible for teachers to participate in such a neighborhood movement.

Such problems led teachers to ask that they be given the right to negotiate with their public employers—a right recognized in the private sector since 1935 with the passage of the National Labor Relations Act (NLRA).

There appeared to be a concurrent readiness on the part of the public for extending such rights to public employees by the early 1960s. The Wisconsin legislature, in 1959, enacted a statute to provide to public employees, including teachers, the right to negotiate with their employers. The act forbade employers to interfere with employees in exercising the rights granted under the statute. Strikes were prohibited by the act, but mediation services were made available on request to the Wisconsin Employment Relations Board.

The following year, President Kennedy issued Executive Order 10988 extending to federal employees the right to be represented by an employee organization of their choice in negotiations of working conditions with their federal employer. This order and the subsequent (May 21, 1963) Standards of Conduct and the Code of Fair Labor Practices in the Federal Service gave federal sanction to the right of public employees to enter into negotiations with their public employers.

Resolutions are adopted annually by the NEA Representative Assembly advocating professional salary levels, academic freedom, and various rights of teachers. The platform that expressed the collective beliefs of NEA members and set the direction for Association programs had from the beginning included a strong recommendation for teachers' salaries "commensurate with the teachers' importance to American society."

For the benefit of those who may not have had the opportunity to observe the NEA Representative Assembly in action, a brief description is in order. The Assembly was created in 1920 in a move to democratize the Association. The chief policymaking body of the Association, it meets annually and is composed of about 8,000 delegates elected by the members of the NEA's 10,000 local and 53 state affiliates. The Assembly is a wide-open democratic body. Microphones are placed throughout the meeting hall, and all delegates are free to raise questions, make proposals, or discuss any matter which comes before the body, subject to the rules of procedure that are presented to the body for approval at the opening session. Obviously, it is difficult to make decisions on complex issues in a limited time with 8,000 participants. However, improvements in procedures and extensive use of closed-circuit TV, telephones, caucuses, state delegation meetings, and other techniques have made decisionmaking easier. The Assembly amazed many observers who had to see it in action to believe that 8,000 delegates could serve effectively as the chief legislative body of a changing, growing organization such as the NEA. It is larger than the conventions of either national political party and is believed to be the largest deliberative legislative body in the world operating under parliamentary procedures.

The Representative Assembly expresses policies of the Association through resolutions proposed by a Resolutions Committee with representation from all states. Following hearings presided over by the committee, the resolutions are printed and distributed to all delegates. Then the committee's proposals are debated in meetings of the individual state delegations and of caucus groups, and in open meetings of the Assembly.

Assembly discussions are regulated by official convention rules and Roberts's Rules of Order. A professional parliamentarian is employed to assist the presiding officer, and the staff operates a bank of telephones on the platform to keep in order the names and locations of delegates seeking recognition.

The resolutions and new business items are taken seriously by the delegates, since they become the expression of policies that guide the action programs of the Association. Discussions are open, frequently intense, and sometimes highly emotional, as will be observed from some of the excerpts from the debates on negotiations and desegregation of the public schools in this and the following chapter.

George Fischer, perhaps the NEA's most flamboyant and controversial president, was fond of saying that "the Representative Assembly never makes a mistake," to give emphasis to its preeminent position as a policymaking body. Whether or not the Assembly makes mistakes is debatable. But as in other democratic institutions, there are mechanisms in place to temper the mistakes until they can be corrected at the next meeting.

The first proposed resolution relating to *negotiation* of salaries and conditions of work came before the assembly in 1960—a year following the passage of the Wisconsin statute and two years before President Kennedy's executive order.

An amendment was proposed by the Michigan delegation to provide for appeal to an education-oriented mediation body if the teachers and school board failed to agree. In the discussion that followed, the New York State Teachers Association expressed concern that such an amendment could sweep teachers under provisions of the state labor laws. On the other hand, Michigan delegates feared that failure to adopt the amendment might force them to use the provisions of the state labor code. The matter was finally referred to the Board of Directors for study, with a request to submit a new proposal for consideration by the 1961 Representative Assembly scheduled to meet in Atlantic City, New Jersey.

The Board of Directors did appoint a committee to study teacher–schoolboard relationships and to submit a report to the Board prior to the Atlantic City meeting. After the report was considered by the Board, the following resolution was drafted to embody the principles recommended by the committee:

> Since boards of education and the teaching profession have the same ultimate aim of providing the best possible educational opportunity for children and youth, relationships must be established which are based upon this community of interest and the concept of education as both a public trust and a professional calling.
>
> Recognizing both the legal authority of boards of education and the educational competencies of the teaching profession, the two groups should view the consideration of matters of mutual concern as a joint responsibility.
>
> The National Education Association believes, therefore, that professional education associations should be accorded the right, through democratically elected representatives, using appropriate professional channels, to participate in the determination of policies of common concern, including salary and other conditions for professional service.
>
> The seeking of consensus and mutual agreement on a professional basis should preclude the arbitrary exercise of unilateral authority by boards of education and the use of the strike by teachers as a means for enforcing economic demands. Professional procedures should be established which can be utilized, when agreement is not reached through joint discussion in a reasonable time, to bring about a resolution of differences.[3]

A proposal was made by George Lauer, president-elect of the Michigan Education Association, to amend the resolution by deleting the last paragraph and substituting the following language: "When common consent cannot be reached, the Association recommends that a board of review consisting of members of professional and lay groups affiliated with education should be used as a means of resolving extreme differences."[4]

Thus amended, the resolution was adopted, and the NEA was committed to a course of action that was to change the character of the Association in respects then unenvisioned.

Another subject to receive intense debate and action at the Atlantic City meeting was the deterioration of the large cities and the implications for teachers and the Association. For almost a decade, the NEA had scheduled meetings at the Representative Assembly for delegates from the big cities to give them an opportunity to discuss the problems unique to the changing urban areas. These centers of population, long regarded as self-sufficient centers of affluence and culture, were now faced with problems so overwhelming it was impossible to deal with them from their deteriorating tax base and outmoded machinery.

As a means of bringing to public attention the urgent needs of the changing urban school population, many big-city teacher groups employed full-time executive secretaries to organize action programs that could involve members and interested citizens in seeking solutions. About forty of the full-time urban association executives, accompanied by officers and delegates from their organizations to the Atlantic City convention, determined to draw the attention of the delegate assembly to their problems.

They had held several meetings with Dr. Karl Berns, assistant executive secretary for field operations, and Dr. Ivan Booker, director of membership, who had arranged opportunities for them to present their requests to Dr. William G. Carr, NEA executive secretary. In February 1961, four officers of urban affiliates—Frank Heinisch, Arthur Simonds, Helen Bain, and Robert Bogen—met with Dr. Carr to request the establishment of an urban division in the NEA. However, they were not satisfied with the meeting and decided not to continue to press for action by the NEA administration but instead to focus on the political route by presenting their proposals directly to the Representative Assembly.

Actually, a number of activities were initiated by the NEA administration in response to the pressure of urban leaders. The first salary consultant, Eric Rhodes, was employed in 1957–1958. Robert McLain was added to the staff when Rhodes was assigned to the Membership Division in 1958 and Irwin Coons and Jack Kleinmann became the third and fourth salary consultants in 1960 and 1961. Kleinmann's assignment was to work exclusively with urban associations. A former member of the staff of the White Plains (New York) school system, Kleinmann was the author of a book on fringe benefits for teachers. In addition to working with individual local associations, the salary consultants participated in leadership training activities sponsored by the NEA, local affiliates, and state associations. Beginning in 1957–58, a national salary school was held annually that dealt with both principles of salary scheduling and developing skills in conducting negotiations with boards of education.

In response to demands for direct economic benefits to members, Newell Walters was employed in 1961 as a consultant for welfare services. In this position he developed group insurance plans, tax-sheltered annuities, and other benefit programs.

The Budget Committee recommended to the 1957 Representative Assembly an increase of $116,970 over the previous year in the allocation for membership problems in the big cities.

Dr. Carr, in his report to the 1958 Representative Assembly, reported that the salary consultants had filled ninety-one field assignments, giving direct assistance to forty-one systems, each of which increased its salary schedule for 1958–59. He also reported that attendance at the 1958 salary school was one-third larger than usual.

Dr. Marston, director of membership, was the first NEA official to recognize the need for special services to big-city affiliates. Bogen quotes Marston's successor, Dr. Ivan Booker, on an experience that sparked Marston's initial interest:

> While Marston was showing a visitor through the NEA headquarters in the early 1950s, they stopped off in the offices of the Division of Rural Service and the Department of Rural Education. . . . When the tour ended the visitor commented that he had not been shown a staff unit dealing with "urban education." As a result, R.B. invited urban presidents to a luncheon meeting at the next two or three conventions. The main topic at these sessions was the question: Should NEA create a separate staff unit . . . for "urban education?"[5]

Booker reported to Bogen that he continued regular contacts with the officers of urban affiliates until 1962, when the urban project was created to deal with urban problems.

The initial efforts of the NEA during the 1950s did not make a significant impact in the urban school systems. The chief reason was that the emphasis was placed on increasing NEA membership rather than on demonstrating how NEA services could aid urban teachers in solving their problems.

Urban leaders at first met informally in meetings organized by the Membership Division. They were later to become organized into the National Council of Urban Education Associations (NCUEA). The NCUEA and the smaller Urban Education Directors Association (UEDA), composed of the executive directors of urban associations, in coalition with minority groups, classroom teacher leaders, like-minded younger delegates, and a few of the more progressive state association leaders, became the agents of change who provided the impetus and leadership to transform the NEA into a growing, vigorous, independent professional teachers' union.

The decision of NCUEA leaders to take their appeal to the political arena paid off. A combination of external developments and the militant campaign of the NCUEA succeeded in making urban problems, teacher–school board relationships, strikes, and sanctions the dominant topics of discussion at the 1961 and 1962 meetings of the Representative Assembly. The zeal with which the urban delegates controlled the microphones caused one state executive secretary to complain about the tactics of the militant "young boys in short pants." Such comments seemed to stimulate the urban delegates to even greater activity. They held daily caucuses, met with the Board of Directors and state delegations, and made proposals to the Budget and Resolutions Committees.

Before the 1961 meeting of the Representative Assembly in Atlantic City, the executive secretaries of urban associations proposed a resolution requesting the Board of Directors to create an urban division to serve the special needs of those local associations in areas with populations over 100,000 and small associations employing executive secretaries. The resolution spelled out some of the services desired from the new unit, including: a newsletter, a staff large enough to assist urban organizations to strengthen programs and structure, a clearing-house service to share promising practices, and communications services to create awareness within the NEA of the needs of urban associations.

Just prior to the assembly meeting, Dr. Carr called a meeting of national, state, and local leaders to discuss this resolution. Urban leaders attended the meeting expecting to present their proposal for an urban services division. Before they had a chance to do so, however, Dr. Carr suggested that a thorough study be made of the needs of the urban affiliates by a nationally recognized researcher, the study to include recommendations on how such services could best be provided. The urban leaders viewed this suggestion as a stalling tactic and left the meeting determined to persuade the delegates to authorize an urban division at the Atlantic City meeting.

The proposals for the creation of an NEA unit to serve urban associations were contained in two motions presented by Eric Hohn, executive secretary of the St. Louis (Missouri) Suburban Teachers Association, and Arthur Simonds, executive secretary of the Montgomery County (Maryland) Teachers Association.

The Hohn motion proposed that the $50,000 provided in the budget for the development of a program for urban school systems be an action project instead of a study project. It also asked that all NEA units be directed to give priority to the needs of urban education. The Simonds motion provided that the Representative Assembly recommend to the Executive Committee and Board of Directors that they create, as soon as possible, a division for urban services.

Since these motions involved a budget item and were made during the Assembly's action on reports of committees, the chairman, Clarice Kline, said they would be held for discussion until the following day, when action on the budget would be taken. The next day, when Simonds was recognized, he asked permission for Dr. Carr to explain to the delegates the implications in the proposed study of services needed by affiliates in urban areas. Dr. Carr then read from a document that had been before the budget committee and added a personal comment:

"Inaugurate a special one-year project for 1961–62 on service to urban members of the profession. This special project should be placed under the supervision of the executive secretary.

"The purpose of that . . . is to give it as much status as possible and, as you have noted, half of all the funds for special projects for the coming year are allocated in this area.

"The purpose of the project would be fourfold:

(a) To begin to render coordinating services to the Urban Executive Secretaries, to study their needs from the national and state education association, and to report on this subject.

(b) To survey whatever differences may exist between the interests and needs of the urban and rural members of the Association.

(c) To catalog the existing services of all staff units of the Association— insofar as these services are specifically concerned with, or directed to, the urban and the rural membership.

(d) To search for some way to coordinate the rural services and proposed urban services, or to propose some better alternative."

I might add that we hope, if this is approved, that it will be implemented in the very near future by the assignment of a full-time staff member, at least one such, to this project, more if they can be recruited, and that one of the high priorities on the time of the staff member will be consultation with state association secretaries and presidents, urban association secretaries and presidents, and representatives of the Board of Directors in order to develop both immediate plans for immediate execution and middle-range plans and long-range plans for the development of NEA service—in the [urban] areas.[6]

Simonds then repeated his motion that the Representative Assembly recommend to the Executive Committee and the Board of Directors that they create as soon as possible a division of urban services or form a separate unit for specialized services to members in urban communities. Seconding and supporting speeches followed by Alan Stratton, president of the Dade County (Florida) Classroom Teachers Association; Gerald Saling, Spokane (Washington) Education Association; Horace Mayo, Minnesota; Joseph Brewer, Delaware; and Earl Kenyon, California.

Only one moderate voice was raised against the motion. It appeared the motion would pass with a good majority. Then Dr. Carr was recognized and made the following statement:

I am very sorry to take your time at this time. I am probably going to be one of the most unpopular people here, not only for taking your time but in asking you to defeat this motion.

Ladies and gentlemen, I do not think it is the correct way to organize a staff of some 900 people for a Delegate Assembly to take precipitate action without any investigation or study and mandate. That is what it amounts to—a recommendation from this body is an order to your servants—a mandate [for] the creation of a particular unit concerned with a particular area of service.

As sure as you and I are here in Atlantic City, if a division of urban services is mandated, there will be a division of suburban services and who knows how many others by geographic areas. The problems of administering the affairs of NEA is complicated enough in all conscience right now without setting up another series of criss-cross arrangements, without at least time to consider.

The original proposal, as far as I am concerned, came to my attention in April. We have worked on it rather diligently since then, stealing all the time we could from the promotion of federal aid legislation and other matters that seemed to be reasonably important at the time.

I hope very much that this Assembly will have confidence in your Board of Directors and in your officers and that you will not pass a motion directing that a particular unit be set up in the headquarters staff. After the year of exploration and the initiation of the service which all the urban secretaries say they want, and which I am sure we will do our level best to provide, I do believe you will then be in a position, if you still think it is essential to create another unit, to make a much wiser decision on a matter of such great importance.

Units, commissions, committees, are very easy to create and awfully difficult to bring to an end. As your chief executive officer, I feel I would be remiss in my duty to you if I did not advise you not to pass this resolution.[7]

After five more speakers—both pro and con—had spoken, Simonds repeated the motion to create a division of urban services and moved to close the debate. The motion to close debate carried, and in a subsequent vote the Simonds motion was killed and the Hohn motion was withdrawn.

Some urban leaders never forgave Dr. Carr for making the statement that killed the motion, and Dr. Carr never forgave Arthur Simonds for attempting to imply that his motion was merely a means of implementing the budget proposal read by Dr. Carr at the outset of the discussion. In fairness to Dr. Carr, I believe he thought at the time that the urban services needed could have been provided by coordinating the efforts of existing NEA units and reordering their priorities. By the time the study was completed, however, that notion had been discarded.

Despite the defeat of the Simonds motion, the urban group had won three significant victories at Atlantic City. First, they succeeded in passing a resolution that approved the study of urban problems and urged the officers and directors, in view of the gravity of urban problems, to intensify their efforts and initiate specific action in crucial areas. Second, they succeeded in creating an urban study with an appropriation of $50,000 to study the problems of teachers and schools in the large urban areas, develop a program of services that could be provided by the NEA and state affiliates, and make recommendations concerning how the Association could organize itself most effectively to provide the services needed. Finally, the resolution on teacher–board of education relationships had been strengthened to recognize the need for a mechanism for impasse resolution independent of labor channels.

Dr. Carr lost no time in implementing the decisions of the Representative Assembly. To conduct the urban study authorized by the Assembly, he appointed Dr. John K. Norton, retired professor of school administration at Teachers College, Columbia University, and the NEA's first director of research.

Collective Bargaining Election in New York City

While the Representative Assembly was discussing the need for better procedures for teachers to negotiate with their school boards, a referendum was being held in New York City to determine whether New York teachers wanted collective bargaining. The teachers voted three to one in favor of developing a collective-bargaining procedure.

A year earlier, in 1960, representatives of eight of the more than seventy different organizations of New York City teachers had met with the NEA to request assistance. (Stinnett established the number of teachers' organizations in New York City at from seventy to ninety.[8] Lieberman and Moscow said there were "at least ninety-three."[9] However, many were based on narrow interests—religion, ethnicity, geography, subject matter—and only a small minority of the organizations was concerned with the broad range of problems troubling New York teachers in 1960.)

At that time, the NEA had 749 members in New York City out of a total teaching staff of about 45,000. Most had joined individually to receive Association publications. Many were in administrative and supervisory positions and held membership in a variety of the seventy-plus local associations in the city. As a result, the NEA had no collective voice in New York. Moreover, no local organization was affiliated with the New York State Teachers Association—the NEA's state affiliate with headquarters in Albany.

When a report of the New York teachers' request for NEA assistance was made to the Board of Directors on June 27, 1960, the following discussion and action took place.

An Oregon director asked what the precise issue was upon which the New York City election was being called. Dr. Karl Berns, NEA assistant executive secretary for field operations, responded, "The conditions under which the election will be held have not been fully determined."

A Michigan director asked whether the leaders were members of the NEA. A Mississippi director said that it mattered less whether they were members than what could be done to involve the profession.

NEA President Walter Eshelman of Pennsylvania said, "The teachers of New York City have shown an interest in the NEA; we should take advantage of the opportunity." The director from the District of Columbia said, "When teachers call for assistance, the NEA should help."

A motion was then passed to support the action of the Executive Committee to open an office in New York City and provide staff assistance to the teachers of that city.[10]

The establishment of an office in the Time-Life Building was authorized, and a budget was approved by the Executive Committee on October 13, 1960. Eric Rhodes, former executive secretary of the Montgomery County (Maryland) Teachers Association, NEA salary consultant, and assistant director of the NEA Membership Division, was appointed director.

Rhodes's assignment was to build a coalition of organizations that could represent New York teachers in a collective-bargaining election. He had no local staff, no consensus among the local organizations he was to represent, a limited budget, and practically no contacts in the 840 New York City schools, and the initiative was with the United Federation of Teachers (UFT).

The UFT had, with the threat of a strike, a commitment from the Board to call a collective-bargaining election if 30 percent of the teachers wanted it. When the Board failed to act, the UFT called a strike in November 1960. It lasted one day, involved fewer than 15 percent of the teachers, and was settled when the Board agreed to the appointment of a fact-finding panel by Mayor Wagner and promised that there would be no reprisals against striking teachers.

The mayor appointed three well-known labor leaders, who recommended that an appropriate collective-bargaining procedure be provided for teachers. Following a series of hearings that produced no clear-cut consensus, the Board named a second group to serve as a commission of inquiry.

The new commission, headed by Dr. George W. Taylor, professor of industrial relations at the University of Pennsylvania, recommended, among other things, that a referendum be conducted in June 1961 under commission auspices to determine whether New York teachers wanted collective bargaining.[11] As mentioned earlier, the outcome was a three-to-one vote in favor of collective bargaining.

The UFT had been formed in 1960 by a merger of the New York Teachers Guild and an aggressive faction of the High School Teachers Association. The merged UFT kept the AFT charter originally held by the guild.

What neither Rhodes nor NEA leaders knew at the time of their commitment to the New York City organizations was that the city had been selected by Walter Reuther's Industrial Union Department (IUD) as a showcase for a nationwide effort to boost labor's sagging membership rolls. Reuther's plan was to organize teachers, other professionals, public employees, and white-collar workers.

According to Robert Braun, David Selden, then an AFT organizer, was sent to New York in the 1950s "with orders to build a strong local, an order unaccompanied by any promise of financial support."[12] Frustrated by the fragmented collection of teacher organizations, the slow pace of organizing, and the lack of resources, Selden appealed directly to Walter Reuther for help. As Braun points out,

> New York was a liberal town, a labor town; if professional unionism wouldn't work here, if teacher unionism wouldn't work here, neither movement had a chance anywhere in the country. But money was needed, and that's where Reuther came in. Walter and his brother Victor, and Zonorich and organizers from the Auto Workers, the Communications Workers, and other unions came to the big town to help lay the foundation for a membership drive for the AFT local.[13]

In addition, when political help was needed, George Meany would be called on to talk with Mayor Wagner. Harry Van Arsdale, New York City Central Labor Council; David Dubinsky, International Garment Workers; Jacob Potofsky, Amalgamated Clothing Workers; and Arthur Goldberg all would intercede at critical points to "pull chestnuts out of the fire" for the UFT-IUD.

Its successes in securing a conditional favorable commitment for collective bargaining from the board of education and then a favorable response from teachers in the referendum gave the UFT a considerable advantage. Although the UFT drew scorching criticism for some of its tactics, teachers faced with frustrations began to see collective bargaining as a possibility for constructive change.

Organizing an election campaign on short notice in a city the size of New York was no small task. In addition, Rhodes had to devote countless hours to meetings after school and in the evenings, trying patiently, amid acrimonious dispute, to put together a coalition of organizations with enough common interests to give the city's teachers an opportunity to be represented by an independent professional organization.

Under the name Teachers Bargaining Organization (TBO), a coalition of nineteen organizations was finally formed, and more than 10,000 signatures were obtained to qualify for a place on the ballot—more than double the number required by the election rules.

Staff was borrowed from state NEA affiliates from California to Connecticut and from Minnesota to Florida to work in the campaign. These staff members were all effective in their own states. But few had ever been more than a few blocks from Times Square in New York, and few had the feel for the city or the background to deal effectively with its issues. Shuttled in and out of New York for one or two weeks at a time, they had little opportunity to keep up to date on developments.

When the mailed ballots were counted on December 15, 1961, the UFT-IUD had won a clear victory with 20,000 votes. The TBO received 10,000, and the independent Teachers Union was supported by 2,500. An estimated 10,000 to 13,000 teachers had not voted.

One of the most significant aspects of the New York City election is the role played by the Industrial Union Department in the operation. The IUD was an association of the CIO unions that became a department of the AFL-CIO at the time of the merger in 1955. Walter Reuther was president. The AFT, an AFL affiliate, changed its affiliation to the IUD following the New York campaign.

Why would the IUD, after a long history of cooperation on legislation with the NEA, now declare war and attempt to organize teachers? There is little doubt that the New York election would have been a different story without the support of the IUD.

In 1961, a plan for an extensive membership drive had been developed by Walter Reuther, as chairman of an AFL-CIO standing committee on organization. Reuther was obviously concerned about the failure of the AFL-CIO to maintain its membership. Between 1956 and 1962, total membership had dropped by 900,000. In 1956, organized labor enrolled 25 percent of the nation's work force. By 1962, the percentage had dropped to 22. White-collar employees comprised 43 percent of the total labor force in 1962, but only 3.2 percent were union members.

Reuther's organizing plan was never implemented by President George Meany. It had been approved "in principle" by the Executive Council of the AFL-CIO, but because one union president disagreed, Meany, according to Victor Reuther, accepted the one dissenting vote as a veto of the entire program.[14]

Lacking AFL-CIO support, Walter Reuther then geared up to implement a modification of this plan through the IUD. The objective was to solve labor's problem by moving into the white-collar and public-employee fields with teachers as the opening wedge.

In his report to the IUD in November 1963, Reuther declared that "the importance of a growing, active teachers' union to all of organized labor cannot be too greatly stressed." Later, Charles Cogen, UFT president, wrote in his column in the January 15, 1964, issue of *The United Teacher*: "The United Federation of Teachers has become a symbol of what can be accomplished in the white collar area." And Nicholas Zonorich, IUD director of organization, asked, "How long will a file clerk go on thinking a union is below her dignity, when the teacher next door belongs?" It was obvious that IUD's plan went beyond the organization of teachers.

The selection of New York City as a showcase was a shrewd decision. New York City teachers, once considered self-sufficient, were ripe for organization. They were suffering from neglect and realized the need for a collective voice that could bring their problems to public attention.

New York was a union city. The Central Labor Council was a major force in city politics. Mayor Wagner owed a debt to labor, and since he appointed members of the school board, they could not ignore a request from him.

It soon became clear to Rhodes and his revolving staff that they were not involved in another routine confrontation with the AFT. Both the tactics and the personnel were different.

Stinnett, writing of the methods used in the New York campaign, pointed out that

> it was as if a precise scenario had been written in advance, as indeed many people believe had been the case. Perhaps there was not actually a written script, but one agreed upon verbally in advance.
>
> The sequence ran like this: a series of demands were made upon the New York City Board of Education involving concessions either already decided upon by the board or impossible of attainment by the board alone. Then came the strike threat, always accompanied by denunciation of the board. Next were sustained negotiations, more threats and bluster, and denunciation of the law against strikes. Somewhere along the line, at the appointed time, the New York City Central Labor Council would join in to reinforce UFT's demands and to announce its unequivocal support of the demands.
>
> Things would get dark, indeed everyone would be quaking at the prospect of closed schools. But the hero would gallop in at the last minute to rescue the teachers' union.
>
> The hero? Who but Mayor Robert F. Wagner?[15]

Those of us who worked in New York during the campaign were aware of forces in the background beyond the capability of the AFT to influence or control, but did not learn until late in the campaign the full extent of the AFL-CIO involvement.

Lieberman and Moscow reported that the IUD contributed $38,500 to the campaign and lent $50,000, to be used for organizing in other areas when repaid.[16]

Dr. Carr related this experience:

> The resources expended by the AFT to achieve its objectives in New York City alone amounted to about a half-million dollars. I obtained this figure from one of the vice-presidents of the AFL-CIO. We were both attending a luncheon and were amicably discussing the outcome of the New York City election. I remarked, and my companion readily agreed, that the Teachers' Union of New York City could not possibly have financed such an extensive campaign. I said that the Teachers' Union must have had available about $90,000 for the purpose. This was a pure, but not guileless, guess on my part. My luncheon companion responded immediately that the actual sum was about $500,000. Besides this substantial cash assistance, the AFT local in New York City received, he told me, various kinds of help from the Auto Workers, the Amalgamatd Clothing Workers, the [Ladies'] Garment Workers, the Machinists, and other unions.[17]

Victor Reuther, an associate in the United Auto Workers (UAW), shed some light on the extent of the IUD's support of the AFT. He said that "the records show that, beginning in 1961, under Walter's presidency, the IUD expended well above $1 million to the organizing campaign of the AFT. Later, the AFL-CIO did respond to the Federation's appeals."[18]

From the foregoing sources, it is not possible to pinpoint the precise IUD expenditure in the New York City campaign. But it was obviously much higher than that reported at the time.

The Meaning of New York for the NEA

Although the NEA had been aware of the problems of New York City and other large cities for at least a decade, it had delayed too long in attacking the problems in a fundamental and systematic way. Its primary interest had been in the potential for Association membership rather than in providing services to teachers that would enable them to solve their problems. And in the clear light of hindsight, one might fault the judgment of NEA leaders in going into New York City in the absence of strong support from its New York state affiliate and time to develop a capable cadre of local leaders.

There is no denying that the New York election was a victory for the UFT, IUD, and AFT and a serious blow to the NEA's prestige. However, the effect of the defeat was not all negative for the NEA. The experience shocked the Association into action. It speeded up the development of a workable policy of organizing and negotiating with school boards. It caused the Association to recognize the need to take a searching look at itself and to streamline its programs and structure to meet the demands of a new day.

Staff and power groups had been pushing for such changes and some were already in progress, but the New York City experience dissipated internal resistance and moved the pace of implementation into high gear.

New York City made it possible for those of us in the NEA who were advocating modifications in structure and programs to accomplish rapidly changes that would have otherwise taken years.

The Urban Project

Within a few days of the New York City election, Dr. Norton completed his urban study and Dr. Carr called a conference for January 20, 1963, to be attended by representatives of urban associations, state affiliates, and NEA leaders for the purpose of reviewing the report and making recommendations for its implementation.[19]

Out of the two days of discussion came two resolutions. Resolution 1 was as follows:

> There is immediate need for the NEA to establish a new and vigorous program of services, which will seek to develop active local association programs in urban areas throughout the country. This program should work with and through state associations when possible, but should not be delayed if the state association is unable to cooperate.
>
> Leadership in this service is so critically important that it must carry relatively high salary and prestige. Staff responsibility should be clearly defined and centered in a special project directly responsible to the Executive Secretary. It is suggested that the Executive Secretary be urged to develop a recommendation to the appropriate policy making bodies of the NEA to achieve the implementation of this program as soon as possible.

Resolution 2 was more succinct: "Great consideration should be given to training for urban association leaders."

In his report to the February 17, 1962, meeting of the Board of Directors, President Ewald Turner spoke of the challenge of the labor unions and the need to change the structure of the NEA. Dr. Carr's report to the Board reviewed the NEA's work in New York City, expressed the need for a more efficient structure for the NEA, and recommended further services to urban members and the development of unified dues, programs, and services of NEA's departments.

The Board adopted the recommendations and created the Urban Project within the office of the executive secretary. Its mission: to coordinate the programs of all NEA units and develop and administer an action program to channel needed services, as revealed by the Norton study, to the urban areas.

I had been a member of the NEA staff for a year as associate director of the Membership Division. Shortly after the Board's action to create the Urban Project, I received a telephone call from Dr. Carr asking me to come up to his eighth-floor office. After the usual pleasantries, he told me he would like me to be his special assistant for urban services to administer the new project. The new assignment, he said, would be both challenging and demanding.

I told Dr. Carr that, if he felt I could serve the Association better as special assistant to the executive secretary, I would welcome the opportunity. I asked what decisions he would expect me to make and what decisions he wanted to be involved in. His reply was "That will depend on you. I will always be available for consultation when you want my judgment, but the responsibility is yours. I do not want to impose an obligation on you which might delay decisions that must be made."

In the action-packed months that followed, I appreciated the confidence and freedom that Dr. Carr's statement implied, and I must say he gave me his full support—even in some instances when he may have had good reason to question my judgment. I did, however, make a conscientious effort to consult with him in advance on all matters involving Association policy, future plans, and the modification of programs previously agreed upon.

The NEA was in an awkward position on teacher–school board negotiations. It had been involved in a campaign to be named bargaining agent in New York City. But the policy adopted by the Representative Assembly could not be stretched to include the industrial model of collective bargaining being considered in New York.

The process of formalizing a procedure considered appropriate for the relationships in the public schools had been under discussion for several months. Concern centered on the following five questions.

1. *What should be the composition of the bargaining unit?* Should the Association negotiate salaries and conditions of work for all professional personnel or for rank and file professionals only? Since NEA membership includes all professional personnel, can it support a more restrictive bargaining unit? Should the unit composition be left optional to fit the variations in local traditions and practices?

2. *What subjects are negotiable?* Under industrial-type collective-bargaining statutes and interpretations by the courts, wages, hours, and conditions of work have been defined as negotiable. There are established precedents for subjects included under this definition. But in public education, the professional literature generally has advocated the active involvement of professional personnel in policy formulation on all matters that affected them. Therefore, should the scope of negotiations be broadened for professional personnel in the public schools to include all matters influencing the quality of education?

Are there some subjects that should be reserved exclusively for decisions by the board of education and the administration of the school system? If so, what are they?

3. *Who shall represent professional personnel?* The negotiation process required that there be spokesmen authorized to speak for each party—the employer and employee. In public education, the employer—the school board—was usually elected by the citizens of the community. School personnel generally belonged to voluntary organizations that they joined because they agreed with the purposes and desired the benefits their programs provided. In some school systems, the professional personnel may have been represented by more than one organization. Should *one* organization represent all employees in the negotiating unit? If so, how should the organization be selected? If not, what workable mechanism could be devised to give representation to multiple employee organizations?

4. *How should disputes between teachers and school boards be resolved?* The Representative Assembly had partially answered this question in Atlantic City in 1961 when it adopted Resolution 17, which said: "When common consent cannot be reached . . . a board of review consisting of members of professional and lay groups affiliated with education should be used as a means of resolving extreme differences." The Assembly preferred to resolve disputes through educational channels rather than use the mechanisms in the state labor codes, which might have established a precedent for dealing with public-sector educational questions by means of procedures and practices adapted to the special needs of industry in the private sector. The adoption of the resolution also revealed the delegates' deep-seated distrust of administrators of the labor laws.

While the resolution recommended an alternative to labor channels for dispute resolution, it provided no guidance to affiliates on possible means of avoiding persistent disagreements through such resources as fact finding, mediation, and arbitration.

Other questions, too, persistently arose. In the absence of a state law, what were the appropriate means of persuading a reluctant school board to engage in negotiations with school personnel? And whose man was the school superintendent? The NEA had taken the position that the superintendent occupied a dual role. He was both the executive officer of the school board and the leader of the professional staff. The American Association of School Administrators (AASA) agreed with this definition. But as a practical matter, the NEA found that when "the chips were down," the school boards disagreed. They insisted the superintendent's role be singular—executive officer of the board—and in many instances, boards instructed superintendents to withdraw from membership in the Association.

5. *Should teachers strike?*   The UFT in New York City was advocating the full-blown application of industrial-type collective bargaining, including the right to strike, although its parent body, the AFT, had a "no strike" policy. The NEA's policy took no specific position on the strike but said that "the seeking of consensus and mutual agreement on a professional basis should preclude the arbitrary exercise of unilateral authority of boards of education and the use of the strike by teachers as a means of enforcing economic demands." Was it ethical for professional personnel to strike? Under what conditions, if any, could a strike be justified? What appropriate alternatives to the strike exist?

The foregoing questions had been the subjects of intense discussion by the NEA staff. What was urgently needed was a coordinated effort to develop a consensus on these questions and put together a procedure designed to serve the special needs of teachers in the public schools.

After consultation with these units within the NEA house, it was clear to me that one of the top priorities of the new project should be to secure the counsel of a competent law firm. The firm should have a specialty in labor law and a desire to assist the Association in the invention of an appropriate procedure for negotiation adapted to the unique character of public employment and especially public education.

Equally important was the need to begin at once to develop vigorous local affiliates in the large cities capable of accepting new responsibilities. Long neglected, too many associations in the big cities had fallen into the hands of entrenched, weak, or self-seeking leaders, and programs had become outdated. Fresh leadership was needed, new service programs had to be initiated, and a more realistic membership dues structure had to be put into operation. Demand by teachers for participation in the formulation of policies that concerned them placed responsibilities on local affiliates that many were not equipped to assume.

I told Dr. Carr I wanted to move ahead immediately on these two priorities. Having done some investigation of the costs involved, I wanted his concurrence before moving ahead. Briefcase and hat in hand, he was about to leave for Friendship Airport, so he asked me to ride there with him in the Association limousine; we could talk on the way.

I proposed we move ahead at once to engage a law firm. I had consulted several persons who were familiar with firms specializing in labor law. I told Dr. Carr I would like to go to New York City and with his approval, to meet with a partner in one of these firms. We discussed the probable expense involved and the extent of our need for their services. Since few subjects had received more attention during the progress of the Norton study than the need to strengthen urban affiliates, that proposal required little discussion.

By the time we reached the airport, I also had the executive secretary's support to move ahead on both proposals as well as his agreement to the transfer of Sylvia Brotman to the Urban Project and the employment of John Carlson as assistant director. Carlson was a former teacher in Grosse Point, Michigan, then a field staff member for the Michigan Education Association (MEA) working with the NEA-MEA affiliate in Detroit. Sylvia Brotman, a former New York City teacher, had been employed in the NEA's Membership Division to work with urban affiliates since 1955.

The following week, I met with Frederick R. Livingston, a senior partner with the New York firm of Kaye, Scholer, Fierman, Hays, and Handler to explore the possibility of establishing a relationship as counsel to the NEA for labor relations. Livingston invited his partner Donald H. Wollett to join us. Wollett had been a member of the law faculty at the University of Washington and New York University before joining the firm. We reviewed the NEA's problems associated with the adaptation of the collective-bargaining process to negotiation with the school boards. I stressed the Association's desire to do some innovative thinking to make the negotiation process compatible with the nature of the teaching profession and the public service. Both men appeared to welcome the challenge of developing modification of collective bargaining to the new frontier in the public sector. I left them with the understanding that they would discuss the possible association with the NEA with the partners of the firm and then contact me in Washington. Within a week or two, a working arrangement was consummated.

Bob Chanin, currently NEA general counsel, was associated with the Kaye, Scholer firm at the time. He left the firm to join the NEA staff as general counsel in 1968. He is now recognized as one of the nation's top authorities on collective bargaining in the public service field.

One of our first actions was to seek a meeting with Walter Reuther to find out how serious were his plans to organize teachers. We also wanted to remind him of the successful cooperation of the AFL-CIO and NEA on national legislation and the possible effects of his actions on its continuing. If feasible, we were prepared to explore new areas of cooperation on matters of mutual concern in lieu of continuing the competition for membership begun in New York City.

A luncheon meeting was scheduled at the Hay Adams Hotel in Washington to be attended by Walter Reuther and his administrative assistant, Jack Conway, Fred Livingston, Don Wollett, and me. To our disappointment, Reuther did not appear for the luncheon, ostensibly because of the pressures of a forthcoming convention of the AFL-CIO in Florida. Jack Conway told us that Reuther's interest was not centered on organizing teachers alone. He saw teachers as one segment of society, along with office workers, minorities, and other public employees, all of whom were involved in a common struggle for social and economic justice. He expressed the personal opinion that plans had progressed too far to be modified to exclude teachers. However, he said he would report our discussion to Reuther and advise us of his reaction.

A short time later, Fred Livingston attended the AFL-CIO convention in Florida and met Reuther during a stroll on the beach between meetings. As they walked together, Fred raised the same questions that we had discussed with Conway. Conway's opinion was confirmed. Reuther's plans were too far along to be changed. The battle for America's teachers had begun. New York City was to be the IUD's model for the nation.

Meanwhile, plans were moving ahead for a methodical effort to strengthen urban affiliates and to rebuild those that had become moribund. For several years, the National Association of Secretaries of State Teachers Associations (NASSTA) had operated an evaluation service for state affiliates. The new service for urban associations borrowed many of NASSTA's successful procedures for evaluating the state organizations, adapting them for use with urban affiliates. The procedures included creating a team of three to five leaders, usually with at least one urban president and one urban executive secretary. The balance of the team might include a leader of a state affiliate, an NEA staff member, or a person with a specialty deemed relevant to the problems of the association being evaluated.

The team made an on-the-site visit to the Association, where they invited members, officers, school officials, and community leaders to discuss with them the work of the organization and the degree to which it was serving the needs of members. Before the visit, forms developed by Urban Project leaders had been completed, giving a concise picture of the organization, its purposes, programs, structure, budget, governance, staff, and general method of operation.

After the visit, a hard-hitting, frank report including recommendations was delivered to the Association and reviewed with its officers by a member of the evaluation team. The report would remain with the Association as a guide for a local self-examination. Follow-up reports were made to keep the Urban Project informed of actions taken to implement the recommendations. The willingness of the Association to accept the recommendations of the evaluation team became the basis of NEA and state association financial support.

Prior to the 1962 Denver meeting of the Representative Assembly, a group of leaders of the urban executive secretaries met in St. Louis to plan their Denver activities. I was delighted to receive an invitation to attend, for it would give me an opportunity to let them know that the Urban Project was off to a running start. I had to win their support to launch the project and its program on a positive note at the Denver convention. I was well aware that this group had been eager to have one of its members head the Urban Project. Bogen expressed the group's feelings this way:

> The urban leaders' grapevine had been humming on the possibility of getting "one of their own" appointed to this new post [special assistant to the executive secretary for urban services]. . . . After all, they reasoned, who would know better how to cope with urban problems? . . . Contacts were made to urge the appointment of an urban oriented staff member to head the new program. When the announcement was made that West was to receive the new assignment, some concluded the urban forces had "won the battles, but lost the war."[20]

At the St. Louis meeting, I was able to report the engagement of a labor relations law firm, plans for the evaluation service, the employment of five staff members, the development of plans to promote state legislation for teacher–school board negotiation, and the existence of an urban task force to coordinate the services to urban affiliates by all NEA units.

Intense interest was expressed in the actions already taken, and a number of valuable recommendations for next steps emerged from the discussion. I left the meeting with the feeling that I had their support and that the Urban Project was beginning to gather momentum.

Dr. Carr's address to the Representative Assembly in Denver in the summer of 1962 was titled "The Turning Point." He recounted how the NEA had responded to four crises in this century, indicating its ability to change to meet new demands. He then described the new crisis of urbanization, the IUD's effort to unionize teachers, and charged the delegates to respond by:

1. Strengthening their local associations
2. Securing a written agreement on professional negotiations with their local school boards
3. Making sure each delegate understands and can explain to others "the difference between a professional association and a teachers' union and why the former is better"
4. Arranging local forums to make certain every member of the association represented at the convention understands why an independent profession is essential
5. Setting a timetable in each state for the achievement of unified, local, state, and national membership with unified collection of dues and a schedule of services and responsibilities at each level
6. Avoiding "unnecessary dissension at this critical time," stressing agreements, and "leaving this one-hundredth convention a militant and united force"

He then concluded his address with the following words:

In the long history of the National Education Association, there have been many occasions when Association policies were under vigorous and even bitter attack. This, however, is the first time in which forces of significant scope and power are considering measures which could destroy the Association. This is the turning point of 1962. This is the convention which must defend or surrender the independence of a profession, with all that this implies for the future of public education and American institutions. This defense is our clear duty, of course, but it is more than a duty. To maintain the professional independence of teaching is also a privilege, made all the greater because none of our predecessors has needed to put his shoulder beneath so heavy a burden.

If, at this hundred-year turning point, we succeed—and we shall not and cannot fail—our professions (unlike Robert Frost's "Hired Man") will have much to look backward on with pride; much to look forward to with hope.[21]

If there were any delegates who questioned Dr. Carr's statements about the IUD's intent to organize the nation's teachers, they only had to wait one day for confirmation direct from the mouth of the secretary treasurer of IUD, James A. Carey. Carey had been invited by President Ewald Turner to participate in a symposium as a representative of labor on the subject "Public Education Tomorrow." Other panel members were Charles A. Percy, then chairman of the board and chief executive of Bell and Howell, and Palmer Hoyt, editor of the *Denver Post*.

Carey began his address in a scholarly fashion. However, by the time he had reached the third page of his typewritten manuscript, he had some blunt words for teachers and the NEA. He said:

> I intend to be critical of the NEA and the teaching profession, and right there is that word "profession" as the best starting point.
>
> One of the prime troubles—if not the chief curse of the teaching industry, is precisely that word "profession." That term, as it is used so frequently here, implies that your craft is somewhat above this world of ours; it implies a detachment, a remoteness from the daily battle of the streets, in the neighborhoods and cities.

Carey went on to say that professionalism among newspapermen was too often used by "multimillionaire publishers as an excuse for paying low wages." When "they found that neither professionalism nor professional societies could save their jobs or the mortgages on their homes or pay for their kids' dental work," they joined unions and gained job security, higher salaries, stronger tenure, better pensions, more holidays, and severance pay better than most teachers have.

"The predicament of teachers today," he declared, "without unionism is not only economic; it is a predicament also of integrity. There is more and more evidence that teachers cannot afford integrity." . . . Pressure from big business and industry, including the preparation and the subsidy of textbooks, was resented by teachers but, in the most part, submitted to."

He disputed Dr. Carr's statement that $500,000 had been spent in New York City by AFL-CIO unions, calling it "a ninety percent exaggeration."

Carey concluded his speech with the following comparison of the treatment of school charwomen and teachers:

> And if I sound shocked because the charwomen in some high schools get a higher rate of pay than the high school teachers, understand it comes from the heart. And if the charwomen in the high schools have more tenure in their jobs and more security than the high school teachers, to me it is a shocking disclosure of the method in which we pay our reward. Or if the charwomen of the schools have sense enough to band together and organize and negotiate contracts, and the teachers do not, I wonder sometimes who should have the degrees.[22]

It is not surprising that Carey's address received more attention in the press than those of his two colleagues at the symposium, who spoke to the topic assigned. This was obviously Carey's calculated intent—to exploit his opportunity by speaking over the heads of the delegates to all teachers through the press, radio, and TV.

One result that may not have been calculated, however, was the effect of his address on the delegates. It was generally given credit for assuring

passage of a new and stronger resolution on the right of teachers to negotiate with boards of education through their "professional" association.

The resolution passed in 1961 in Atlantic City was entitled "Teacher–
Board of Education Relationships."

While teachers had for years carried on a wide variety of procedures to
negotiate with their employing boards, they had felt little need to define a
standard procedure and give it a label until the Wisconsin law was passed
making collective bargaining legal for teachers and other public employees. A strong feeling was held by teachers, school boards, and many
industrial relations authorities that the industrial term "collective bargaining" should not be attached to the process applied in the public sector
because the conditions in private industry and public service were so different.

The Taylor Committee, in its New York City report, referred to the
process not as collective bargaining but "collective negotiation." The
committee's report said: "It is much too early to be dogmatic about anything in the field of employer-employee relations in the public service because we know too little about it." There existed, among educators especially, a resistance to the use of the legal and governmental channels for
the administration of the labor law. The chief reason for this was the fear
that those who administered the labor law held union stereotypes and
possibly pro-union prejudices as a result of their experiences that would
make it difficult for them to distinguish between a professional organization and a labor union. More important, they saw the possible danger of
public administrators and courts applying precedents from industrial collective bargaining to the administration of the public sector—and specifically to school problems—which may require added insights and specialized knowledge.

As a result of these concerns, the search continued for a suitable label.
The first proposal to emerge was "cooperative determination." This was
rejected as being too academic or benign.

After consultation with state and local affiliates between the 1961
meetings in Atlantic City and the 1962 meeting, the NEA staff developed
a concept that was defined and given the label "professional negotiation".
It was developed under the leadership of Martha Ware and Jack Kleinmann working with the NEA's Field, Urban Project, and Professional
Rights and Responsibilities staffs.

The effort was motivated by an enthusiastic idealism. We were developing a procedure tailored to the unique relationships in education and
recognition of the special conditions existing in public-sector negotiations.
We were developing the "collective bargaining for the future" for public
employees.

The resolution on negotiation passed by the 1962 Representative Assembly in Denver was titled "Professional Negotiation." That was the first time the term had appeared in an NEA official publication.

Strikes and Sanctions

In the early 1960s, strikes and sanctions were popular topics of discussion among educators. The New York City campaign by UFT-IUD was designed to demonstrate the efficacy of the strike. The problem was that few school systems had the political conditions that existed in New York and made the strike appear to be effective. It was not the strike but the ability to influence the decisionmakers that led to the victorious result. However, to those not close to the situation, what was communicated was the impression of the invincibility of the strike. But New York City was a showcase, selected and staged for the purpose, and it was an effective showcase at the time.

There were three views expressed on the strike at the Denver convention. All were by leaders with stature and influence with the delegates. Dr. Carr stated in his address: "I think I can say on your behalf to school boards, as well as to parents and other citizens: the members of the National Education Association, whatever others may do, will constantly strive to improve their qualifications and the quality of service they render; they will keep their pledged word; and *they will never walk out on the students in their charge*" [emphasis added].[23] This statement was applauded by the delegates.

Later in the discussion of the Resolution on Professional Negotiation, the Connecticut delegation proposed a substitute that would have the effect of adopting a "no strike" position, as opposed to the proposal submitted by the resolutions committee. The committee's proposal included the following statement: "The seeking of consensus and mutual agreement on a professional basis *should* preclude the arbitrary exercise of unilateral authority by boards of education and the use of the strike by teachers." The Connecticut delegation's proposal would, among other changes, substitute the word "must" for the word "should" in the resolution proposed by the committee.

Dr. Fred Hipp, executive secretary of the New Jersey Education Association, had expressed his position on the strike in a previous discussion:

> Since 1944, the New Jersey Education Association has provided its teachers with a professional program of field service to appear before boards of education on behalf of teachers' salaries, welfare benefits, and to settle grievances of one type or another. We have 18 years of experience in negotiating with boards

of education. . . . I would like to emphasize throughout the years we have been able to help resolve problems between teachers and boards of education because we could operate flexibly and perform as occasion demanded. We wish to continue to have this right in the future.

On several occasions, we were called in after the local association had decided to strike. . . . Much as we regretted the conditions which brought this about and the injustices which caused our several local associations to resort to direct action, no strike endured more than two days. . . . We want the freedom to call upon the NEA for assistance in difficult situations, and we want the NEA to be free to come in and help—without being bound by a restrictive resolution which could deny that privilege to our national office.[24]

When the Connecticut substitute proposal came before the assembly, Dr. Hipp again took the floor to oppose what would be the equivalent of a "no strike" position for NEA. Speaking for the New Jersey delegation, he continued: "I would like to point out to the Representative Assembly that the adoption of this particular paragraph could make it impossible for the NEA to work effectively in certain tense situations. . . . We should like to have freedom to act in those situations. I urge you to vote against this substitute resolution."

This statement was also greeted with applause from the delegates. Many could identify with Dr. Hipp's position. They did not want to be placed in a position in which they would be prevented from going to the aid of a local affiliate that was in trouble. And it would be difficult to say to the leaders of a local affiliate—even though they may have been mistaken in going on strike—"Sorry, you're on your own." The Connecticut proposal was defeated, and NEA was on record as making every effort to avoid strikes but not specifically opposing their use.

The third speaker on the strike issue was Dr. Arthur Corey, executive secretary of the California Teachers Association. He had spoken to an open meeting of the Educational Policies Commission, and a number of the delegates who heard the presentation requested President Ewald Turner to permit all delegates to hear Dr. Corey's views on a topic of vital concern.

At the third business session, the president asked for and received the delegates' unanimous consent to have Corey address the Assembly. "To strike or not to strike," said Corey, "is no longer an academic question." Between 1941 and 1961, there had been 105 teacher strikes in the United States, not including "the recent unpleasantness" in New York City. Substantial data, available on only fourteen of the strikes, indicated, he said, the loss of 7,691,400 pupil days of school.

Corey denied that the strike could be separated from the balance of the collective-bargaining process. "No matter how much sheep's clothing we wrap around the wolf, the fangs are still present under the masquerade," he said.

He declared: "The strike, as a weapon for attaining economic and professional ends by teachers, is first, inappropriate; second, unprofessional; third, illegal; fourth, outmoded; and fifth, ineffective."

Corey then discussed each of his five arguments in some detail, pointing out under the first heading that the strike, while appropriate in the private sector because it can impose financial losses on the employer, actually saves money in the public service. Moreover, he argued, "it is axiomatic that in civilized society the integrity and continuity of government must be maintained."

Referring to his second point, Corey maintained that "professional ends may not be attained by unprofessional means." Holding that a professional's first obligation is to the pupil, he said, "Teachers cannot hope to gain professional ends by using children as pawns in the struggle."

To support his argument on the illegality of the strike, he quoted legal scholars and the teachers' obligation to uphold the law as an example to students.

On the strike as an outmoded technique, Corey quoted Adlai Stevenson's comment following the steel strike of 1959–1960 in which he branded the strike as "irresponsible private power which endangered our beleaguered society." He also quoted George Meany, president of the AFL-CIO, and George W. Taylor, a director of the American Arbitration Association, on the need for guidelines and new social inventions to avoid a repetition of such costly struggles.

Finally, Corey recognized the need for a more effective alternative to the strike by which teachers' organizations faced with unsatisfactory conditions could appeal to public opinion—the ultimate arbiter. He recommended that "a system of professional sanctions be instituted by which the collective influence, not of just a local group but of the whole profession—state-wide and nation-wide—be brought to bear upon a school district which refuses to correct unsatisfactory conditions in its schools."

Corey concluded his presentation with a description of a sanctions action against the Little Lake School District in Los Angeles County then in force by the California Teachers Association. Describing the procedures used in that case, he said a local unit may request the imposition of sanctions. The state association would then study the causes of the action and make recommendations for correction, and then allow a reasonable time for corrective action by local school authorities. After the foregoing procedures had been exhausted, if conditions had not been corrected, the personnel standards commission of the state association, could recommend to the association's board of directors that sanctions be applied to the district.

The state association by this action declares officially that conditions in such a district are not conducive to professional service of its teachers. The information is distributed widely through the news media, the placement service of the association is denied to the district, and all private placement services are notified of the sanctions and the reasons why such action was taken.

So persuasive was Corey's presentation that the Assembly passed the following resolution on professional sanctions.[25]

> The National Education Association believes that, as a means for preventing unethical or arbitrary policies or practices that have a deleterious effect on the welfare of the schools, professional sanctions should be invoked. These sanctions would provide for appropriate disciplinary action by the organized profession.
>
> The National Education Association calls upon its affiliated state associations to cooperate in developing guidelines which would define, organize, and definitely specify procedural steps for invoking sanctions by the teaching profession.[26]

The Denver convention was, in fact, a turning point. It dissipated much of the reluctance, apathy, and outright opposition to the use of formal negotiation procedures by teachers. The Assembly passed Resolution 18, which insisted on the right of local teachers' associations to negotiate with their school boards on policies of common concern, including salaries and other conditions of professional service. It included a provision for appeal through educational channels when agreement could not be reached, and it called upon NEA members and school boards to seek state legislation that would clearly and firmly establish these rights for the teaching profession.

Local affiliates were urged to return home and, together with their school boards, formalize those negotiation procedures already in use by preparing written documents recognizing the right of teachers to negotiate with their employers and outlining the procedures by which the negotiation should take place. Further, local affiliates were requested to file copies of the signed agreements with the NEA.

Immediately following the Denver meeting, the Urban Project staff returned to Washington and began developing a prototype state statute appropriate for implementing the policy adopted by the Assembly. The purpose of the statute was to serve as a guide for state affiliates in preparing proposals to the forthcoming meetings of their state legislatures.

The "model bill" contained a complete procedure, including: a preamble expressing the general policy of shared responsibility by employer and employee for the success of the school program and recognition of the right of teachers to participate in the formulation of school policies; a section on definition of terms; provision for the fair administration of the act by a state educational services board; a section that spelled out the rights of professional educators to participate through organizations of their own choice; rules of procedure defining unlawful acts; definition of negotiating units and nature of representation; provision for resolution of disputes; and provision for a grievance procedure.

State-Urban Conflict

In the fall of 1962, the executive secretaries of state education associations and the urban executive secretaries and elected officers held their annual meetings on the same dates in Miami Beach, Florida. This was not accidental. In their efforts to bring the problems of urban areas to NEA attention, some state leaders felt the state affiliates had been bypassed. The response of urban leaders was that they had been unable to secure the services and resources needed from the state associations, so they were forced to appeal to the NEA.

Since the new demands on the Association required the combined resources of all three levels, the leaders of both groups were encouraged to hold the meetings at the same time and place. To help improve relationships, some joint meetings were planned and free-time activities were scheduled to provide opportunities for informal interaction.

Some progress was made at Miami, but feelings were so strong that it was obvious more time would be required to heal all of the wounds. A number of urban leaders considered the state executive secretaries conservatives whose sole interests were in state legislation. On the other hand, some state association executives looked upon the urban leaders as troublemakers whose activities were inimical to the primary concerns of members of the state associations.

One anomalous incident occurred in Miami. The progressive California Teachers Association (CTA) recognized the need to strengthen its affiliate in Los Angeles. The local affiliate was an all-inclusive organization enrolling as members all professional personnel. The CTA felt, given the climate in 1962 and the prospects of competition for exclusive representation, that a unit of classroom teachers only would give them greater strength. The local affiliate insisted on remaining all-inclusive and criticized the state association for interfering in the internal affairs of the local. Los Angeles leaders asked for the support of their urban colleagues to resist the state association's action. To complicate matters, the executive secretary of the Los Angeles local affiliate was a former NEA staff member and a leader in the urban movement. Failing to persuade the local association to reorganize, the CTA had proceeded to organize a competing Los Angeles Association composed exclusively of classroom teachers. This became one of the hottest issues at the Miami meeting, and it split the urban group wide open. After much debate, the matter was disposed of by appointing a team of five urban leaders to make an on-the-site investigation of the Los Angeles situation and make a report of their findings. This committee, which had hoped to produce unity, failed to achieve its objective. The effect of the investigation was to give tacit approval to the CTA plan to organize a classroom teacher unit in Los Angeles.

Model Negotiation Bill

We decided the Miami meeting would be an appropriate place to unveil the "model bill" for professional negotiation. Since the state association executive secretaries were the chief legislative advocates in the states, Don Wollett and I felt the logical forum in which to introduce the proposed statute would be at their meeting. Don Wollett made the presentation. He stressed the content of the preamble, which expressed the common aims and obligations of both employee and employer. Then he presented the proposed statute section by section. The bill included all the elements of a collective bargaining bill plus the guiding philosophy of the professional negotiation procedure advocated by the Association.

When he finished, the fireworks began. The measure had few supporters and many vocal critics, who asked for a commitment from us that the proposed bill not be presented to any other group and that it be marked "for discussion only" and buried in a well-secured file in the second basement of the NEA headquarters building.

So concerned were they that a committee was appointed to meet with Executive Secretary Carr and members of the Urban Project staff in Washington the following week to reinforce their concerns.

At the meeting, after the committee had made its presentation, Dr. Carr and I both assured the committee members that the proposed statute would be used with discretion and explained our desire to provide resources in advance of their perceived needs rather than the opposite.

Within the following three years, all of the members of the committee had requested copies of the model statute for their use in drafting bills to be presented to their state legislatures.

The Movement for State Negotiation Laws

One fact sustained us during the early days of negotiation for teachers. All the evidence indicated that teachers overwhelmingly favored it. Opinion surveys by the NEA Research Division revealed this support. Reports from the field staff also showed widespread teacher support. It was just a matter of weeks and months in most states for this message to influence the decisionmakers. As might be expected, states with large industrial cities were in the vanguard. The movement to formalize negotiation procedures that began with the 1962 Denver convention was to provide much of the impetus for the achievement of negotiation statutes in thirty-one states by 1980.[27]

Some of the early laws limited the coverage to public school personnel. As experience was gained, however, the trend was toward state laws covering all public employees, including teachers. Two factors accounted for the trend. First, teachers' associations found they could secure fair treatment from the public administration agencies. Second, the added support of other public employees could be helpful in securing the approval of the governors and state legislatures to get the proposed laws enacted.

By 1965, ten state negotiation laws had been enacted and more than 350 formal negotiation agreements had been filed with the NEA. As we began to get experience under the laws and agreements, problems appeared. The problems arose in situations in which some school personnel held membership in an NEA affiliate and some were members of an AFT affiliate. In such cases, procedures had to be agreed upon for selecting one organization to speak for all school personnel. The NEA took the position that certified membership records should show which organization represented the largest number of school personnel. The AFT consistently asked for an election. This was the usual procedure under collective bargaining in the private sector. Also, it gave an advantage to the minority organization—usually the AFT group. A referee called in from the American Arbitration Association or from some other source would fix the rules. This customarily resulted in an election.

The next question to arise was who would be eligible to vote in the election. The NEA took the position that all professional personnel should vote. The AFT attempted to restrict eligibility to classroom teachers. This would eliminate a large segment of NEA members, including all central office administrators, and school principals. Generally, all personnel with any supervisory authority or authority to evaluate teacher performance were declared ineligible to vote.

This result was not influenced only by precedents borrowed from private-sector collective bragaining. A concurrent force was developing from the school boards and school superintendents. School boards generally rejected the "dual role" concept for the superintendent and insisted his role be restricted to executive officer of the board. In turn, superintendents, feeling isolated, insisted that principals also be removed from the negotiating unit.

The NEA was forced to give some consideration to what these developments might mean for the future of the organization. To assist in the analysis, we invited a few of the top authorities in the fields of economics, public administration, labor, and industrial relations to attend a two- or three-day informal "think session" in Washington's Shoreham Hotel.

The authorities were Dr. George Shultz, then dean of the School of Economics, University of Chicago, who served as chairman; Dr. Charles M. Rehmus, co-director of the Institute of Labor and Industrial Relations, Ann Arbor, Michigan; and Dr. John Dunlop, professor of industrial relations at Harvard Business School. NEA participants were Executive Secretary William G. Carr; Allan M. West, assistant executive secretary for Field and Urban Services; T. M. Stinnett, assistant executive secretary for Professional Development and Welfare; Arnold Wolpert, director of Urban Services; and Frederick R. Livingston and Donald H. Wollett of Kaye, Scholer, Fierman, Hays, and Handler, NEA's legal counsel.

The discussions were informal. There were no prepared speeches. For two full days, we picked the brains of the experts; secured their views on the limits of our ability to make adaptations in the collective-bargaining process to make it fit the unique conditions of the public sector; and received their judgments on the likely impact of collective bargaining on the NEA. No group conclusions were formulated, but NEA staff members left the conference with a clearer understanding of our limitations in attempting to adapt the collective-bargaining process to then-existing NEA policy. We found little encouragement for our efforts to broaden the bargaining unit to include middle-management school personnel, but we were encouraged to consider streamlining the Association structure. We realized we were irrevocably committed to a process likely to make substantial changes in the traditional relationships among school personnel and the character of the NEA. We were also certain that the NEA's survival as the dominant voice for American teachers depended upon our ability to win the representation elections and outnegotiate the AFT.

Between January 1, 1963, and June 30, 1965, representation elections were held in thirty-six school systems involving 51,000 eligible voters. While NEA affiliates won 23 and AFT won 13, the number of votes cast for each organization was almost equal—22,500 for NEA affiliates and 21,600 for AFT affiliates.

Milwaukee

Because of their strategic character and timing, further information on two of these contests may be helpful—one that the NEA won and one that it lost. The first large city selected for organizing by the IUD after New York City was Milwaukee, Wisconsin. As indicated earlier, the Wisconsin legislature had passed a negotiation law that was probably a large factor in the selection. The Milwaukee school system had a teaching staff of 4300. Nicholas Zonorich, IUD director of organization, was assigned to run the Milwaukee campaign. The AFT had organized the Milwaukee Vocational School with a staff of about 250 in the summer of 1963 as a warmup for the campaign to organize the city schools.

The leaders of the NEA affiliate, the Milwaukee Teachers Education Association (MTEA), were Eileen Cantwell, president, and Don Baer, executive secretary. The NEA state affiliate, the Wisconsin Education Association (WEA), named Ed Gollnick and NEA assigned John Carlson and Dick Dashiell to Milwaukee to serve as advisers to the local officers. Gollnick was a WEA field staff member, and Carlson and Dashiell were members of the NEA urban and field staff. Campaign funds were provided by the NEA, WEA, and MTEA in proportions agreed upon in advance.

The decision to have the campaign run by the local officers proved to be a wise one in contrast to the IUD campaign run by a nonresident and noneducator, Zonorich.

The MTEA campaign emphasized local control and branded the union campaign as a self-serving campaign by Walter Reuther to use teachers to solve the problems of organized labor. When Reuther appeared to address a citywide meeting organized by the AFT-IUD campaign director, it was interpreted by Milwaukee teachers as a confirmation of the MTEA campaign charge. MTEA leaders urged members to boycott the Reuther address, which was scheduled on the day before the balloting. As a result, only 325 teachers attended.

Eileen Cantwell and Don Baer were tough, effective leaders. Both had a keen understanding of the city, the school system, and the problems faced daily by teachers in the Milwaukee classrooms.

In one respect, conditions in Milwaukee were the reverse of those in New York City. In New York, the NEA was the outsider. In Milwaukee, IUD bore that disadvantage.

The NEA won the election 2,250 to 1,650. Stanley Elam later sized up the national picture in an article for *The Nation*:

> The Milwaukee election, won by the NEA after a wicked battle, may turn out to be the most significant of the recent series, in which the AFT won only four out of eleven . . . but got representation rights for nearly 11,000 teachers, including 10,000 in Detroit. To the NEA's total of 7,000, Milwaukee is significant because it proved the wealthy AFL-CIO Industrial Union Department to be relatively ineffective in influencing teachers. The IUD poured money and men (including Walter Reuther) into the campaign, but only about 200 teachers switched to the union camp.
>
> Milwaukee suggests that the NEA can, if it continues to accelerate its current program, eliminate the AFT except in the largest cities where unionism is a way of life. There is little doubt that NEA means to do just that.[28]

The Milwaukee victory was a morale booster for Association leaders, but there was little time to savor the victory. Other contests loomed in a half-dozen cities selected by the unions as being most vulnerable.

Philadelphia

Having won the Milwaukee election, the NEA expected to win in Philadelphia as well. The old-guard leadership had been replaced by young and attractive leaders. Marion Steet, an intelligent, articulate teacher, had just been elected president. The members of the new executive committee were enthusiastic and representative of the ethnic composition of the city.

Walter O'Brien, an able staff member of the New Jersey Education Association, was named executive secretary. John Carlson, who had given effective leadership in Milwaukee, represented the NEA on the Philadelphia campaign team.

The campaign went well in the early stages and was timed to peak just before the election date.

The Philadelphia Teachers Association (PTA) had 4,400 members and the Philadelphia Federation of Teachers (PFT) 3,400. The campaign was well financed, and the morale of the staff and officers was high.

The Philadelphia election was a bitter battle. Efforts were made to exploit racial prejudice and religious differences. Campaign materials were modified to change their meaning, and malicious charges were made against individuals. The chief campaign theme of the AFT went like this: The NEA has been in the majority in Philadelphia for many years, and conditions in the schools have deteriorated; now it is time to give the AFT a chance. An effort was also made to appeal to black teachers by charging the NEA with racism for tolerating dual affiliates in some southern states.

An incident occurred during the final week of the campaign that could have made the difference between success or failure for the NEA. A letter purportedly from Martin Luther King, Jr., was read at a public meeting, praising organized labor and collective bargaining and giving implied support to the AFT in the election. NEA leaders who had known and worked with Dr. King were first shocked, then suspicious that the letter was a fake. Their efforts to reach Dr. King were delayed. When they did reach him, they found he knew nothing of the letter but said he would look into the matter. Meanwhile, the election was over and the damage had been done. It was learned shortly after the election that the letter had been authorized by Dr. King's assistant, the Reverend Andrew Young, in Dr. King's absence.

Twelve years later, NEA was to endorse Andrew Young for election to a congressional seat from Georgia. Such are the vicissitudes of politics.

Status of Collective Bargaining

Earlier in this chapter, I reviewed some questions confronting the Association as it attempted to develop a negotiation structure appropriate for use by teachers and school boards. Several of those problem areas are still major concerns; on others, substantial progress has been made.

One of the early problems involved the role of school administrators. Should they be members of the same bargaining unit as teachers and other personnel whom they supervised? Early experience removed the top administrators, but the most difficult problem centered on the principals, vice-principals, department heads, deans, and other middle management.

This question is now largely resolved. The trend in recent years has been to separate units for administrators in those states which extend bargaining rights to administrators. Several recent statutes, including those of Oregon, and Rhode Island, exclude supervisors from coverage entirely.[29]

Exclusive recognition, a disputed issue in the early days of collective bargaining in education, is now generally accepted. The California collective-bargaining statute initially provided for bargaining councils composed of representatives of more than one employee organization. It was later (in 1975) amended to provide for exclusive representation. According to Chanin, exclusive representation is now "almost as well accepted in the public sector as in the private sector."[30]

As previously mentioned, there is a strong trend toward state bargaining statutes covering all public employees rather than restricting coverage to teachers only.

Answering the question what subjects should be bargainable has involved some problems and will probably continue to do so in the foreseeable future. There was wide variation in the "scope of bargaining" in the early statutes covering teachers. The Washington law provided for bargaining on curriculum, textbook selection, in-service training, student-teacher programs, personnel, hiring and assignment practices, leaves of absence, salaries and salary schedules, and noninstructional duties. On the other hand, the Minnesota law limited collective bargaining to the "economic aspects relating to terms of employment." Provisions of the other statutes fell between these two extremes.

Recent statutes, according to Chanin, have tended to use the language of the National Labor Relations Act—"wages, hours, and other terms and conditions of employment"—or some similar phrase. The problem now is to determine what subjects can reasonably come within the limits of "terms and conditions of employment."[31]

While this problem is common to both private and public employment, it is highly probable that teachers would have an interest in a broader range of subjects than would be found among most employees in private employment. "Experience in the private sector," says Chanin, "indicates the problem probably will have to be dealt with on a case by case basis with judgments made in particular factual contexts."

In a 1969 study of four urban school systems, using thirty-seven subjects, one researcher found that there was greater agreement among school board members, school superintendents, and teachers on the bargainability of subjects classified as working conditions than on those classed as personnel policies or curriculum and instruction. The author also observed that two-thirds of school board members and superintendents thought more of the thirty-seven subjects *should* be negotiable than were then being negotiated. This suggests that teacher organizations desiring a broader range of subjects eligible for negotiation should continue to press their cases with employers.[32]

Another problem relating to the scope of bargaining is the existence of separate statutes that contain specific provisions dealing with subjects that are clearly bargainable under the collective-bargaining act. In such cases, how shall the conflict be resolved? Which statute shall take precedence? These questions have yet to be resolved. While the courts have rendered decisions in specific cases, no guides for general application have yet emerged. Accordingly, this matter will probably continue to be a source of difficulty.

The Right to Strike

Some representatives of teacher organizations continue to advance the argument that denying teachers the right to strike, while recognizing the right of private employees to strike, violates standards of equal protection under the Fourteenth Amendment.

It has also been argued that strikes by some public employees have a much more serious impact on the public than others. For example, Burton and Krider argue that strikes in such "essential services" as the police and fire departments should be considered illegal, while those engaged in less essential services should be allowed to strike in the same manner and for the same reasons as in the private sector.[33]

Despite these arguments, state laws that uniformly prohibit teacher strikes have consistently been upheld by the courts as constitutional.

The most significant progress in litigation recently, according to Chanin, is in the issuance of court injunctions. The first significant case was a Holland, Michigan, case before the Michigan Supreme Court in 1968. In that case the court sustained the constitutionality of the law banning strikes but said a judge should not as a matter of course issue an injunction, even though the law had been violated.

In returning the case for further action, the supreme court directed the trial court to inquire whether the school board had refused to bargain in good faith as charged by the teachers' association. If so, the court said, consideration would be given to whether an injunction should be issued at all, on what terms, and for what period, based on the complete record. Some courts have accepted this approach. Others continue to issue injunctions based only on the illegality of the strike.[34]

The participation in illegal strikes by teachers and teacher organizations in recent years has involved heavy fines and the jailing of teachers and organization leaders, and has caused serious cleavages between strikers and nonparticipants.

Impasse Resolution

An important feature of most state bargaining laws is that which defines some mechanism for resolving disputes short of a strike.

The early statutes included some type of mediation in which a neutral mediator assisted the two parties to reach agreement. If this failed, the matters in dispute were referred to "advisory arbitration" or "fact finding with recommendations." This process resulted in a recommendation of a neutral third party, which might or might not be acceptable to both parties. If the recommended settlement was not accepted, the teachers' only alternative was to engage in an illegal strike.

Experiences in the past decade have brought forth some new procedures. Some state laws provide for mandatory binding arbitration. One state, Nebraska, refers impasses to an industrial commission for binding decision. A Nevada law authorizes the governor to make binding the advisory recommendations of a fact finder. Other statutes encourage but do not require that such procedures be used.

A provision of a 1975 Iowa statute has initiated some experimentation with a variation of the arbitration process known as "final offer selection arbitration." It is designed to dissipate the chief objection to arbitration— that it reduces the incentive of the parties to make concessions in the regular course of negotiations which could weaken their position later if referred to an arbitrator.

"Final offer selection arbitration" limits the options of the arbitrator. He must select the final position of one party or the other and cannot propose a compromise settlement at some point between the two positions. This method encourages the parties to refrain from taking extreme stands.

Chanin describes a procedure used in Hawaii known as "med-arb" in which the mediator attempts to have the parties reach agreement voluntarily on as many disputed items as possible but has the power to make decisions on those remaining.[35]

The trend in 1980 is toward some form of arbitration for resolving impasses. Continued experience and experimentation will undoubtedly lead to the sharpening of present techniques and the invention of other alternatives for resolving disputes short of going on strike.

State Laws

The Vermont legislature approved a bill in 1969 that allows a teacher strike to be enjoined only if it can be demonstrated that the strike poses a clear and present danger to a sound program of school education and that preventing it would be in the public interest.

In 1970, statutes were enacted in Pennsylvania and Hawaii extending the right to strike to public employees, including teachers, under certain conditions. The Pennsylvania law permits the court to issue an injunction only if it can be shown that a strike "poses a clear and present danger or threat to the health, safety, or welfare of the public. The Hawaii statute refers only if it is found that there is 'imminent or present danger to the public health or safety.' " It also provides that public employees may strike after other statutory procedures have been exhausted. Oregon, Minnesota, and several other states also legalize strikes under certain circumstances. Montana is the only state in which public employees have a virtually unlimited right to strike.[36]

There were thirty-one states with some type of collective-bargaining law covering teachers in 1980. The provisions of the laws vary widely. Each state has adapted its statute to what the legislature perceived to be the needs of that particular state or, perhaps more likely, how far the legislature could be pursuaded to go toward the achievement of an adequate collective-bargaining law. The result is a patchwork of laws varying both in quality and uniformity of their provisions. This explains why the NEA and public employee organizations have proposed a federal statute that would establish a basic national right for teachers and other public employees to bargain with their employers under a more uniform and adequate set of procedures.

Organizational Security

Organizational security clauses in a collective-bargaining contract protect the employee organization against employees who are willing to share in the benefits of negotiation but unwilling to share the cost of the service.

In private employment, employees are often required to become members of the employee organization as a condition of employment. While not completely unknown in public employment, this concept has not been widely accepted. The agency shop is generally favored in the public sector. It does not require membership in the employee organization but does require the payment of an amount equal to the membership dues or a fee sufficient to cover the organization's per capita cost of representing the employee in the negotiation process.

Agency shop clauses do not exist in those states having "right to work" laws. Even in those states that do not have "right to work" laws, several questions have been raised on the agency shop provisions in teacher collective-bargaining contracts. It has been charged that the agency shop violates state "right to work" laws, which exist in almost half of the states; that it interferes with an employee's right to refrain from participating in organizational activities; that it would be unlawful to enforce by discharging employees who do not comply; and that it unlawfully encourages membership in the employee organization.

Attempts have been made to surmount some of these objections, Chanin points out, by promoting legislation that explicitly authorizes the agency shop; by recognizing an employee's right to refrain from joining the employee organization; or by limiting the agency shop fee to the actual costs of representation in collective bargaining. Problems remain with organizational security clauses, however, and challenges can be expected in the future both to their legality and to the appropriateness of the concept as a matter of public policy.

Federal Collective-Bargaining Bill

Executive Secretary Sam Lambert, in his report to the 1969 Representative Assembly, announced that an NEA-developed federal teacher–school board negotiation act had been unveiled in the U.S. Senate on April 19, 1969, by Senator Lee Metcalf (D., Montana). "If enacted," he said,

> this bill will set forth an entire new field for teacher–school board negotiations.
>
> I will admit right off that the bill legalizes the work stoppage in education.
>
> But on the other hand, it forces the parties to a dispute to go through both mediation and fact-finding to reduce the danger of deadlock and massive confrontation and the resulting injury to education.
>
> In my opinion, the bill will reduce rather than increase the number of strikes in education. But more important, it will provide for teachers a meaningful role in policy development and an opportunity to make their influence felt in the whole range of educational decision making.
>
> Lest there be some misunderstanding, NEA firmly supports professional negotiations for our own welfare and for the good of education generally.[37]

The 1969 bill covered only school personnel. Subsequent bills have included all public employees, including teachers.

In 1968, when the original NEA proposal was drafted, the U.S. Supreme Court had just issued a decision in the case of *Maryland* v. *Wirtz*. That decision involved the constitutionality of the 1966 amendment to the Fair Labor Standards Act. The Court rejected the challenge, which argued that the act's provisions broadening the minimum wage and maximum hour provisions to certain employees of public institutions, including schools, infringed upon states' rights in violation of the Tenth Amendment to the Constitution.

The Court rejected the claims of the plaintiffs and sustained the amendments as a valid exercise of congressional power under the Commerce Clause. It appeared that this decision opened the way for federal intervention into other aspects of the employer-employee relationship. Consequently, the NEA and other public employee organizations filed bills and organized lobbies to promote the enactment of a federal statute that would extend collective-bargaining benefits to public employees.

Since the decision in *Maryland* v. *Wirtz*, the Supreme Court decided two additional cases involving this issue: *National League of Cities* v. *Usery* and *State of California* v. *Usery*. In these cases, the Supreme Court held that Congress had exceeded its authority under the Commerce Clause and overruled *Maryland* v. *Wirtz*.

Thinking that this action by the Court would appear to offer slight hope for the enactment of the pending collective-bargaining bills, which might be considered to intrude into states' rights to a greater extent than the provisions rejected by the Court in the *League of Cities* case, employee organizations have reconsidered their previous proposals. The NEA decided to modify its proposal to make it constitutionally acceptable without sacrificing its effectiveness in achieving collective bargaining for teachers.

Problem areas involved the right to strike, possible conflicts with state laws, such as those dealing with retirement and tenure, that fell within the definition of the scope of bargaining under the National Labor Relations Act (NLRA) and impasse procedures.

Chanin believes that the revised NEA proposal deals with the three problem areas. He contends that the proposal would not violate the principles expressed by the court in the *League of Cities* case, and would still provide an adequate collective-bargaining procedure for teachers.[38]

The effect of passage of the NEA bill would be to extend to all teachers in the nineteen states presently without a state negotiation law the right to engage in collective bargaining and would strengthen the bargaining rights of teachers in the thirty-one states having laws.

IMPACT OF COLLECTIVE BARGAINING ON THE NEA

Departure of National Affiliates

When the NEA decided to promote the enactment of state legislation governing employer-employee relations in the early 1960s, a continuing discussion on the role of school administrators began. This subject was a special concern of the American Association of School Administrators (AASA), an NEA national affiliate. At each convention of the AASA during the 1960s and early 1970s, this question was discussed. And at each discussion, the intensity of feeling was escalated to a higher level. Dr. Lyle Ashby and I represented the NEA in several of these sessions, taking the position that the education profession was sophisticated enough to be able to disagree on matters involved in the bargaining process and still cooperate on the many areas of common concern, such as state and federal school legislation, school public relations and matters involving the curriculum and instruction. However, as experience with collective bargaining was gained and superintendents of schools found themselves excluded from the bargaining unit, they asked why they should continue to be members of the Association or to continue as an NEA-affiliated organization.

The Constitutional Convention meeting in 1971–72 adopted new standards for the affiliation of national organizations, requiring that at least 75 percent of the members of the affiliated organization also be members of the NEA. After a decade of dialogue on the subject, the AASA held a referendum in 1972 and a majority of their members voted to delete all references to NEA affiliation from their governance documents. On January 16, 1973, I reported the AASA decision to the NEA Executive Committee. I also advised them of the intention of the AASA, the Association of Elementary School Principals, the National School Public Relations Association, the National Association of Education Secretaries, and other national affiliates to move their offices from the NEA headquarters building.

Although the new standards adopted by the Constitutional Convention and the limited office space were contributing factors in the decisions of the school administrator affiliates, the underlying cause of their disaffiliation was the adversary relationship inherent in the collective-bargaining process. The nonadministrator affiliates, however, were probably influenced more by other factors.

In recognition of the many common interests of the former affiliates and the NEA, an effort was made to make their departure an amicable separation rather than a divorce. This effort succeeded, and by 1975–1976 only four nongovernance national affiliates remained.

While there were losses from the breakup of the NEA family, the departure of these affiliates clarified the NEA's public image, simplified its organizational structure, and made it more efficient and easier to administer. It also made possible the development of a continuing relationship with the former affiliates on matters of mutual concern uncomplicated by membership and housekeeping problems.

Financial Requirements

Since 1957, NEA annual membership dues have increased—from ten to forty-two dollars. The Association budget has ballooned from $5 million in 1957 to $67 million in 1979–80—a thirteenfold increase.

The entry of the Association into collective bargaining has required the addition of 1,200 full time local and regional skilled personnel to train local leaders, develop information resources, organize representation elections, and perform a variety of other services necessary for local affiliates to accept their new responsibilities.

Legal services were required to assist associations to win bargaining rights, to resolve legal disputes with school boards and other employee organizations, and to protect the rights of members.

The NEA learned early that representation elections and crisis situations involved in collective bargaining require the accumulation of resources beyond those anticipated for the ongoing programs of the Association.

Relations with Affiliates

From the beginning, the strength of the NEA has been built on its nationwide network of strong state associations. With the advent of collective bargaining, the organizational center of gravity has shifted toward the local association. Such shifts always cause some relationship problems.

NEA Status as an Organization

The NEA was incorporated under a special act of Congress on June 30, 1906, as a nonprofit, charitable, tax-exempt association. Later, as the NEA became more assertive, the Internal Revenue Service (IRS) began to raise questions about the Association's eligibility to accept grants from private sources in view of its new thrust. The grants were being claimed by donors as tax-deductible contributions. Accordingly, by agreement with the IRS, the NEA agreed to give up its tax-exempt status under Section 501(C)(3) of the Internal Revenue Code and accept the classification of a Business League under Section 501(C)(6); it was subsequently classified under Section 501(C)(5) a Labor Organization. To continue to receive tax-deductible grants for special education projects, the Association in 1969 established the National Foundation for the Improvement of Education (NFIE) with an IRS classification under Section 501(C)(3).

In 1979, a legal action in the U.S. District Court for the District of Columbia held that the NEA must comply with the provisions of the Labor Management Reporting and Disclosure Act (Landrum-Griffin Act) unless it terminates forthwith all activities with regard to the representation of private-sector employees.

The U.S. Department of Labor had been making periodic investigations of the NEA's activities since 1963 and also those of some of NEA affiliates. When contacted by the Department of Labor, the NEA admitted it represented some employees in collective bargaining in private institutions but claimed exemption from the act on the basis that they comprised a negligible proportion of the total and should be exempt, under the legal maxim *de minimus non curat lex*. For example, the Iowa Education Association (ISEA), also a party to the recent court case, represents 32,000 employees in dealing with their employers, and of this number only 33, or one tenth of 1 percent, are private-sector employees. Nevertheless, the court ruled on January 12, 1979, that "the *de minimus* maxim was not applicable and ordered NEA and ISEA to comply with the Landrum Griffin Act 'unless they terminate forthwith all activities with regard to private sector employees.' "[39]

In seeking exemption from the provision of the Landrum Griffin Act, Executive Director Terry Herndon explained that the act had many desirable features to which the Association had no objection, but that certain restrictions imposed administrative burdens and limited the operational flexibility of the Association.

The most troublesome features concerned the NEA's guarantees to minority members and membership rights of certain paraprofessional members and education secretaries.

The NEA had guaranteed minority representation in the Representative Assembly at least equal to the proportion of identified ethnic minority populations in each state, and had various other minority guarantees in its governance operation. Some of these guarantees were rendered invalid by coverage under the Landrum Griffin Act and were modified. The Association has indicated that an effort will be made to encourage the minority representation as in the past although prevented from enforcing it. However, other minority guarantees for representation on committees and other nongovernance bodies were not affected.

Paraprofessional and education secretary members and associate members employed in school districts, colleges, and universities had not been extended the right to be delegates to the Representative Assembly or to seek and hold NEA office. Coverage under Landrum Griffin requires that these membership benefits be extended to all members in good standing, subject to "reasonable qualifications uniformly imposed." This language appears to extend these benefits to the foregoing personnel.

Despite the discomfort and change of status brought about largely by the Association's decision to engage in collective bargaining, it is my conviction that the decision was both beneficial and irreversible.

Some practitioners tend to overemphasize the importance of collective bargaining and to create unreasonable expectations. An orderly process for reaching agreement by educators was overdue—one that recognized the right of employees to participate as equals with their employers. But to be effective in delivering economic benefits, it must be accompanied by effective, well-organized, and well-financed legislative and political action programs in the state and national capitals, for collective bargaining takes place in the local communities, which are the level of government least able to respond to the financial needs of today's schools.

CHAPTER FIVE

Equality

The 1957 convention was held in Philadelphia, the city of the NEA's birth a century earlier. The occasion provided an opportunity to look back with pride and forward with hope. Dr. Carr selected as the topic for his annual report to the Representative Assembly "The Past Is Prologue."

After observing that prophecy is risky, he declared that in the NEA's first century the battle for quantity had been won. "Our frontier for the next twenty years," he said, "is quality. As *quantity* was the primary goal for the first century, so will *quality* be our chief aim for the second. We have been concerned that every child get into school. Now we must ask how much each child gets out of school." Among Dr. Carr's suggestions for achieving excellence were: more time for teachers to help individual children; better salaries for teachers with recognition for superior service; modification of what is taught and how it is taught; greater emphasis on music, art, and literature; improvement in the use of modern teaching materials; renewed diligence and skill in preparing for citizenship; and better financing of the schools.

A special centennial issue of the *NEA Journal* was published in which Dr. Francis S. Chase, chairman of the Department of Education, University of Chicago, was invited to express his dreams about what lay ahead for American public schools.

Dr. Edgar B. Wesley presented a 400-page centennial history of the NEA to President Martha Shull and related to the Assembly some interesting vignettes from the past.

The convention met three years after the Supreme Court decision in the case of *Brown* v. *Board of Education*. Yet Dr. Wesley's history made no reference to this landmark decision, which would plunge the schools into the center of a controversy that had not yet run its full course. And neither Dr. Carr nor Dr. Chase viewed desegregation of the schools as a problem worthy of mention as they attempted to visualize the shape of things to come for the NEA and the public schools in the first two decades of the second century.

The centennial issue of the *NEA Journal* did present a list of landmarks in American educational history, which included the 1954 Supreme Court decision, and the 1957 Representative Assembly adopted a resolution on integration in the public schools.

THE CLIMATE FROM 1954 TO 1964

To put the following discussions of actions of the Representative Assembly in context, it is necessary to recall the turmoil of the decade following the 1954 Supreme Court decision ruling that racially separate schools are inherently unequal and a violation of the Fourteenth Amendment.

1955. Eleven southern senators, on March 12, signed and presented to the Congress a paper that became known as "The Southern Manifesto," declaring the decision of the Supreme Court a clear abuse of judicial power.

The Supreme Court ordered that the 1954 decision be implemented "with all deliberate speed" on May 31.

At an emergency NAACP conference convened in Atlanta on June 4, branches in every state were authorized and urged to file petitions with school boards requesting prompt action to comply with the Supreme Court decision to achieve integration in September.

On November 7, the Court extended its desegregation ruling to cover public parks, playgrounds, and golf courses, and on November 25, the Interstate Commerce Commission ordered an end to segregation on interstate trains and buses.

The Alabama bus boycott occurred in December when Rosa Parks refused to move to a rear seat in a Montgomery bus.

1956. On March 7, a Virginia Constitutional Convention amended its state laws to permit the use of public funds for the payment of private school tuition fees.

The Supreme Court, in a case involving a black student who was denied admission to graduate school on racial grounds, ruled on March 12 that the University of Florida could not delay in admitting qualified blacks to such programs.

In a case resulting from the Rosa Parks incident, the Supreme Court, on December 13, ruled unconstitutional the Alabama law requiring blacks to occupy rear seats in public transportation facilities.

1957. Nine black children were scheduled to enter Central High School in Little Rock, Arkansas, on September 3, in accord with a desegregation plan worked out by the local school board in compliance with decrees of the local federal court. Governor Orval Faubus of Arkansas created a national issue by calling out the National Guard to frustrate the school board's plan. President Eisenhower responded by issuing an executive order authorizing the use of federal troops to enforce the federal court's order.

The U.S. Congress on September 9 enacted the Civil Rights Act of 1957, establishing a nonpartisan Civil Rights Commission to gather evidence on voting rights violations. The act also strengthened the civil rights provisions of the U.S. Code.

1958. On August 23, the chief justices of the state supreme courts adopted a motion critical of the trend of recent decisions of the U.S. Supreme Court, saying that such a trend threatened the concept of a "government of laws and not of men."

High schools in Little Rock were closed on September 12 by order of Governor Faubus. Classes were taught by television. The governor's action was in response to the refusal of the Supreme Court to approve a delay in the implementing of the school desegregation plan.

On October 5, an integrated Clinton, Tennessee, high school was demolished by explosives.

The U.S. Department of Health, Education, and Welfare released a report on December 1, indicating that one million school days were lost in 1958 because of schools closing to avoid desegregation.

1959. The schools of Norfolk and Arlington, Virginia, were integrated peacefully in compliance with the decision of the Virginia Supreme Court.

1960.   The sit-in became an accepted method of protest when, on February 1, four black students from the North Carolina Agricultural and Technological College staged a sit-in at a segregated lunch counter in Greensboro. This action led to the integration of lunch counters at chain stores in more than one hundred southern cities.

Efforts by blacks to desegregate the Biloxi, Mississippi, beaches on April 24 ended in a race riot.

President Eisenhower signed a Civil Rights Act on May 6, to strengthen the 1957 act by authorizing the federal judges to appoint referees to supervise voter registration.

1961.   Citizens in the District of Columbia received the right to vote for president and vice-president upon ratification of the Twenty-third Amendment by Kansas on April 3.

In May, "freedom riders" organized by the Congress of Racial Equality met with violence in Anniston, Birmingham, and Montgomery, Alabama. A bus was burned and a number of riders were injured. In Jackson, Mississippi, riders were arrested for disturbing the peace.

1962.   James Meredith was refused admission to the University of Mississippi on September 10, when Governor Ross Barnett had himself appointed university registrar and refused to obey a federal court order. On September 30, President Kennedy issued a proclamation demanding Mississippi's compliance, and under the protection of federal marshals, Meredith was enrolled.

1963.   The U.S. Supreme Court on February 25 overturned the convictions of 187 blacks arrested for disturbing the peace during a demonstration two years earlier in Columbia, South Carolina.

Martin Luther King, Jr., president of the Southern Christian Leadership Conference, led demonstrations in April and May protesting injustice toward black people in Birmingham. The use of fire hoses, tear gas, and police dogs against the demonstrators caused widespread indignation as demonstrations spilled over into other cities. President Kennedy provided the services of a mediator to assist in bringing about a peaceful resolution of the problem in Birmingham.

A confrontation similar to the Meredith case in Mississippi occurred in Alabama on June 11 when Vivian Malone and James Hood attempted to enroll at the University of Alabama. Governor Wallace attempted to block the enrollment but was frustrated in the effort by an order of the U.S. District Court.

Medgar Evers, NAACP field secretary, was assassinated in Jackson, Mississippi, on June 12.

Following the University of Alabama incident, on the evening of June 11, President Kennedy addressed the nation on television. The following excerpt from his address will help to recall the climate of the period:

> The fires of frustration and discord are burning in every city, North and South, where legal remedies are not at hand. Redress is sought in the streets, in demonstrations, parades, and protests which create tensions and threaten violence and threaten lives.
>
> We face, therefore, a moral crisis as a country and as a people. It cannot be met by repressive police action. It cannot be left to increased demonstrations in the streets. It cannot be quieted by token moves or talk. It is a time to act in the Congress, in your state and local legislative body and, above all, in all of our daily lives.
>
> It is not enough to pin the blame on others, to say this is a problem of one section of the country or another, or deplore the fact that we face. A great change is at hand, and our task, our obligation, is to make that revolution, that change, peaceful and constructive for all.
>
> Those who do nothing are inviting shame as well as violence. Those who act boldly are recognizing right as well as reality.[1]

The president went on to say he was asking the Congress to enact legislation giving all Americans the right to be served in public facilities, including hotels, restaurants, and theaters, retail stores, and similar establishments.

The legislation to which President Kennedy referred became the Civil Rights Act of 1964, enacted by Congress after his death.

1964. President Johnson declared his "War on Poverty" and submitted a comprehensive plan to Congress on January 8, designed to provide employment for youth, assistance to Appalachia, improved benefits for the unemployed, the organization of a national service corps, and the extension of other existing programs.

With the adoption of the Twenty-fourth Amendment by South Dakota, the poll tax was abolished on January 23.

The Civil Rights Act of 1964 was passed by Congress and signed by President Johnson on July 2.

Blaustein and Zangrando described passage of the Civil Rights Act as

> The most comprehensive piece of civil rights legislation ever proposed. A bipartisan majority had passed the bill in the House on February 10, and the nation watched with intense fascination as the Senate made the measure its chief order

of business for the next four months. On June 10, supporters of the bill rallied sufficient votes to choke off the extended southern filibuster. This was the first time since 1917, when the Senate had initially adopted rules for limited debate, that cloture was successfully invoked for a civil rights measure. Indeed, cloture had been voted only five other times, up to that point. The fact that northern Republicans were willing to abandon their traditional coalition with southern Democrats made cloture possible, and Senate Majority Leader Everett Dirkson of Illinois explained his party's action by proclaiming, "This is an idea whose time has come. It will not be stayed. It will not be denied."[2]

Such was the climate in which the NEA Representative Assembly struggled to deal fairly with the most important domestic problem to confront the nation and its school system. It was a struggle to give leadership for the achievement of school integration without sacrificing the unity of the organization in the process.

THE NEA AND SCHOOL DESEGREGATION

The 1957 resolution of the Delegate Assembly on school desegregation is significant, both for its content and for the actions of the assembly in dealing with it.

In 1954 the Assembly had adopted a general resolution that recognized integration to be a national problem of concern to all states; urged all citizens to approach the matter in the spirit of fair play, goodwill, and respect for law; and expressed confidence that all problems of integration of the schools are capable of solution at the state and local levels by reasonable, intelligent persons working together in the interests of national unity.

A similar resolution was adopted by the Representative Assemblies of 1955 and 1956. Amendments were proposed and defeated in 1955 to put the Association on record as approving and supporting the Supreme Court decision rather than simply expressing concern. In 1956, no substantial change was made.

Philadelphia—1957. The resolution was introduced by the Resolutions Committee for a fourth year at the 1957 convention, whose theme was "An Educated People Moves Freedom Forward."

When the resolution came up for consideration, George M. Snyder, a delegate from California, stated that he considered the matter of desegregation an important one and felt the Association should do something more than "passing an innocuous resolution and that we resolve as teachers to do something about it." He then proposed the following amendment:

> Believing that integration of all groups in the American public school is a part of the concrete task of that education which moves freedom forward, the Association recommends that all teachers assume special responsibility for study, discussion, interpretation and democratic action with regard to problems of group conflict; that state and local organizations serve as agents of reconciliation in the resolving of differences; and that the good offices of NEA and its departments be used in every possible way to promote the good will and understanding necessary to peaceful change.

Paul Whitehill of New York spoke in favor of the amendment saying "I , for one, do not wish us to ride the fence on this issue."[3]

At that point, Walter Eshelman of Pennsylvania was recognized by President Shull. As immediate past chairman of the Resolutions Committee, he asked the delegates to defeat the proposed amendment, giving three reasons: the resolution was passed at the three previous conventions; he personally felt, and believed that a large portion of the delegates felt, that this statement had been instrumental in holding the NEA together as a united force in the solving of a very perplexing problem in our society; and the problem of school integration was a national, not a regional problem, which involved several different minority groups. He closed with a personal appeal for defeat of the amendment.

The question was called for; the amendment was read and President Shull called for the vote.

The amendment failed.

Paul Whitehill then proposed a second amendment, to substitute five words for two words in the original resolution. The proposed change would have the effect of putting the NEA on record as seeking integrated schools in all states and territories of the nation. The motion was seconded by Gladys Belon of Oregon. George H. Deer of Louisiana, a member of the NEA Board of Directors, was recognized and made the following statement:

> I hope earnestly that this convention will not adopt this amendment, and I make my plea to you on this basis, that it will not help to solve the situation where it is most critical. May I say, while I am on the floor, that this problem is a serious one and the solution cannot be found in resolutions passed by national conventions. No outside resolution, no outside discussion can help. The truth is, they can do a great deal of harm. If you were in the midst of this problem, working with it, as many hundreds of people are trying to work, on the basis of good will, on the basis of professional concern, on the basis of educational commitment, then you would realize how much harm can be done by outside groups who do not really understand the problem.

The solution of this problem will have to come slowly, evolve gradually, be dealt with by the people who know it and understand it. I hope you will vote down this amendment.[4]

The amendment failed and the resolution as originally presented was approved.

Those who attended the annual meetings for the next four years were to hear a repetition of such discussions between those who sought a more aggressive role for the NEA in school desegregation and those who resisted NEA "interference" or honestly felt a more active role would divide the Association and weaken its ability to advance the common interests of members. However, as these debates continued, other events took place—in Congress, the courts, state legislatures, government offices, school board meetings, and the streets—that influenced members' opinions.

Cleveland—1958. The resolution adopted by the Representative Assembly in 1957, with minor technical changes, was introduced in 1958.

The delegates advocating a stronger position on school desegregation did not attempt to amend the resolution. However, on the final day of the convention, an item of New Business was introduced, proposing a study of the problems of integration, with a report to be presented to the 1959 meeting of the Representative Assembly in St. Louis. Since the proposal came near the close of the last business session, many delegates had left the hall. A quorum call was requested, delegations were polled, revealing the absence of a quorum, and the meeting was adjourned without taking action on the motion. So the resolution that had now been adopted by five meetings of the Assembly remained as the expression of NEA policy on school desegregation.

St. Louis—1959. Dr. Ruth Stout of Kansas became president of the NEA at the conclusion of the 1958 Cleveland convention. Having observed the growing intensity of feeling exhibited in the debates on desegregation, she moved to prepare the way for acceptance of the 1958 resolution by the 1959 Representative Assembly in St. Louis.

In her address to the Assembly at the first session, she read the resolution to the delegates, pointing out that it made it possible for the NEA to devote its full resources to the support of affiliates attempting, under difficult circumstances, to prevent the closing of the public schools; to preserve the unity of the Association; and to maintain the strength necessary to wage other campaigns vital to all the teachers' interests in the Congress. She thus placed the prestige of her office behind the Resolutions Committee's proposal. Five days later, when the resolution came before the Assembly for action, Ben W. Kellner of California, chairman of the Resolutions Committee, in a departure from the usual procedure, made the following statement:

> Madam President, because of the deep concern of every delegate on this subject, and because of the countless hours the Committee has spent on it, the Chairman wishes to make a statement on behalf of our Committee. We have considered the resolution on integration carefully and even prayerfully. We have been fully aware that what we say on the subject of integration may have far greater effect than is usually associated with the statements of the position of NEA.
>
> Some of our most respected colleagues may be exposed, by the actions we take on this floor, to personal damage and even to personal danger. For this reason, we sought and received the guidance of the Board of Directors in drafting this resolution. The deepest conviction of the Resolutions Committee and of its Editing Committee has been that we must so conduct our affairs and so compose our resolutions as not to increase the difficulties of those who are now bearing the major burdens imposed by the process of integration.
>
> At the same time, we have noted that as a result of the process of integration in certain parts of the South, schools have been closed and teachers have been unfairly treated. We are not and we cannot be indifferent to these developments. Accordingly, in preparing the proposed resolution on integration we considered including these two statements specifying that the public schools must remain open and that the professional and political rights of teachers must be safeguarded.
>
> In our early discussions, we approached these two matters primarily from the point of view of the difficulties connected with integration and we, therefore, thought of associating these statements with the resolution on that subject. We soon came to realize, however, that the acts we were opposing would be just as objectionable if done on any other pretext. We oppose the closing of public schools not only on grounds of integration, but on any grounds whatsoever.
>
> From our point of view, the public schools are simply not expendable.
>
> We oppose unfair treatment of teachers, no matter what excuses may be offered. The Committee concluded, therefore, that it would be best to speak out against school closing and unfair treatment of teachers in general rather than only in relation to integration.
>
> It was for this reason that the new paragraph was added to the resolution entitled Public Education in America. That paragraph says that the schools should stay open, no matter what the reason for closing.
>
> For the same reason, we spoke vigorously against unfair treatment of teachers in the resolution entitled The Teacher As a Citizen, whether the unfair treatment be connected with integration or any other matter. This is why the resolution which I am about to place before you does not mention these two important matters; they have already been acted on in this Assembly and there is no need to act on them specifically in this context.[5]

Immediately following the reading of the resolution, which was seconded by Charles F. Deubel of New York, the matter was open for discussion.

Walter Ludwig of New York then proposed a substitute motion the scope of which went beyond any proposal heretofore made to the Assembly on the subject of integration in the schools. It would place the Association on record as supporting the Supreme Court decision of 1954, call for respect for law, commend those who had already moved to integrate their schools, and recommend that dual state affiliates of the NEA be integrated.[6]

In the discussion that followed, the chairman of the New York delegation pointed out that the New York delegation had voted 133 to 2 to support the resolution proposed by the Resolutions Committee.

The lack of support by the New York delegation, the active role played by President Stout and the Board of Directors, and the efforts of the Resolutions Committee to strengthen related resolutions were responsible for the defeat of the substitute motion.

A series of amendments was then proposed by Maxine Smith in behalf of the Oregon delegation. The debate on the amendments was intense. The following excerpts, both pro and con, from the discussion of the Oregon amendments reveal the issues and convey the flavor of the debate.

FORREST ROZZELL [Little Rock, Arkansas]: I intend to say nothing and I hope nothing can be inferred from anything that I say to impugn the motives of a single person who represents local organizations or others on the floor of this Delegate Assembly. As for me, I am certain that those who support the amendment coming from Oregon are as sincere and dedicated and courageous as I am, or anyone else who happens to be on the opposite side of this issue. I am not appearing before the Delegate Assembly to defend the evils of segregation, whether that segregation be practiced in Little Rock, in New York, California, or in St. Louis. You know as well as I that the evils of segregation and other evils which we face in our society cannot be resolved by the mere passage of a resolution on the floor of the Delegate Assembly here. If we could resolve the issues which we face in Little Rock by the passage of a resolution, I would be happy to leave and the whole Arkansas delegation would leave and let you write your own resolution. But we know the problem will not be solved that way. The problem that you face as responsible members of the organized profession is to think about this question: What action can this Delegate Assembly take which might be of some assistance to us who are on the front line of this struggle in Arkansas?

There are those who have expressed an opinion that this resolution will be of assistance to us, and I don't doubt their sincerity; I know that they have an abiding conviction that what they say is true. However, on the basis of our experience in Little Rock and in Arkansas, we believe the judgment of the Resolutions Committee is to the best interest of what happens to public education in Arkansas and through the South.

It is inevitable that if you see fit to turn down the proposal of the Resolutions Committee, which has the support of the professional leadership in the South, we must conclude by that action that you are repudiating our leadership. We must conclude that you have concluded that we have defaulted in the assumption of our professional responsibility, and we have not. On May 18, 1954, the day after the Supreme Court decision, we made the statement to the press and to the people of Arkansas that the teachers of Arkansas would abide by the laws as defined by the Supreme Court. We had a struggle in the general assembly in 1955, keeping off extreme pro-segregation measures. By 1956, the situation was becoming more acute. We announced publicly and privately in everything we did in the assumption of our leadership in Arkansas, that we would be guided by these three principles: first, the public school system is not expendable; second, the principle of local autonomy must be respected; and third, whatever is done by any group must be done according to due process of law. Those opinions have undergirded every action that we have taken. . . . I feel this: if you have faith in the integrity of your professional leadership as represented by the Resolutions Committee, and in the leadership in Arkansas and the rest of the South—if you have confidence in the judgment of that leadership, you will vote to reject all of these proposed amendments and stand by the recommendations of the Resolutions Committee.[7]

KEITH GOLDHAMMER [Oregon]: I would like to say in behalf of the Oregon delegation that we are presenting this amendment to the resolution on the floor of the convention in behalf of the Representative Council of the Oregon Education Association, which has so instructed us to do. . . .

As one who was in Arkansas at the time preceding the crisis which arose, I have a deep sympathy for the people, the educators in Arkansas, for the manner in which they have continued to struggle in behalf of the public schools. Certainly every educator in the United States, if not in the world, can take pride in the courageous leadership that Mr. Rozzell and other members of the Arkansas profession have given not only in this crisis but in the battle for good schools preceding the crisis. . . .

However, I think it is also necessary for us to recognize that there are many inarticulate voices in many parts of the country who, too, have the same privilege or are granted by the Constitution of the United States the same privilege of speech, yet who at the present time do not dare to speak out in behalf of their convictions.

At this time, it is the feeling of our delegation that although we generally concur with the resolution of the Resolutions Committee, the time has come for the NEA and professional educators to stand up and take the leadership in this issue which the people of the United States are certainly looking to us to assert. Certainly, if there were a bond issue or a budget election, the educators would be expected to make their stand known unequivocally; similarly, in this crisis, the educators of America have a responsibility to be heard. We do not feel that in any way we impinge upon the freedom of action of any state to act as it so chooses, if we merely state that as the NEA we stand firmly on the belief that the problems of integration must be solved with deliberate speed and that the present generation of children growing to maturity have the same right of equality of educational opportunity as have other children throughout the country.[8]

WILLIAM L. GREENE [North Carolina, speaking as an individual]: I have to use that designation in order to have my right before this microphone; but I shall speak to you as the other voice from the South. Since 1950, when we met in St. Louis, Missouri, there is a group of about 30,000 southerners with you now who were with you then only in token numbers. By 1952 in Detroit, Michigan, a pattern of second affiliates in southern states had been processed; at that time there were 21 second affiliates. That number has dwindled to 11. Why then should those of us who still comprise the majority of these NEA members in the South be deprived of the benefits of better human fellowship that have occurred to 10 of our neighbors? It has been the leadership of President Eisenhower, the school board and superintendent in St. Louis, Missouri, Louisville, Kentucky, in Washington, D.C., and Baltimore who have taken the initiative in doing what they did, while NEA said, "We are afraid of what might happen."

Now, we are not going to say anything about withdrawing from the NEA or diminishing our enrollment effort. We are not in that category, but we are saying to you as members of the NEA, "You promised us expanded services and you are welshing on the deal." We fought this battle against discrimination through other organizations until 1952 and you told us, through your Platform, before you got into this business of special resolutions, that our right to fair treatment and advocacy against discrimination qualified us. You said you would fight for us, and when we declare war, you hold up the white flag; it is not a square deal.

As the other voice from the South, I appeal to the conscience of the organized profession. . . . The voice you heard from the South before my speech was not the voice of educational leadership—it was the voice of compromise and political intimidation.[9]

All four of the Oregon amendments failed, and the resolution proposed by the Resolutions Committee survived for another year.

Los Angeles—1960. Early in the Los Angeles meeting of the 1960 Representative Assembly, it appeared that those desiring a more agressive policy on school integration were stronger and more confident. Discussions involved a greater variety of participants.

The procedure followed the pattern of the St. Louis meeting, with an opening statement by the chairman of the Resolutions Committee, Elizabeth Ann Meek. In her opening statement Meek said that the committee was guided by three general principles:

1. The right of children to public education must be respected and maintained.
2. The professional rights and status of teachers must be respected and maintained.
3. The action of the NEA must be such as will be helpful in dealing with the problem of integration.

President Eshelman then introduced George Deer of Louisiana, a member of the Executive Committee, who made a strong appeal for adoption of the resolution without amendment, which had now been approved in substantially the same form by the last six Assemblies.

The first two amendments were proposed by the Arizona delegation. One would add to the Resolutions Committee's proposal the following sentence: "Resolved, that the National Education Association pledge continued support of the United States Supreme Court Decision on school integration."[10] After a lengthy debate, this amendment was approved by a roll-call vote of 1,933 to 1,780.

The second Arizona proposal sought to amend the resolution by adding a sentence commending those communities that had made progress toward ending the practice of segregation in the schools. It passed on a voice vote.

Then Charles Deubel of New York proposed an amendment that would be a substitute for the entire resolution as amended. This amendment, which had been rejected earlier by a narrow margin by the Resolutions Committee, was nearer to the original proposal than the two amendments just adopted. After the adoption of the two Arizona amendments, the Deubel amendment was supported by the Association officers, the Resolutions Committee, and some delegates who preferred to go partway but not as far as the Oregon proposals. The substitute was approved on a voice vote.

With the adoption of the Deubel substitute, the two Arizona amendments were killed and the final product after hours of debate left the resolution only slightly stronger than the one originially presented by the Resolutions Committee. Nevertheless, the growing dissatisfaction with the desegregation resolution at the Los Angeles convention made it clear that the Association leadership would not be able to avoid open support of the 1954 Supreme Court decision much longer. Moreover, delegates from large cities began to demand more attention for the growing problems of big-city schools resulting from poverty, racial discrimination, archaic financial machinery, and a shrinking tax base.

Separate meetings had been held for urban leaders beginning with the 1956 Representative Assembly to give them an opportunity to discuss problems unique to urban areas. This urban group understood the problems of black teachers. Both groups were seeking greater recognition from the NEA. The informal beginning of cooperation among the urban group, black leaders, and northern and western liberals was evident in Los Angeles. This coalition was later to be formalized into the National Council of Educators for Human Rights (NCEHR). This group, by skillfully using all of the forums available to it within the NEA to keep the pressure on, became the chief catalyst for accelerating the pace of change in the NEA on civil rights matters.

Atlantic City—1961. The following summer at Atlantic City, a new resolution was presented that had been drafted by the Resolutions Committee and agreed upon in advance by representatives of both black and white groups in the South as a resolution they "could live with." At this meeting, the activist groups and their supporters succeeded in amending the resolution to include a pledge of continued support of school desegregation.

The Atlantic City meeting of the Representative Assembly marked a conclusion to the overriding annual debates on the NEA's policy on school desegregation. The ideological battle had been won. The NEA was now committed to the active support of the Supreme Court decision on desegregation of the nation's public schools.

In the following decade, the delegates would turn more of their attention to implementing the desegregation decision with action programs; the merger of the NEA and the black American Teachers Association (ATA); the merger of the dual state affiliates; and collective bargaining.

Denver—1962. Only one amendment was adopted to the resolution on school desegregation, and it was of minor importance. Chief concerns in the 1962 meeting were urban problems, collective bargaining, strikes, sanctions, and the efforts of the Industrial Union Department of the AFL-CIO to organize teachers, white-collar workers, black people, and the poor.

Detroit—1963. Significant was a motion proposed to the 1963 assembly by the Board of Directors and read to the delegates at the opening meeting of the Representative Assembly by Treasurer Lyman Ginger. The motion called upon state and local associations to establish consultative committees and to organize seminars and other human-relations activities to facilitate the removal of racial membership restrictions, and offered the "good offices" of NEA to assist them.

The motion also requested the joint committee of the NEA and the ATA to consider whether and under what conditions it would be desirable and feasible to merge the two associations. It called upon the committee to report its recommendations in one year or less.[11]

The motion was presented, Dr. Ginger said, with the understanding that it would be brought before the delegates for action the following day.

This action by the Board of Directors and the Representative Assembly set in motion a program of action bridging fourteen years and leading to one of the most important recent achievements of the NEA: the elimination of separate affiliates nationally for black and white members in the remaining eleven states.[12]

The Board of Directors, by taking the initiative, had succeeded in Detroit in securing passage of a motion calling on affiliates with dual associations for black and white members to merge into a single united organization. At the conclusion of the discussion, Peter Goudis, a leader of the National Council of Educators for Human Rights (NCEHR), posed a challenge to the leadership by speaking in favor of the Board's motion after several efforts to strengthen it had been voted down. Goudis said:

> I support the resolution as presented by the Board of Directors through Lyman Ginger. I had hoped that we would have much stronger and more exact wording. However, fellow delegates, I believe that this is a stronger resolution than many people suspect.
>
> Bear with me for a moment and see if my logic is in agreement with yours. We have had the Board of Directors of the NEA say to us late in the convention, "This is the principle. We wish to desegregate our locals." We all want this. No one has spoken against it. The Board of Directors has told us, "This is the way it can and should be done."
>
> I say let them prove it. I say give them their resolutions. I say I will be at the next convention. I want to hear that their sentiments as our leaders were correct and that mine, and perhaps yours, in wishing for something stronger, were incorrect.
>
> And the proper way to desegregate, the easiest way to desegregate, the quickest way to desegregate, is through the resolution which they, in their consultation, present to us. They have, in effect, gone out on a limb. They have told us, the body delegate, and recommended to us that this is the way to do it. I say let's accept it and then let's see what their report tells us next year. If, by integrating the locals, they mean that we will have one in State A, one in State B, three in State C, I know what I will say. If, however—and hopefully—they prove me and the people who feel as I do incorrect, I will be the first one to applaud their decision.
>
> I ask you to tell them by supporting the motion that has been made by the Board, "We want you to show us, as leaders, that you were correct, and we will await the final decision at the next convention." But that will be the time when we who want this done strongly and now will prevail.[13]

Seattle—1964. As promised by Goudis, the urban group and the NCEHR joined with western and northern liberals, and a growing number of young NEA leaders and staff members, at the Seattle meeting and succeeded in passing a mandate to affiliates with specific deadlines for compliance.

The action, referred to from that day to the present as Resolution 12, was voted by the NEA. At the same time, another debate was approaching a climax in the U.S. Senate—the debate on the Civil Rights Act. Thus, Resolution 12 was adopted by the NEA in the same week the United States Congress approved the Civil Rights Act of 1964.

By adoption of Resolution 12, the Representative Assembly instructed the officers and directors of the associations to:

1. Require the removal of all restrictive membership provisions dealing with race, creed, or ethnic groups
2. Take immediate action to develop plans to effect the integration of all affiliates—state and local where separate affiliates exist
3. Set July 1, 1966, as a deadline for revising constitution and bylaws, and taking other actions to remove racial restrictions, and for presenting a plan for the complete integration of the associations

The Executive Committee was given the responsibility for enforcing compliance and discretionary power to deal with those failing to meet the time schedule.

NEA CIVIL RIGHTS ACTIONS

NEA concern for equality for minorities has a long history. In the early 1960s, however, the NEA's role with regard to problems of black teachers and black children began, haltingly at first, to change to one of advocacy. As early as 1943, the Representative Assembly had voted not to meet in a city that did not provide equal accomodations to blacks and other minority-group members.[14]

In 1959, the public schools in Prince Edward County, Virginia, were closed rather than comply with the Supreme Court's 1954 decision to desegregate the public schools. In the 1963–1964 school year, the Prince Edward Free School Association was organized to serve the black children of that county and any white children whose parents desired that they attend. The administrator of the Free School Association asked the NEA's assistance. The NEA agreed to invite Association members to make contributions through its network of affiliates. Since it would take time to raise funds from members by mail, NEA staff members made the first voluntary contributions. Contributions of the staff and members came to $75,000. In addition, Association attorneys filed a memorandum in the case with the U.S. Supreme Court, and the NEA assisted in recruiting teachers for the Free School Association. The superintendent of the Free

School Association later told the NEA staff the schools could not have opened without the NEA's prompt assistance.

Voting Rights

Prior to the 1965 Selma-to-Montgomery, Alabama, march led by Dr. Martin Luther King, Jr., the Selma teachers appealed to the NEA to support them in a voter-registration effort. The NEA did support them in organizing and participating in a campaign that adopted the slogan "Fit to Teach—Fit to Vote." The successful campaign won the right for Selma teachers to vote. This action became the opening wedge for all black people to win that right in a subsequent campaign led by Dr. King.

The NEA's black local affiliate in Selma was led by Fred Reese, who was also the chairman of the Selma Improvement Association—the organization spearheading the voter registration campaign.

When the local affiliate asked the NEA for assistance, an effort was made with both the black and white local groups working together to form a united front. The NEA flew the officers of both the black and white affiliates to Washington and the effort was a success. But at the conclusion of the victorious Selma to Montgomery march Fred Reese's teaching contract was not renewed for the following year. Over fifty members of the local association did not sign their contracts until the deadline date for returning them to the school board office, and, then, only after Fred Reese insisted that they do so.

As of this writing, Fred Reese is a member of the Selma City Council.

Minority Participation

As the NEA's dual affiliates merged, the need was recognized to encourage black members to be more than nominal members by preparing them to become active participants in Association programs. A forum was organized in the NEA Department of Classroom Teachers in 1967 to acquaint minority members with Association programs and opportunities and to encourage their participation. Training materials and programs were developed and seminars were scheduled in cooperation with state and local affiliates. Administration of the program became the responsibility of the Center for Human Relations, established by the Representative Assembly in July 1968.

Under this program, a variety of activities developed that made it possible for the Association to bring thousands of minority members quickly into active participation in Association programs. Minority programs carried on by the black associations have been continued, expanded, and made more effective by the larger multi-ethnic association. Opportunities had been opened up for minorities to influence policy decisions through the formation in 1970 of minority caucuses where positions could be defined, differences resolved, and strategies developed. The caucuses negotiated opportunities with NEA officers and governing boards. President Don Morrison, in an effort to expand and speed up the effort, organized a series of Minority Involvement Conferences to include all minority groups. The conferences served to give impetus to the caucus movement. By 1980 there were eleven recognized caucuses formed to influence Association policies. They included the four ethnic caucuses: the American Indian/Alaska Native, the Asian/Pacific Islander, the Black, and the Chicano/Hispano groups. Other interest groups that had formed caucuses were: Women, Campers, Higher Education, Teachers, Special Education, Veterans, and Vocational. Training programs were organized to enable minority members to sharpen their leadership skills, and special internships were established to help train and place minority members who desired staff positions.

When the new NEA constitution was approved in 1973, it contained ethnic guarantees for representation of minorities in the Representative Assembly, the Board of Directors, the Executive Committee, and all of the Association's appointed committees. Since the new constitution became effective, minority representation has consistently exceeded the constitutional requirements, indicating acceptance of the principle by members of the Association.

In 1957, 90.7 percent of NEA staff members were white. Of the remaining 9.3 percent, all were in the clerical and administrative support, technical support, or trade and craft categories.

In 1979, largely owing to the NEA's efforts to bring minority members into full participation in Association programs, 42 percent of the 562 NEA staff members were minority members. Moreover, 28 percent of minority members held executive, managerial, or professional positions. In addition, the NEA's governance, which was virtually all-white in 1957, had been transformed into one in which minority members comprised 22 1/2 percent of the membership of the Board of Directors, 44 percent of the membership of the Executive Committee, and 17 percent or more of the delegates to the Representative Assembly. One in four members involved in NEA-funded action programs were minority group members.

By 1975–76, the NEA and forty-four state affiliates had formally adopted affirmative action programs, and by 1979, all affiliates had taken such action.

Histories of the Dual Affiliates

When the black American Teachers Association merged with NEA in 1966, a part of the agreement provded that the NEA would preserve the histories of both the black and white state associations and carry on the cooperative relationship begun by ATA and the Association for the Study of Afro-American Life and History. Through the Center for Human Relations, the NEA has fulfilled this obligation. A history of the American Teachers Association has been published, as well as histories of the seven black state associations in Florida, Mississippi, Tennessee, Texas, Virginia, South Carolina, and West Virginia. The NEA has contracted with the authors, selected by the state associations involved and the Association for the Study of Afro-American Life and History, and has assisted with distribution of the books. Authors have been selected and histories of the black associations in Alabama, Georgia, and Arkansas are in preparation. Plans are under way to write the histories of the white affiliates in Mississippi, Louisiana, and South Carolina.

Recognition of Individuals and Organizations

A feature associated with the annual meeting of the Representative Assembly since 1967 has been the Human Relations Dinner. The program for the annual dinner has been the presentation of awards in recognition of worthy efforts to promote human rights and advance human relationships. The dinner and awards were initiated by the American Teachers Association and carried on as a feature of the annual convention of the ATA. Since the merger of the ATA and NEA in 1966, the program has been continued as a part of the annual meeting of the NEA Representative Assembly.

NEA Center for Human Relations

The Center for Human Relations was established in 1968 in response to a recommendation of a special task force on human rights. The recommendation proposed that the center be created to carry on the work of the Professional Rights and Responsibilities subcommittee on Civil and Human Rights of Educators. The action also created a racially balanced Human Relations Council, and staff advisory committee. Sam Ethridge, the first administrator of the center, was made an assistant NEA executive secretary. The center operated until 1972. It promoted the establishment of Human Relations Councils in the NEA's fifty state and 10,000 local affiliates. It also sought to inject a human-relations element into all facets of the NEA program.

With the reorganization, the Center for Human Relations, the Commission on Professional Rights and Responsibilities, the Committee on Professional Ethics, and the Fund for Teacher Rights were combined to form a single unit coordinating all programs relating to human relations and the rights of teachers.

Through the Teacher Rights Unit and its predecessor agencies, the NEA has engaged in a variety of activities to advance equality and protect the civil rights of members. It has sponsored an annual national conference on civil and human rights attended by leaders in educaion, religion, civil rights, government, and other concerned areas. The conference programs have featured the most pressing problems facing local communities, the states, and the nation. In addition to the obvious advantages of keeping the participants up to date with current conditions, they have provided opportunities for the Association to meet the leaders of other groups and to form cooperative relationships and engage in activities of common interest.

Studies have been made on the desegregation progress, the displacement of minority educators, personnel policies, urban field studies, the treatment of minorities in textbooks and encyclopedias, curriculum guides for ethnic studies, minority pupil dropouts, unfair treatment of minority teachers, and related subjects.

Publications, filmstrips, and tapes have been produced and distributed through the NEA's network of affiliates for use by teachers and school-related groups. A data bank has been developed containing pertinent information on minority educators.

Workshops and seminars, too numerous to mention, have been held on such subjects as voter registration, student rights, racism, preparing for faculty desegregation, displacement of minority educators, and personnel policies.

Mississippi Task Force

The U.S. Supreme Court on October 29, 1969, ordered thirty Mississippi school districts to desegregate immediately. This action understandably flooded the NEA with requests for help. Nick Duff, chairman of the Commission on Professional Rights and Responsibilities, met with the Executive Committee on January 9, 1970, to request the assignment of a number of staff members to Mississippi to give concrete evidence of NEA concern, to coordinate NEA efforts with those of other organizations, such as the National Association for the Advancement of Colored People (NAACP) and the American Civil Liberties Union (ACLU), to collect facts on the developments as districts attempt to integrate their schools, to provide data to state and federal agencies, and to work with local and state affiliates to observe developments and help bring to public attention reports of progress and problems involved in the effort.

Duff emphasized the urgency of dealing, before school would open in the fall, with such matters as the displacement of black educators, discrimination against black pupils in the process of integration, testing as a basis for selection of teachers, and the establishment of all-white private schools.

Executive Secretary Sam Lambert organized a task force of twenty-five staff members to make a survey of the situation in Mississippi and recommend a course of action. The task force visited twenty-seven of the thirty districts affected by the Court order and another twenty-four systems yet to be integrated. The members met with officers of NEA affiliates, teachers, principals, superintendents, Parent-Teacher Association members, and newspaper, radio, and TV reporters.

Some members met with the state attorney general, who served Sam Ethridge, NEA assistant executive secretary for Teacher Rights, and Jim Williams, NEA's regional manager, with nineteen injunctions in an effort to prevent their monitoring activities.

Within a month, the leaders of the task force made their report and recommendations to the Executive Committee in Washington. They reported that black educators were being dismissed, demoted, or pressured to resign from desegregated school systems. White parents were withdrawing children from the public schools and enrolling them in private, all-white schools to circumvent the Supreme Court order. Churches and public facilities were being used to house private schools. Two schools were burned to delay integration.

Jim Williams cited one case to illustrate how school districts were using legal means to accomplish unethical, if not illegal, results.

The district planned to integrate its schools in February. Teachers were surveyed to find out if they would agree to a transfer to teach in an integrated school. Teachers' annual contracts specified the school to which they were assigned. Reassignment without the teacher's approval would be a breach of contract. Ninety percent of white teachers refused to agree to a transfer, while 80 percent of black teachers agreed. The school board thus might be obligated to pay salaries for the remainder of the year to reassigned teachers who refused to accept transfers. The teachers would then be free to teach in private schools at lower salaries.

The task force recommended and the Executive Committee approved nine legal and legislative actions, six federal-level actions, and eleven actions involving lay and related organizations. Among the major recommendations approved were the following:

1. Provide prompt legal assistance to Mississippi educators who were dismissed, demoted, or unfairly treated.
2. Bring court actions in the local districts and the state capitol, either separately or in cooperation with organizations such as the NAACP Legal Defense and Education Fund (LDEF) and the ACLU, to protect educator rights; to prevent the sale or transfer of public school property, equipment, and materials to private, segregated schools; and to prevent the state of Mississippi from giving state financial support to private schools.
3. Encourage and support the enactment of a compulsory attendance law by the Mississippi legislature.
4. Publish a legal handbook to inform educators of their rights and available resources.
5. Request a meeting with the President of the United States to discuss the task force findings and request his active support to carry out the recommendations.
6. Communicate the findings of the task force to HEW and the Department of Justice.
7. Urge NEA-affiliated school administrator organizations to take appropriate action against administrators guilty of unfair treatment of educators and children and to protect those who were acting fairly and responsibly.
8. Call upon the churches to refuse the use of their facilities for private, segregated schools; local community and business leaders to initiate constructive programs to prepare communities for peaceful school integration; the National School Boards Association to establish programs to help local school boards provide community leadership for orderly desegregation; and accrediting agencies to take strong positions to preserve high standards for accreditation of both public and private schools.

Louisiana Task Force

Responding to an urgent request from the Louisiana state affiliate on February 11, 1970, the NEA sent a second task force to monitor the desegregation process in Louisiana resulting from the Supreme Court's immediate desegregation order.

At the March meeting of the NEA Executive Committee, Jim Williams, reporting for the task force, described these conditions in Louisiana in the early spring of 1970:

> Virtually all of the desegregation that has occurred in Louisiana public schools has been implemented since September, 1969. Prior to that date, only one school system could fairly be described by state officials as "totally desegregated." In September, 1969, court-ordered desegregation plans were introduced in 15 Louisiana school systems. Eighteen additional systems were ordered to be desegregated effective February 1, 1970. Desegregation suits have been filed in 59 Louisiana districts as of February, 1970. Today, in Louisiana 34 of the 66 school systems can be classified as totally desegregated; in addition, 3 systems have signed compliance agreements with HEW and are therefore committed to total desegregation. In these 37 systems, there are 290,133 White children and 160,145 Black children, a total of 450,278 children registered in totally desegregated systems. This is roughly double the amount of desegregation that existed only a month ago. The most immediate casualties of school desegregation in this state, as in Mississippi, are the Black administrators, counselors, department heads, coaches, and band directors. It is a frequent practice for school officials to name the principal of the formerly all-Black school to the position of "coordinating principal" or "coordinator of instruction" between the two desegregated schools and to name White educators as principals of the paired schools. In the 18 Louisiana school districts, desegregated as of February 1, 1970, approximately 5,300 White students have withdrawn from the public schools. In some parishes, the exodus is critical: One small system lost 69 percent of its White students; another small system lost 51 percent; three others lost between 20 and 30 percent of the White students. Four of the 17 reported no loss. In a number of districts, it was reported, public school buses are used to transport private school students.

Williams stated that "the Task Force concludes its report with an urgent request for an effective NEA presence in Louisiana."[15]

The task force submitted fifteen recommendations for action to be taken in Louisiana with NEA leadership and support. They concerned legal actions similar to those recommended for Mississippi, including financial assistance to members involved in legal actions to protect their rights; specific actions needed on the federal level with the appropriate federal agencies; and community actions to be stimulated by the NEA affiliates with NEA support. The Association responded promptly with manpower, money, and legal resources.

Both the Louisiana and the Mississippi task forces were motivated by three principles: (1) educators whose school positions are placed in jeopardy by desegregation must be protected; (2) the establishment of private schools to circumvent the integration of public schools is both ethically and educationally wrong; and (3) NEA resources must be made available to assist local affiliates to achieve integration in a fair and peaceful way.

Since the Courts did not appoint monitors to perform the service, the Association accepted the responsibility.

The information gained was communicated to Congress at hearings before the Mondale Committee on Equal Educational Opportunity. It influenced the guidelines for the administration of the Emergency School Assistance Act and helped to strengthen the provisions of the act itself.

Task Force III

A third NEA task force was appointed to observe seventy school systems in Mississippi and Louisiana during the early weeks of school in the fall of 1970. Its charge was to continue the work of the first two task forces, which visited seventy-five systems in the months of January and February, and assess the progress and problems remaining eleven months after the original Court order was issued. In its report to the Association and the public, released on November 12, 1970, in New Orleans, the task force said it had observed promising developments as well as serious remaining problems. Unfortunately, the latter outweighed the former.

Among the positive signs observed were the peaceful opening of most school systems, a reduction in the number of supposedly integrated schools with segregated classes, the improved racial balance of the school staff as a result of Court orders, major strides in some schools toward the acceptance of integration, the reinstatement by Court order of a number of black teachers who had been arbitrarily dismissed or downgraded, the return of white pupils from segregated academies to the public schools in several school districts, some reduction in the use of the National Teacher Examination as a means of eliminating black teachers, evidence of growing teacher association influence on racial and educational policy issues, and the emergence of constructive leadership with courage and determination to make integration work.

The task force spelled out many specific examples in both states of unfair treatment of black students and teachers, principals, band directors, and coaches, cases in which reductions in force were not carried out in accord with the procedures set forth in Court decrees.

Violations of the spirit of the Court order were uncovered by the task force and included such practices as having separate lunch periods for black and white pupils, separate school dismissal times, segregated classrooms, and segregated seating within single classrooms.

Institute on Nonviolence

The NEA has been a partner with the Martin Luther King, Jr., Center for Social Change in supporting the Institute on Nonviolence every summer since its inception. The institute is held each summer for a full week and involves approximately 150 participants from all sections of the nation.

Legislation to make January 15—the birthday of Martin Luther King, Jr.—a national holiday has had the active support of the Association.

John Ryor, NEA president (1975–1979), served as chairman of the education division of the Campaign to Construct Freedom Hall at the King Center in Atlanta. Freedom Hall is the permanent home of the Institute on Nonviolence.

Legal Assistance

Unfair treatment of teachers occurred in the United States for many years simply because teachers lacked the resources to secure legal redress through the courts.

In the spring of 1943, three teachers of Muskogee, Oklahoma, learned through the local newspaper that they were not reappointed for the following school year, 1943–44. They had received no written or oral notice. No hearing had been held. No statement of charges had been made. The three teachers were Kate Frank, Mrs. R. P. Chandler, and Mrs. Mabel Runyan.

Kate Frank was a teacher of commercial subjects in the Muskogee high schools with twenty-three years of service in the same position. She held a bachelor's degree from Southwest Missouri State Teachers College and a master's degree from the University of Missouri. She had completed graduate study at the Gregg School of Business and the University of Chicago. She had served as president of the Muskogee Classroom Teachers Association and of the Oklahoma Education Association.

In 1942, the Board of Education had reduced the school term from nine to eight and one-half months for lack of funds. Thanks, in large part, to Kate Frank's efforts, Muskogee teachers succeeded in winning the two weeks' pay due them under their contracts. After payment was made, $9,000 remained in the budget, indicating the Board could have kept schools open for the full term.

The Board did not appreciate Miss Frank's exposure of these facts. A coalition of community groups formed to ensure full school terms for the future. It decided to support an independent slate of candidates for three vacancies on the Board in April 1942. One of the coalition's candidates and two candidates supported by the Board were successful in a difficult election in which teachers were coerced into supporting the candidates openly opposed by Miss Frank. At its meeting following the election, the Board voted not to reappoint Miss Frank and her two colleagues.

A twelve-member committee named by the NEA volunteered to raise funds from Association members to support the three teachers. Their goal was $3,600. They raised $3,795.60. It was used to pay Miss Frank's salary for the year and a half that she was out of work.

The matter was brought to the attention of the NEA Representative Assembly in the summer of 1943. The delegates referred the matter to the Executive Committee with the direction that every resource of the Association be directed toward the best settlement of the grievance.[16]

The Executive Committee accepted the recommendation of the Committee on Tenure and allocated $10,000 for pursuing the case. The Committee on Tenure charged the Muskogee board with dismissal without just cause, failure to give the teachers a statement of the charges against them, and failure to exercise due process.

Kate Frank was restored to her position in the Muskogee schools, and the $984.39 unspent at the conclusion of the case became the beginning of the Dushane Fund for Teacher Rights, which at present spends well over $2 million annually to protect the civil, human, constitutional, and professional rights of educators.

NEA state and local affiliates have over the years established similar funds for the protection of members. In the mid-1970s, an integrated program was developed, with common policies and procedures financed jointly by the NEA in partnership with the affiliates.

The policies governing the administration of the Dushane Fund and the volume of cases have changed dramatically since the fund's establishment in 1944. In 1957, the annual expenditure for the protection of teacher rights was $82,620. In 1978–79, expenditures were $2.6 million, not including state and local shared funds. The number of active cases handled by the Dushane Fund in the four years from 1975 to 1979 increased from 1,743 to 15,614. Much of the increase can be accounted for by the unification of the NEA service with the programs of its state and local affiliates in 1977. But the number of cases handled at all levels has grown steadily since the fund was created. The increase in the volume of cases has been due to the greater need for protection against the risks inherent in the collective bargaining process, civil rights, pupil violence, the increased exercise of constitutional rights by members, and the increased tendency in society to initiate legal actions for dispute settlement.

The NEA has supported legal cases involving individual members and class actions in which groups of members have a common interest. The Association has also supported nonmembers in cases that could set precedents affecting members.

Among the hundreds of cases supported by the NEA each year, many have dealt with racial discrimination in which large numbers of minority members were treated unfairly in the process of desegregating schools.

Many have involved actions relating to dismissals of teachers for engaging in organizational activities, exercising their constitutional rights of free speech, using controversial teaching materials or methods, or engaging in community activities frowned upon by the administration and school board.

Other cases have involved dismissals of teachers for wearing beards, mustaches, sideburns, turtleneck sweaters, or dresses deemed to be too short. Declining enrollments in the colleges and universities and the competition for tenured faculty positions have triggered a sharp increase in cases by higher education personnel in the 1970s. Many involved academic freedom, the administration of tenure, promotion, and termination policies.

Cases have also been supported that had effect upon such fundamental public policies as providing equal school opportunity for all children.

The nature of the NEA's participation varies. In some cases participation has been via interest-free loans, grants, or legal assistance to the member. In other cases the Association has initiated legal actions or intervened in ongoing actions. In many cases the NEA has filed briefs as "Friend of the Court" to secure the court's consideration of its views in addition to providing direct assistance to the member.

THE MERGER OF NEA'S REGIONAL AND STATE AFFILIATES

The passage of the Civil Rights Act was a very persuasive force for modifying the attitudes of white resisters. However, this welcome development was partially offset by the growing black separatist movement. Many blacks were having second thoughts about integration because of disillusioning experiences. Having won the right to be equal, they did not feel accepted as equals. Separatists argued that by remaining separate, blacks would have greater power and could bargain more effectively for conditions that would ensure true equality. Unfortunately, examples existed which reinforced their arguments.

The rise of the separatist movement was an example of the changing nature of the problem faced by the NEA. The sentiment among black members in the late 1950s and early 1960s was "Open the door and let us in"; but after the doors were opened, a period of disillusionment set in. Blacks accustomed to seeing black leaders then saw only whites or token blacks in the less important positions, and they began insisting on full participation in the affairs of the new organization. This included the right to hold office and serve in policymaking positions.

This separatist movement would have been understandable if the differences in emphasis of the programs of the black and white organizations were considered. The white teachers' associations sought to improve schools and conditions of work for teachers by influencing state school legislation. This included drafting proposals, securing sponsors, and persuading legislators to vote for them. The legislative process also included defeating proposals that were educationally unsound or would weaken existing school programs and engaging in political action.

On the other hand, the black teachers were experienced in the art of defending the civil, professional, and human rights of their members, their pupils, and their pupils' parents. Teachers typically comprised the largest group of educated persons in the black community. The major preoccupation of black people for generations had been the problem of securing the right to participate in their communities on the basis of equality with whites. One teacher described it to me as the "one big problem complicating life in America for black people. All other problems are viewed by blacks in terms of their impact on that one big problem."

It was important that the role of the black teachers' associations be understood. They were organized to provide better school opportunities for black children and to improve conditions for black teachers. Unlike the white organizations, historically the black associations had not been a part of the power structure. Thus they had to use different methods and possess different skills to achieve their objectives.

The overriding problems of discrimination and limited social power were an integral part of every problem the associations had to deal with. Collective action was recognized as absolutely essential for the protection of members. Such protection, if effective, caused members to place a high value on association membership and nurtured intense loyalties to the organization. At the same time, black association leaders had developed skills in using the political process, the courts, and various other means of achieving their objectives. These skills were then proving valuable to the merged organizations—more valuable than many white members originally believed. After all, there was not much difference between the skills required to win the right to vote and those required to win the right to engage in collective bargaining with the school board.

When the merger of the dual associations was first proposed, the reaction of many black teachers was to accept membership in the white association at once. Later, they viewed merger in terms of two conflicting desires—equality with white teachers by membership in one professional organization and use of their collective power to come into the new organization on terms that would assure black members the protection of their civil, professional, and human rights. The black teachers acknowledged that the white teachers' organization would continue to represent them in winning economic benefits from the predominantly white legislatures and the white school boards. But the question that troubled the black teachers was whether the new organization would go to bat for them before the white school board and in a white courtroom in personnel cases involving the protection of their rights as teachers and citizens.

These conditions posed different problems for the executive directors of the two merging organizations. The white executive had the problem of leading the members to do the right thing by fulfilling the constitutional promise of equality. White leaders also persuaded their colleagues to see the benefits of a larger membership, which meant greater power to win victories for schools and all teachers. But they had to exercise care not to cross the line between "white leader" and "black advocate" or they would cease to be leaders.

On the other hand, the black executive had the problem of restraining the members from stampeding into the new organization and giving up their power to negotiate conditions of entry that would ensure the new group's responsiveness to the needs of black teachers.

As the mergers proceeded, weaknesses began to appear in the merged organizations. Some black leaders in the early mergers were honored initially as pioneers and heros but quickly became "whipping boys" accused of "selling out" their black constituents. As a result of changing conditions and attitudes, each time a merger was approved, the price went up for the next one in terms of protection demanded by the black associations. Another factor influenced this trend: the rapidly changing public opinion among whites in favor of equality for blacks in the mid-1960s. The racial climate of the mid-1960s was quite different from that of 1957. These factors didn't make the merger negotiations any easier, but I am confident they helped us to produce mergers that have a greater chance to survive and serve better all members, both black and white.

Merger of NEA and ATA—1966

The struggle for equality for black schools and decent working conditions for black teachers has been a long and frustrating one, and despite the gains made in recent years, much remains to be done before equality is achieved fully.

The first problem was to secure the opportunity for black children to attend a public school. Then, after the Supreme Court upheld legal segregation in *Plessy* v. *Ferguson* in 1896, the problem became that of obtaining for blacks school opportunities equal to those provided to whites.

Teachers in the black schools needed a forum in which to discuss problems, set directions, and engage in collective action. An organization to serve these functions was formed in 1904. Originally called the National Colored Teachers Association, it changed its name three years later to the National Association of Teachers in Colored Schools to avoid the appearance of excluding white teachers who were teaching in black schools. In 1937, the name was changed again, to the American Teachers Association, the designation remaining until the ATA merged with the NEA in 1966.

State organizations of black teachers had been in existence as early as 1861, but until 1904, no formal national organization existed to deal exclusively with the problems of black schools and black teachers.

The first direct joint activity between the NEA and the National Association of Teachers in Colored Schools (NATCS) came in 1926. In that year, NEA President Mary McSkimmon appointed a Committee on Problems in Negro Education and Life.

The committee's first efforts were aimed at securing the accreditation of black high schools using the same standards that were being used for white schools. The objective was partially achieved when the Southern Association of Schools and Colleges agreed to make inspections and judgments on black high schools. However, there was a general feeling among black educators that "standards were more lax for judging the black high schools, thus making it appear that the two groups of schools—Black and White—were more nearly equal qualitatively than they really were."[17]

While the committee in its first year did not achieve its full objective, Perry evaluated the result of the first year's efforts in these words:

> It is certainly not overstatement to observe that the negotiations of NATCS . . . had the strengthening influence of NEA behind them. This added substance to the requests, and it bolstered the morale and determination of Trenholm, Robinson, and the other suppliants to be certain that the larger, more prestigious body recognized the validity, even the necessity, for the future of American education, to bring the Negro into the mainstream of educational opportunities

and policies. The joint committee . . . played a substantive role in the efforts . . .
as did some individual NEA members.[18]

As a result of this first cooperative effort of NEA and NATCS, the joint
committee included in its first report a recommendation that the committee be made permanent.

The recommendation was approved, and programs related to the problems of black schools and teachers have been carried out on a continuing
basis ever since. Many of the concerns and activities of the joint committee have been expanded and given greater emphasis since the merger of
the NEA and ATA in 1966 as a result of policy changes and greater resources.

During the forty years from 1926 to 1966, the committee engaged in a
wide variety of activities and became the conduit through which the special problems of black educators and schools were brought to the attention of the NEA and ATA for their consideration in developing action programs. Some of these activities, gleaned from the annual reports, include:

Making surveys on the status of Negro education and the health of Negro schoolchildren[19]

Encouraging research studies related to the special problems of Negro
education

Encouraging greater participation of minority-group members in all
activities of NEA

Working with publishers to improve the content of encyclopedias and
textbooks with more adequate, unbiased material concerning minority contributions to science, art, history, and the general culture of
the nation

Promoting the use of more minority-group members in NEA films and
printed materials

Holding conferences, workshops, and seminars on principles of race relations, human relations, and intergroup understanding

Developing film presentations on the history of Negroes in America, de-
picting their struggles, accomplishments, and contributions to society both in war and peace times

Encouraging the participation of prominent Negroes on NEA convention programs (As a result of the committee's recommendations,
many black educators were invited to address NEA conventions.
However, as early as 1884, the NEA had provided Booker T. Washington his first platform to outline his views on the educational needs
of black people, eleven years before his famous Atlanta address,
which catapulted him to national prominence.)[20]

Working with the U.S. Congress and federal agencies for programs of
federal support that would equalize school opportunities for black
and white children

Encouraging the establishment of centers for training doctors, dentists,
and nurses to serve the black people

Preparation and distribution of kits of materials on intergroup relations

In its later years, more and more emphasis was given by the committee to
the immediate problems of implementing the 1954 Supreme Court order
for the desegregation of schools.

The committee's forty years of work on problems of concern to both
black and white teachers developed the faith and confidence that enabled
it to recommend in 1966 the merger of the NEA and ATA. But it was not
the committee's history alone that made this recommendation possible.
The social climate of 1966 helped to create the appropriate moment for
racial unity in the teaching profession.

Representing the ATA on the committee at the time of merger were Edward Brice (Washington, D.C.), Joseph T. Brookes (Atlanta, Ga.),
Joseph C. Duncan (Yanceyville, N.C.), Rupert Picott (Richmond, Va.),
and Walter N. Ridley (Petersburg, Va.).

Members of the committee representing the NEA were Malvin Bowden
(Austin, Tex.), Walter L. Gordon (Camden, N.J.), William Lehr (New
Castle, Ind.), Katherine McCormick (Wheatridge, Colo.), Wallace Mc-
Crae (Pendleton, Ore.), and Ivan A. Booker (NEA staff contact).

In his address to the 1966 Representative Assembly, Dr. Carr reported
the merger of the NEA and ATA in these words:

> The American Teachers' Association was founded in 1904. In 1927, a joint
> committee of NEA and ATA was established to improve the opportunities of
> teachers and pupils of minority groups. In 1963, the NEA Representative As-
> sembly asked the joint committee to "consider whether and under what condi-
> tions it would be desirable and feasible to merge the associations."
>
> The joint committee agreed quickly on the desirability of unity. Details were
> formulated at a series of meetings of representatives of both associations; final
> points were resolved last October.
>
> Last week, the delegates to the American Teachers' Association annual meet-
> ing voted favorably on unification with the NEA. The NEA Executive Commit-
> tee and Board of Directors approved the resolutions which will come before you
> later. Your ratification will be the final step, except for the formal signing of
> papers. Among other conditions, the NEA will—
>
> 1. Accept all annual members of ATA currently in good standing.
> 2. Accept as NEA life members all ATA life members whose ATA fees are
>   fully paid.

3. Credit ATA life members whose fees are partially paid toward NEA life membership.
4. Employ the staff of ATA in the Southeastern Regional Office of NEA in Atlanta.

This decision will strengthen the entire profession. . . . When this document is signed, bringing into the National Education Association all annual members of ATA in good standing, the Association will have a million members.[21]

Dr. Carr's statement was greeted with enthusiastic applause, and the unification resolution was approved unanimously on June 28, 1966, in Miami Beach.

Elmer Hawkins, a past president, trustee, and director of the ATA, gave an eloquent, moving introduction to the resolution and moved its acceptance. It was seconded by Ed Henderson, executive secretary of the Florida Education Association. Then came an unprecedented action. In rapid sucession, seconds were offered by the delegations from New York, Ohio, Noth Carolina, Connecticut, Massachusetts, the District of Columbia, Oregon, Pennsylvania, Puerto Rico, Maine, the Overseas Education Association, South Carolina, Virginia, Colorado, Oklahoma, Missouri, New Jersey, California, Delaware, Rhode Island, Wisconsin, Florida, and Kentucky.

Then a motion was made, by Ed Henderson of Florida, who pointed out that time would be saved by casting a unanimous ballot. But President Richard Batchelder ruled that the matter was sufficiently important to require a precise vote. Thereupon the seconding continued until every state delegation had seconded the motion to approve the resolution. Nevertheless, the president called for a standing vote of the delegates before ruling the resolution had received the necessary two-thirds. He then declared that unless objection was heard, he would rule the vote to be unanimous.

A unification certificate was signed by the presidents and executive secretaries of the two associations at the evening session, while the 8,900 delegates sang "Glory, Glory Hallelujah," concluding with a standing ovation. Present and past officers of the ATA, who were seated on the platform, were introduced individually, along with members of the joint committee representing ATA.[22]

I have attended twenty-nine NEA conventions during my career in organization work and have never witnessed a more enthusiastic and spontaneous response from the delegates.

It would be misleading to conclude the story of this significant event in the life of the ATA and NEA without observing that it was not achieved without some pain, soul searching, and anxiety. It took three years to reach agreement on the merger conditions. For months, negotiations were at a standstill lacking satisfactory answers to such questions as: How shall the support of the NAACP Legal Defense and Education Fund (LDEF) be continued? The ATA had for years given generous support to the fund, which has been an effective defender of black civil rights. This question was resolved when the NEA Board of Directors on June 26, 1966, voted to initiate, and promote, a campaign to raise a special fund of at least a million dollars to protect the rights of teachers by providing legal and other assistance. An agreement was also made with the LDEF for the NEA to cooperate by accepting the responsibility for cases involving the defense of teacher rights. This would relieve the LDEF of financial obligations approximately equal to former ATA contributions.

The NEA also agreed to cooperate with the Association for the Study of Afro-American Life and History and to carry on the traditional support given that organization by the ATA.[23]

Perhaps the greatest obstacle to the NEA-ATA merger was the pervasive feeling of frustration by many black leaders at the time the merger talks were in progress. Eleven years had passed since the Supreme Court ordered desegregation of the nation's schools, but only one black child in a hundred was attending an integrated public school in the deep South. Black state association leaders saw little evidence that the experience gained by black teachers could have much impact on programs of the combined organization. These were some of the problems that, up until the last meeting of the ATA in Miami Beach on June 24, 1966, threatened to deny the unification. However, the final vote was 172 for the merger and 3 against. An interesting sidelight is that one of the three negative votes was cast by Dr. Horace Tate, who was then executive secretary of the Black Georgia Teachers and Education Association. He was later appointed executive secretary of the merged Georgia Association of Educators which position he held at the time this book went to press.

Fortunately, the NEA Executive Committee provided for periodic evaluations of the merged state affiliates based on criteria for successful merger. The criteria were developed as experience was gained with mergers. The evaluations enabled NEA officers and staff to assist affiliates in correcting some of the shortcomings of the early mergers and in sharpening sensitivities to the needs and resources of all members of the new organization.

Perhaps the overriding positive force for merger was the faith and confidence developed among leaders of both organizations through forty years of experience gained by working together on common problems in the joint committee of NEA and ATA.

The trend toward merger in the early sixties is described by Thelma Perry as irreversible.

> For more than three decades, the two groups had communicated, from tenuous beginnings in 1926 to a sure-footed common purposefulness and goal-oriented consensus about the rightfulness of educational democracy for America by 1960.
>
> It would nevertheless be wrong to suppose that ATA used most of its . . . energies in pressuring NEA for admittance . . . the progression of both associations toward merger was continuous though gradual and perhaps unacknowledged or even undetected by the parties until the time had ripened.[24]

Merger of Dual State Affiliates

When the NEA Executive Committee suspended four state affiliates and refused to issue credentials for them to attend the Philadelphia convention in 1969, some viewed the action as self-destructive. But those close to the committee saw the action as an expression of the deep conviction of committee members that the time had come for the NEA to give leadership to eliminate racial prejudice in the nation's schools.

In May and June 1969, the Executive Committee suspended its white state affiliates in Louisiana and Mississippi and its black state affiliate in North Carolina. This action came as a shock to critics and supporters alike who regarded NEA as an organization created by the states to serve the interests of the states. By this forthright move, the NEA demonstrated its determination to serve the interests of the teaching profession nationally when the national interest was at stake. In the intervening years since 1969, experience has supported the wisdom of the action, which later enabled President John Ryor to declare, "The doctrine of separate but equal has no place in the teaching profession," as the last merger of state affiliates was recognized at the Minneapolis convention in 1977 with the unification of the two associations in Louisiana.

When the Seattle meeting of the Representative Assembly adopted Resolution 12 in the summer of 1964, the District of Columbia and six of the original seventeen states with dual associations had merged. Those with racial membership restrictions simply removed them from the constitution and bylaws and invited their black colleagues to join the formerly all-white association. The six, all border states, were Missouri, Maryland, West Virginia, Kentucky, Oklahoma, and Delaware.[25]

Unmerged in 1964 at the time of the Seattle convention were Florida, Texas, Virginia, Tennessee, South Carolina, Arkansas, Alabama, Georgia, North Carolina, Mississippi, and Louisiana.

Two significant events occurred in 1965 which carried great influence on the events of the next few years.

The joint committee of the NEA and ATA had urged for some time that a regional office be opened in the South. The need for such an office was recognized in April 1965 when the NEA's sixth regional office was established in Atlanta. Similar offices already existed in Boston; Trenton, New Jersey; Minneapolis; and Burlingame, California.

The following summer at the Miami Beach convention, Dr. Irvamae Applegate was elected vice-president/president-elect of the Association.

Appointed to head the regional office was James H. Williams, a native of the deep South who had trained for the ministry but after graduation found he preferred the classroom to the pulpit. His religious training, along with a unique set of personal qualities, fitted him well for the problems he would face in the next fifteen years. He lived with the problems of race relations in the South twenty-four hours a day during one of the most turbulent periods in the nation's history. Williams was intimately involved in the merger negotiations in the eleven remaining unmerged states and played a key role in the process. John Lawton, principal of a black school in Statesboro, Georgia, was named associate director of the regional office. On completion of the NEA-ATA merger, Dr. Joseph T. Brooks, ATA executive secretary, and Eloise Sykes, ATA administrative assistant, also joined the staff of the regional office.

When NEA established the Southeast Regional Office, a biracial advisory committee was appointed. At its first meeting, held early in 1965, I wanted to be certain no racial incident would occur to mar the spirit of harmony that we were seeking to promote. When I learned that ours was the first racially mixed meeting to be held in the Atlanta hotel we had chosen, I was even more determined to plan carefully, anticipate problems, and provide for safeguards in advance. We met with hotel personnel and secured a firm commitment that there would be no discrimination, that our entire group would be served in the main dining room, and that equal accommodations would be provided in the same section of the hotel.

All went well until the luncheon break. When we arrived in the dining room, we found the tables reserved for our group completely surrounded by portable screens setting us apart from the other guests. This did not happen again. For the balance of the meeting, we dined together in the open without either protection or incident. This meeting thus broke a longstanding tradition that blacks and whites socialize separately.

We did have another problem, though. When the black members entered the dining room, they entered together and sat together. Williams and I developed strategies to integrate the tables, with only modest success. At the second meeting, however, we reserved a large meeting room with a folding partition, enabling us to hold our meetings at one end of the suite, then reassemble at the other end for our mid-day meals. In a few months of dealing with common problems and associating in out-of-meeting activities, both groups relaxed, racial barriers were dissipated, and such arrangements were unnecessary.

Dr. Applegate, dean of education at Saint Cloud (Minnesota) State University, when elected NEA vice-president/president-elect, announced that her aim was to promote excellence in American education. She soon became involved in the merger of the NEA and ATA. Through that experience, she became convinced that the Association must give more aggressive leadership to the merger of the dual affiliates if the mandate of the Representative Assembly was to be realized. She "picked up the ball and ran with it," taking the initiative in matters involving the implementation of the mergers from the executive secretary, Dr. Carr. The following year, when she became president, she announced that the Executive Committee would name a compliance committee to supervise the implementation of merger plans. She named herself chairman. Other members were NEA president-elect Braulio Alonso; the immediate past president, Richard Batchelder; and one additional member to be named by and from the Executive Committee.

The following year, when Braulio Alonso became president, the personnel of the committee was expanded to include Irvamae Applegate, Thelma Davis, Elizabeth Koontz, Clarice Kline, Lyman Ginger, Mabel McKelvey, and Baker Thompson.

I think Dr. Carr sincerely believed the Association was pursuing a dangerous course in putting pressure on the southern state affiliates to merge by setting deadlines and appointing a compliance committee of Association officers to monitor progress. He would have preferred to go about it more slowly, using persuasion rather than threats of force. His style was to listen to the executive secretaries of the state associations and members of the NEA Board of Directors, most of whom represented the state viewpoint. In the early stages, Dr. Carr seemed to see school desegregation as society's problem, rather than a school problem, and felt the Association should remain aloof from the battle. On the other hand, the Executive Committee was elected by the delegates to the Representative Assembly. Through their election campaigns, they became aware of the priority issues of the delegates.

In the mid-1960s, the Executive Committee, feeling confident it had a better reading on the desires of the members than either the executive secretary or the Board of Directors, seized the initiative and moved ahead to implement the policies that it had helped to push through the Assembly.

In urging caution lest the unity of the Association be upset, Dr. Carr was viewed by some as blocking progress on a problem the members wanted to see solved. So they moved into what they perceived to be a vacuum left by the administration.

With dual affiliates in nine states still unmerged in 1966, black leaders began to become discouraged. At discussions in meetings of the National Council of Officers of State Teachers Associations (NCOSTA), there was growing concern about the types of merger that had been taking place. The names of the new organizations were all a continuation of the names of the former white groups. Black leaders lacked confidence that the merged organizations would provide the type of aggressive defense of their professional and civil rights to which they had become accustomed in their own separate organizations. Meanwhile, black members, anticipating merger, began joining the white organizations, thus eroding the power base of the black groups.

Vernon McDaniel, executive secretary of the Teachers State Association of Texas, declared at the New Orleans NCOSTA meeting: "Unification, Yes; a coalition of first- and second-class professionals, no." He said, "Unification should guarantee unrestricted opportunity for professional advancement, consideration for elective and appointive offices free from racial stigma, and security of employment for *all* teachers."[26]

Horace Tate, executive secretary of the Georgia Teachers and Education Association, voiced the feelings of some other black leaders when he said:

> The aim of many who are administrators . . . of associations that have previously served all white members, is not to merge, unify or integrate with the associations directed by Negroes but to eliminate them. . . .
> Mediators or joint committees charged with the responsibility of bringing the state-wide education associations together must understand and operate under a premise that it is not enough just to get two groups together, but they must be gotten together on an equitable, dignified basis.[27]

These feelings on the part of black leaders led to their insistence that the NEA set some standards for what constituted an acceptable merger.

NEA officers and staff had no precedents to follow. We learned from experience as we went along. I remember vividly a meeting of officers of both black and white associations in Atlanta in which questions relating to the need for standards were raised by black leaders. Members of the compliance committee, Jim Williams, John Lawton, and I spent most of one night between meetings drafting some tentative guidelines. When they were presented to the meeting the following morning, sharp objection was voiced to the use of the word "guidelines." In the South, that was a dirty word identified with the federal bureaucracy. We changed the title to "Criteria for Evaluating Merger Plans."

By the time the criteria were adopted, four states—Florida, Texas, Virginia, and Tennessee—had merged. Some leaders may have perceived the direction that future negotiations were to take and moved rapidly to avoid the new conditions.

The influence of the criteria will be apparent in the following state-by-state summaries of the procedures, issues, and conditions of merger. The summaries are in sequence according to the dates on which the mergers took place.

Florida—1966

The Florida merger became effective on July 30, 1966, before merger criteria had been established. However, the agreement contained a provision for a committee on human rights to monitor the merger and to be a mechanism through which members could present grievances if they felt the merger was not serving their needs properly.

The white Florida Education Association (FEA) and the black Florida State Teachers Association (FSTA) were supporting an FEA member—a Florida principal, Braulio Alonso—for the office of NEA vice-president/president-elect at the Miami Beach convention. The effective date of the merger fell in the same week as the meeting of the Representative Assembly. The timing of the merger gave impetus to the merger movement, motivated members to move ahead on the merger, and obviated any opposition that might have arisen if the associations had been unmerged at the time of nomination.

The chief issue in the merger negotiation was job security for members of the staff of the minority association. Gilbert Porter, FSTA executive secretary, noting the erosion of membership in FSTA as merger talks progressed, accepted a position as special assistant deputy superintendent of public schools in Dade County in 1965. At the time of Porter's resignation, merger was imminent. Therefore, some assurance of continued employment was necessary to attract an able successor. Alvie A. Benton, who served as FSTA president in 1964–65, took over as executive secretary and held that position until consummation of the merger. At that time, he became a member of the field staff of the FEA.

The disposition of assets and the selection of a name for the unified organization were also issues. For many years, black people could not own property. Accordingly, the headquarters building of FSTA was a prestigious symbol that was highly prized by the members who had, with considerable sacrifice, constructed the $100,000 brick and glass structure in 1961. Upon completion of the building, Gilbert Porter said, "Now, for the first time in the seventy-one year history of our Association, we can begin to hold up our heads and stick out our chests, for when this structure is completed, the membership of FSTA will have a new sense of pride, unity, and accord."[28]

Obviously, it was a wrenching experience for FSTA members to give up their exclusive identification with the headquarters building within the short period of five years from the time of its completion. Nevertheless, the FSTA not only agreed to make the sacrifice to achieve the promise of added strength through unification, but called upon its members to pay off the $15,266.88 mortgage on the building so they could "enter into the merger agreement free of . . . indebtedness." The members came through, the mortgage was paid off, and the merger took place on schedule.

At the Miami Beach convention on July 1, 1966, Ed Henderson, FEA executive secretary, said to the NEA Representative Assembly, "It is my privilege to report to you and to this Delegate Assembly that since yesterday the status of our delegation has changed. Yesterday, we represented two state associations. Today, we represent one."

He then introduced the presidents of the two associations. Marion Shannon, FSTA president, said: "The members of the former Florida State Teachers Association are proud of this day. . . . We recommend our efforts as a beginning for our sister states, and we pledge to this union our sacred trust that we will make it work." Bob Jones, FEA president, spoke in a similar vein, saying: "We urge and pray that elected and employed leaders of our neighboring states will follow a similar course and mind."

Texas—1966

The Texas merger, which became effective on December 30, 1966, provided that net assets of the former black affiliate, the Texas State Association of Teachers (TSAT), be turned over to the Commission on Democracy and Human Rights, which was created by TSAT to protect the civil, professional, and human rights of black educators in Texas. This action reflected the anxiety black teachers felt in giving up the organization they had relied upon for protection through years of struggle for equality.

No guarantees were given except for the written assurance of the executive secretary of the Texas State Teachers Association (TSTA) that "there will be no racial restrictions in employing future employees" for the TSTA.[29]

The TSTA removed racial membership restrictions on November 30, 1963, and an estimated 2,900 TSAT members joined following the announcement.

The rationale for the TSAT action included the following points:

1. Texas had progressed more rapidly than other southern states in desegregating its schools.
2. Passage of the Civil Rights Act of 1964 made separate organizations untenable, given the requirement of integrating teachers and pupils.
3. Dual membership caused the attrition of members, weakening the ability of TSAT to provide needed services.
4. Freedom of decision gave the state associations greater flexibility than might exist later when national guidelines might be implemented.
5. The association anticipated a federal mandate for desegregation of school faculties.

Proceeding under the foregoing rationale, the Executive Committee of TSAT initiated merger talks by directing a telegram to the TSTA Executive Committee on September 21, 1963, proposing that the two associations take exploratory steps toward merger. The following month, the TSAT Executive Committee recommended a position statement to the Delegate Assembly which was approved by the delegates.

As talks about unification progressed, TSAT membership continued to decline. The membership of 10,036 in 1964–65 dropped to 7,306 in 1965–66, thus eroding the ability of the TSAT to either provide the quality of programs required to serve black members or to bargain effectively for merger conditions related to the special needs of minority members.

In January 1966, the Executive Committee, in accord with the action of the Delegate Assembly, drafted a resolution to terminate the association no later than September 4, 1966. At a special convention on the following August 12–13, TSAT members voted without a dissenting vote to dissolve the association.

A certificate of dissolution of TSAT was filed with the secretary of state on December 30, 1966. A certificate of incorporation for the Commission on Democracy in Education had been issued four months earlier to assure TSAT members they wouldn't be without protection after merger.

Virginia—1967

In the Virginia merger, the chief issue blocking agreement was employment of the staff members of the 8,500-member black affiliate, the Virginia Teachers Association (VTA). This problem was resolved when the Virginia Education Association agreed to name Fitz Turner, president of VTA, to the position of director of special services in the new organization and Dr. Rupert Picott, VTA executive secretary, was employed by NEA.

Tennessee — 1967

The issue in Tennessee was similar to that in Virginia—the employment of staff. In both cases, the primary issue was the black executive secretary, who because of his leadership position had been aggressively and prominently involved in the push for civil rights. There was agreement that the merged associations must have a racially balanced, integrated staff. But it was difficult for whites to overlook feelings generated over a period of years. It was equally difficult for black members to see their leaders sacrificed to achieve merger. In both states, the problem was solved by the black executive secretary's acceptance of other employment. George W. Brooks, executive secretary of the Tennessee Education Congress (TEC), was employed by the Tennessee State Department of Education, and Harper Johnson, another black leader, was later named to the position of field representative on the staff of the merged association.

South Carolina — 1968

The merger plan in South Carolina was developed by a committee composed of six members from each association. The plan called for a one-year transition period during which a new constitution would be developed.

The governance structure provided for the present president-elect of the white South Carolina Education Association (SCEA) to become the first president of the merged association. The vice-president would be the president of the black Palmetto Education Association (PEA), who had served one year of a two-year term.

The executive secretary of the merged association would be the white executive secretary of the SCEA. The Black executive secretary of the PEA would become associate executive secretary of the combined association for special services.

The interim Board of Directors would be the combined Executive Committees of the two organizations, composed of eighteen PEA members and twenty-one SCEA members. An Executive Committee of seven would include the president and three members from each former association appointed from members of the two boards.

The plan provided for proportional representation on committees and a minimum number of PEA members. Exceptions were made to give the PEA, among other exceptions, the chairman plus equal representation on the balance of the membership of the Committee on Professional Rights and Responsibilities. This is the committee that would deal with the protection of members' rights, in which the PEA had both a special interest and years of experience.

The effective date of merger, under the plan, was to be April 1, 1968, after which there would be no ethnic guarantees. (This provision was modified in 1971 and 1972 to guarantee for nine years at least two PEA members on the nine-member Executive Committee, three PEA members of nine at-large members on the Board of Directors, and inclusion of the past presidents of the PEA, the SCEA, and the merged association as voting members of the Delegate Assembly.)

PEA representatives on the merger committee sought to achieve four objectives:

1. A guarantee that the $40,000 Teacher Defense Fund of the PEA would be reserved for that purpose
2. A name for the new association that would establish it as a completely new association
3. Agreement that the PEA president would become president-elect of the new association and move automatically to the presidency the following year
4. A two-year interim period with equal representation on boards and committees

Only the first objective was achieved. Voting on the merger committee was by a simple majority. The plan was approved by a 7-to-5 vote. SCEA members persuaded the PEA president to vote with them to break a tie. The SCEA Delegate Assembly ratified the plan in March 1967. The PEA delegates rejected it. However, in a special meeting on April 1, they reversed their initial action and approved the plan by a vote of 72 to 38.

The former PEA president ran for president of the merged organization for 1968–69 and was defeated by a white school superintendent.

The PEA president, Ellen C. Watson, felt she had a tacit understanding with SCEA members on the merger committee for SCEA support in her campaign for president of the merged organization. This was disputed by SCEA members on the committee. This misunderstanding and the merger committee's failure to define clearly in advance the duties and responsibilities of the former PEA executive secretary, Walker P. Soloman, created feelings of distrust that took the edge off the sincere efforts of leaders to launch the new organization in a climate of goodwill, unity, and faith in the future. These incidents did serve to emphasize to both state associations and NEA leaders the importance of developing clear understandings of merger conditions and the critical need to record agreements in written documents for discussion prior to action. Elaine Marks, NEA state director, agrees. "Being an early mover," she said, "we have suffered from our own mistakes, from which other states could profit."

On the positive side, in a personal meeting with leaders of the SCEA in September 1978 in Washington, D.C., I was informed that the association has elected two black presidents in two years—Edward E. Taylor (1975–1976) and Agnes H. Wilson (1973); adopted racial guarantees for membership on the boards and committees; and scheduled a survey of attitudes of nonmembers as a basis for building membership.

Criteria for Merger Approved

The criteria for evaluating merger plans, developed initially in Atlanta with the participation of the associations affected, provided the standards for all mergers occurring after October 10, 1968.

At that time, the merger issues centered on the following questions: What should the name of the new organization be? How shall racial balance be achieved for elected officers? For boards of directors? For staff? How shall the assets and liabilities of both associations be shared? How can the basic programs of each organization be continued and strengthened? How can the traditions of the two organizations be preserved?

The criteria, a combination of minimum standards and general principles, were designed to assist affiliates in negotiations on those questions. In addition, for the first time, they provided for third-party intervention in dispute settlements. This made available the services of persons with specialized training to assist the two parties in reaching agreement through biracial mediators, fact finders, and arbitrators.[30]

At the same meeting in which the Executive Committee approved the criteria, E. B. Palmer, immediate past chairman of the National Committee of Educators for Human Rights, urged the Executive Committee "to take immediately the necessary action to achieve one organization in each unmerged state."

Dr. Applegate reported to the Executive Committee in January 1969 that mediation efforts were proceeding toward agreement in Alabama, Louisiana, and North Carolina. Following her report, the committee

Directed mediation efforts to continue in the three states where negotiations were in progress and should be initiated immediately in Arkansas and Mississippi

Asked that all inquiries relating to merger be referred to the office of the Associate Executive Secretary

Declared that the Executive Committee was concerned about the pace of mergers in the five remaining states, and called upon those states to agree to merger terms through mediation or binding arbitration in time to submit their agreed-upon plans to their delegate bodies or membership votes prior to the June 1969 meeting of the Philadelphia convention

Put the state affiliates on notice that the Executive Committee would consider merger progress on a state-by-state basis at its February 1969 meeting

At the conclusion of the Executive Committee meeting the six states of Alabama, Arkansas, Georgia, Louisiana, Mississippi, and North Carolina remained unmerged. The deadline for merger of all affiliates left only five months to reach agreement and go through the process of ratification by the membership or state representative assemblies.

The mediation sessions were moving slowly. Both associations, in most cases, had taken positions from which they could not retreat without losing face. Daily warnings were being received. Those whose chief concern was "preserving the unity of the association" warned against bringing in "outsiders" to solve the "internal problems" of a state.

Those whose primary interest was "merger now" warned that unless the Executive Committee assumed the leadership to force one association in each state, the Representative Assembly would take matters into its own hands at the June meeting in Philadelphia.

Obviously, new procedures were called for. The compliance committee asked me to send weekly reports of progress to keep them up to date with developments.

It was agreed that the only way to complete the task was to put greater emphasis on the mediation and arbitration function. There was an obvious need for a skilled third party who could propose solutions without committing either of the parties to a specific position. There was also a clear need for trained neutral persons who could press both parties to examine their own positions.

Special care was given to the selection and assignment of mediators because the conditions in merger talks differed sharply from those involved in the usual labor dispute settlements. Strong pressures of immediate self-interest that provide motivation for agreement in labor-management disputes were not present.

Inexperience with negotiation techniques, the nagging fear of whites that whatever agreement was reached might be rejected later by their constituents, and the sensitivity of blacks to the possible charges of "Uncle Tomism" posed additional problems requiring sensitivity, skill, and understanding on the part of the mediators.

At first, there was strong opposition to mediation. However, with experience and with persistent prodding by NEA, all of the remaining six states agreed to accept the assistance of a mediator. Usually, a two-member team was used—one black and one white. A different black mediator, recommended by the Center for Dispute Settlement of the American Arbitration Association, was assigned to each state by the NEA after consultation with state leaders.[31]

Black mediators and the states to which they were assigned were: Romulus Murphy, a Raleigh, North Carolina, attorney (North Carolina); Dr. Sam Proctor, a dean at the University of Wisconsin (Alabama); and Frank Williams, former U.S. ambassador to Ghana and head of the Urban Center, Columbia University (Louisiana).

Frederick H. Bullen, a partner in the New York City law firm of Kaye, Scholer, Fierman, Hays, and Handler, was the white mediator in North Carolina, Georgia, Alabama, and Mississippi. Peter Fishbein, a member of the same law firm, was the white mediator in Louisiana; and I, by agreement with the two associations in Arkansas, assisted in resolving the final differences in that state, and served as NEA staff coordinator in my position as associate executive secretary.

Elizabeth Duncan Koontz was the first black person to attain a major NEA leadership position when she was elected to head the Association's largest department—the Department of Classroom Teachers—in 1965. She then went on to become president-elect of the NEA in 1967 and president the following year. Through the force of her personality and the prestige of her positions, she was able to intervene effectively at critical points in the merger negotiations. Her influence, often subtle and low-key, was a major factor both in keeping merger talks moving in a constructive way and in achieving equitable results.

Resolving the Issues

The Executive Committee, following an executive session on February 12, 1969, strengthened the hands of mediators by approving recommendations of the Compliance Committee which gave two options to associations that had not reached agreement by March 1, 1969:

> *Option one*—accept fact finding by a fact finder selected by NEA, after consultation with the parties. The fact finder would make a study of the issues after a hearing, and submit a report and recommendations to both parties and NEA. If the recommendations of the fact finder were not accepted by both parties, the NEA Executive Committee would draft a proposed plan that, in its judgment, would be equitable to all parties.
>
> *Option two*—accept binding arbitration on all remaining, unresolved issues by an arbitrator selected by the NEA after consultation with the officers of the two state associations.

The committee reaffirmed its previous action requiring ratification of merger agreements before the close of the 1968–69 school year and agreed to share the cost of a special meeting of any association's Delegate Assembly if such a special meeting were necessary to meet the deadline.

In the event the two parties failed to agree to accept the arbitrator's decision, the recommendations of the mediator, or the plan recommended by the Executive Committee, the Executive Committee would call a hearing to secure information and recommend a plan of its own. The hearing would be held before June 30, 1969, and the parties could submit briefs and oral arguments.

In a formal motion, the Executive Committee indicated it would take whatever action it believed to be appropriate with regard to compliance, including disaffiliation of one or both organizations in a state or by recognizing an entirely new organization.

Georgia—1969

The Georgia merger agreement is one of the most comprehensive, and its development involved a longer and more intense period of negotiation than was required in most of the previous mergers. Issues included the disposition of assets; the name of the new association; representation on boards, committees, and commissions; elected officers; and the designation of an executive secretary and the salary relationship of the executive secretary to the associate executive secretary.

In some merger negotiations, the name for the new association became a major issue. In others, it was a bargaining point to be traded for concessions on more substantive issues. In Georgia, it was not a major issue. But there were strong feelings about the use of the name of either of the merging associations. Therefore, early in the negotiations, it was agreed the new organization should have a completely new name. This conformed to a philosophy expressed first by John Lucas of North Carolina in a meeting of the NEA Board of Directors. Lucas made an eloquent appeal for a new association based on the concept that it not be a continuation of anything that has existed in the past. Rather, at some point, both merging organizations cease to exist and an entirely new organization is created unlike either of its antecedent associations. This concept was received warmly by the Board and Executive Committee and influenced several of the remaining merger negotiations on the issue of finding an appropriate name to promote the "Lucas concept."

Having made the decision for an entirely new name, all that remained was finding a combination of words which was acceptable to the merger committee. The name that finally received the committee's approval was the Georgia Association of Educators.

There were other questions more difficult to resolve. For example, how shall boards, committees, and commissions be racially balanced? Customarily, white merger committee members pushed for the "one man, one vote" principle, with racial membership on boards and committees determined according to the ratio of white to black members. Black members, having observed the disappearance of black faces from among the officers and board and committee members in the early merged associations, held out for fifty-fifty representation.

Blacks conceded that after an interim period long enough for the two groups to get acquainted and to develop respect for each other, such guarantees would be less important.

In early merger discussions, it was painfully clear that blacks and whites who lived in the same geographic communities did not know each other, and the communities were structured both physically and socially to perpetuate the estrangement. Initially, the black members were reluctant to disagree openly with the white members. It was not until differences could be expressed openly that we began to make progress.

Another familiar factor complicated the discussion of representation. The black and white organizations provided different services for their members, requiring different programs and staffs with different skills. In such activities as the defense of a member's constitutional rights, black negotiators wanted majority representation on the committee responsible for this activity. In addition, they wanted assurance that adequate budgets would be available to implement the committee's recommendations. A term was coined for this need in negotiating matters relating to the distribution of power within the association structure. The term was "determinative power." At certain critical points, black negotiators insisted on determinative power to do what had to be done to carry on activities heretofore provided by the black associations. They also needed the power to block an action such as might occur if the committee were to defend a black teacher in an action against a white administrator who may be a member of the former white organization.

In the Georgia merger agreement, questions involving the distribution of power were resolved by providing for nine-year guarantees of the following:

1. The presidency of the new association would alternate for the first two years. Thereafter, there would be a black president every three years for three three-year cycles. For the first year, the president would be of the race opposite to the race of the executive secretary.

2. The Board of Directors would be comprised of ten white and ten black members for the first three years. In the second three years, Board membership would include twelve white members and eight black members. In the third three-year period, the black membership would be reduced to six and white membership would increase to fourteen.

3. The Executive Committee would include three white members and two black members for the nine-year period.

4. Committees and commissions would have equal representation of black and white members for the first three years and minimum ratios thereafter.

5. The Professional Rights and Responsibilities Committee would serve the same function as the NEA committee with the same name.

6. Adequate staff and budget would be provided.[32]

Another issue that became a major problem for the committee was the disposition of properties owned by the two associations. At one point, this problem threatened to wreck the entire merger. Both associations owned headquarters buildings. Both saw the building as symbolic of the strength and stature of the organization.

The black Georgia Teachers and Education Association (GT&EA) had conducted a drive to pay off the mortgage on the building just months before the merger talks began.

White members of the committee took a firm position that the assets of both associations should become the property of the new association at the time of merger. Black members had doubts about the ability of the new organization to endure and insisted that the buildings not be disposed of but retained until it was known whether the merger was to survive. In the event the merger were to fail, black members saw the building as a place to which they could withdraw.

White members saw retention of the building as a hedge that could be a continuing threat to the merger, providing a refuge to which black members could retreat if the new organization faced difficult problems. They therefore insisted that all "bridges be burned" and all assets of both associations be turned over to the merged organization.

Through skillful negotiation by Fred Bullen and Jim Williams, and some statesmanship by leaders in both groups, a compromise was arrived at. It was agreed that the new association would not occupy either headquarters building.

Immediate steps would be taken upon consummation of the merger to purchase a site and design a new headquarters building adapted to the functions and size of the new association. Each association would advance $25,000 for the purchase of a site and to cover initial architectural fees to develop a building plan and specifications. Construction of the new building would commense as soon as possible after merger.

It was agreed that the properties of both associations would be transferred to two separate groups of trustees for a five-year period. At the end of the five-year period, the properties would be transferred to the new association. With the approval of three-fourths of the trustees of each trust, the property could be transferred before the end of the five-year period. Provision was made for mortgaging the property, if necessary, to pay construction costs of the new headquarters with the majority vote of both groups of trustees.

Until such time as the new structure would be completed, it was agreed that both the executive secretary and the associate executive secretary would occupy offices in the same building.

Of all issues in the Georgia merger negotiations, the most stubborn was the appointment of the executive secretary and the associate executive secretary and the fixing of salaries for both positions.

White committee members argued that white members of the merged association would outnumber black members by three to one; any agreement would have to be ratified, and it was unlikely that a merger agreement would be ratified if the white executive secretary were not selected.

Black members argued that the GT&EA executive secretary should have the position because of his ten years of experience as an association executive, compared with one year the white executive secretary.

After long and often emotional discussions, it was finally agreed that the appointment of the executive secretary would be made by a three-member selection committee—one member selected from each association and the third member, who would be chairman, to be named by agreement of the first two. Finding the third member was not easy. After unsuccessfully canvasing the South for a person acceptable to both sides, the negotiators finally agreed upon Dr. Theodore R. Sizer, dean of the Harvard College of Education. Sizer took the task seriously. He organized a biracial group of graduate students to dig into the backgrounds of both executive secretaries. Interviews were held with members of both associations, NEA officials, and others. Both candidates were interviewed by the committee.

Meanwhile, a new issue developed. Carl Hodges was receiving a salary of $25,000 as executive secretary of the white Georgia Education Association (GEA), and Horace Tate's salary as executive secretary of the GT& EA was $22,500. What difference should exist between the salaries of the executive secretary and the associate? The negotiators couldn't agree, so they referred the question to the Selection Committee. NEA criteria required that both executive secretaries of the present associations be the nominees for the position of executive secretary of the merged association; the one not selected to head the merged association was to be assigned an appropriate position reporting directly to the executive secretary, with a salary at least equal to the person who was second in command.

The Selection Committee, with Dr. Sizer playing a key role, selected Carl Hodges for the position of executive secretary. The committee set Hodge's salary at $27,000 and Tate's at $25,659, a 5 percent difference to be maintained in future years.

With the settlement of the thorny questions of selecting the executive secretary and of fixing the salaries, it appeared an agreement was assured. On January 1, the negotiators took the agreement to the Boards of Directors of the two associations for ratification.

The agreement was approved by the GEA Board and rejected by the GT&EA. This outcome shocked the GEA and left the negotiators frustrated and discouraged.

Through the mediation skills of Fred Bullen, Sam Ethridge, and Jim Williams, the negotiators were persuaded to return to the negotiating table for one final effort to reach agreement. The GT&EA Board had a legitimate criticism of the agreement: it lacked a procedure through which members could file grievances after the expiration of the nine-year period. Bullen persuaded the GEA to modify its position, and this one further compromise put the agreement back together.

Twice a year, a Grievance Committee of twelve members—six white and six blacks—would review how the merger was working and consider complaints concerning violations of the merger agreement. It was agreed that after the nine-year period there would continue to be black members on the Board of Directors, on committees, and among the officers. If such representation did not occur, the committee would report to the Representative Assembly and Board of Directors and make recommendations for correcting the situation.

The merger plan was approved on March 8, 1969, and ratification by the two delegate bodies was scheduled by the GT&EA on March 27 and by the GEA on May 17. The ballots cast by the GT&EA delegates were impounded in an Atlanta vault, to be opened and counted at the same time as those of GEA.

The ballots of both groups were counted in an "impeccably integrated situation—a small conference room at the Macon Coliseum, with officials and poll watchers of both races present."[33] The final count showed a substantial majority in favor of the plan by the delegates of both organizations. The GEA approved by a vote of 803 to 172, and the GT&EA voted for approval 313 to 73.

In the achievement of the Georgia merger, a number of heroes emerged. Among those whose commitment to the principles of equality sustained them through a three-year sequence of meetings requiring endless patience, sensitivity, and understanding, Clyde W. Kimball, Jr., Atlanta school principal and GEA president in 1966–67, was a key figure in the negotiations. One participant described his contribution by declaring, "Without Clyde Kimball there would have been no Georgia merger."

GT&EA members whose leadership contributed in a substantial way to achievement of the Georgia merger were Charles A. Hicks, GT&EA president, 1968–69, and NEA directors R. J. Martin (Macon) and Charles L. Butler (Augusta). Sam Ethridge, NEA assistant executive secretary for human relations, assisted in a variety of ways. Franklin Shumake, GEA president and chairman of the merger committee, played a key role in solving the sensitive balance-of-power question.

The Georgia merger was not only one of the most complex but was made more difficult by the personal relationships and provocative developments during the merger talks. For example, in the summer of 1968, while the talks were taking place, the GEA abruptly accepted the resignation of Executive Secretary Frank Hughes, who was within two years of retirement, and replaced him with Dr. Carl V. Hodges, the fifty-six year old superintendent of schools in Waycross, Georgia. He had earned his doctor's degree at the University of Georgia and had been engaged in school work all of his working life.

With the imminent retirement of Frank Hughes, Horace Tate obviously nurtured the expectation that, if not appointed initially, he would succeed to the executive secretaryship when Hughes retired. It is easy to understand why Tate would see the replacement of Hughes with a man whose academic qualifications were more nearly comparable to his own as a ploy to pave the way for Hodges to be appointed to head the new association.

Horace Tate, a naturally aggressive person, became more aggressive. Tate was the first black man to receive an earned doctorate from the University of Kentucky. He had served as a member of the Atlanta school board, had run unsuccessfully for mayor of Atlanta, had become state vice-chairman of the Democratic party, and was elected to the state senate. When Carl Hodges resigned, Horace Tate was appointed executive secretary of the merged association, a position he holds as of this writing.

It was a standing procedure in the South to open all meetings with an invocation. Fred Bullen, recalling some of his Georgia experiences with the merger committee, said, "After bowing our heads together in prayer, the members of the committee spent two hours ripping one another apart, in a courteous manner, of course, before the mediators could even be introduced. By that time the parties were talking about plans for adjourning, and returning to their homes located in scattered communities throughout the state."[34]

Jim Williams added that "one night it was decided to forgo the prayer and to read aloud the Twenty-third Psalm, but when we reached the passage which reads, 'Thou preparest a table before me in the presence of mine enemies,' members of the committee could not keep a straight face."[35]

During merger talks in the spring of 1968, the NEA Board of Directors held a meeting in Atlanta. During the meeting, separate invitations to cocktail parties were received from the GEA and the GT&EA. The parties were scheduled for different evenings at the state headquarters buildings of the two affiliates. When the invitations were delivered to President George Fischer, he called Jim Williams, manager of the NEA regional office, and told him the NEA doesn't want to participate in "separate but equal" cocktail parties and asked him to see if he could persuade the two organizations to cooperate in hosting a joint party.

This incident occurred at a time when the two associations were having difficulty agreeing on merger conditions. But when Jim Williams delivered the president's message to the executives of the two associations, they responded as one. Carl Hodges of the GEA said it was hardly fitting or gracious for the guests to inform the hosts how to organize a party. Horace Tate of GT&EA said, "Next they will be telling us what to serve." However, Williams, in characteristic fashion, persuaded them to cooperate by jointly hosting the venture. But they insisted on two parties instead of one. One was held at the GT&EA headquarters building and the other took place in a downtown Atlanta hotel.

Arkansas—1969

Agreement was reached on conditions of merger by the joint committee of the black Arkansas Teachers Association (ATA) and the white Arkansas Education Association (AEA) on March 1, 1969, to take effect on the following July 1.

Prior to merger the AEA had a membership of 18,000 compared to 3,500 for the ATA. Largely due to the foresight and statesmanship of the leaders of both organizations, efforts had begun for merger of the two organizations prior to the adoption of the NEA's merger mandate in 1964.

Issues included representation, the utilization of property, the reorganization of the staff, preservation of the history and continuation of the traditions of the merging organizations, and the selection of a name for the new organization.

It was agreed that the new, merged association would take the name of the former white affiliate—the Arkansas Education Association. The president, president-elect, and past president of the black ATA would be members of the thirty-six member board of directors. In addition, the constitution of the new organization authorized five directors elected from the state at large to represent the former ATA members.

Committee membership was to be in the same proportion as the relation of black to white members in the total membership of the new association. However, additional representation for black members was provided on the Commission on Professional Rights and Responsibilities because of the special concerns of black members for the work of that commission.

It was agreed that representation on delegations to state regional and national meetings would be representative of the racial composition of the membership of the merged association, and the alternate member of the NEA Resolutions Committee from Arkansas would be of a different race from that of the committee member.

The joint committee of the two merging associations was continued for a period of five years to resolve differences that might arise in the application of the merger conditions.

Upon merger, the AEA building became the headquarters of the merged organization. Also, the ATA building became the property of the new association. It was agreed, however, that it would not be disposed of without the advice and consent of a building board of supervisors composed of four black and three white members. (The ATA building was sold on July 1, 1970, with the approval of the building board of supervisors. The proceeds from the sale—$45,000—were invested to finance a living memorial to the Arkansas Teachers Association. The annual earnings of approximately $3,600 support undergraduate scholarships to qualifying black students enrolled in accredited teacher education programs in Arkansas, and an annual in-service grant is awarded to an association member to pursue an appropriate research study for the advancement of black educators.)

The executive secretary of the white AEA was named executive secretary of the meged AEA, and the executive secretary of the black ATA became assistant executive secretary for human relations. Position descriptions and salary schedules were agreed upon for all staff positions.

In order to demonstrate that the new association was a product of both the AEA and ATA, it was agreed to display the pictures of all past presidents of both organizations in the board room of the merged association.

Presidents of the two associations at the time of merger were Maurice Dunn (AEA) and York W. Williams (ATA). Forrest Rozzell was executive secretary of AEA and T. E. Patterson was the executive secretary of ATA.

In an interview in Washington, D.C., on September 27, 1978, Sherry Price, AEA president; Peggy Thompson, NEA state director; Kai Erickson, executive secretary; and, T. E. Patterson, associate executive secretary, told me the merger in Arkansas had improved services for both black and white members. Pressed for tangible results, they pointed to the election of their first black president, Joe Key, who would take office in 1979; "white members," they said, "were better protected than ever before; black members with 20% of the membership held 33% of the positions on the board of directors; and the association had voluntarily extended the original guarantees of black representation for an unlimited period."

Alabama—1969

The major issue in the Alabama merger centered on the protection of the rights of teachers. The stickiest aspect of the problem involved assurances that court actions already filed would be pursued to a conclusion. The white affiliate did not have a history of defending the constitutional rights of its members. Since the defense of members' rights was of prime concern to the black members, their representatives wanted to be certain the new organization would not circumscribe the traditional role of the

Alabama State Teachers Association (ASTA). If the merged organization failed to pursue the cases, the black association wanted assurance that the NEA would assume the responsibility. This issue developed late in the negotiations and for a time threatened to upset the entire plan. I shall return to a more complete discussion of this issue after reviewing other facets of the Alabama agreement on which negotiators had reached a meeting of the minds.

Representation and Officers. It was agreed that the president of the merged association would be the president of the white Alabama Education Association (AEA) elected at the last election. The president and president-elect of the black ASTA elected at the last election would become presidents in the second and fourth years. No guarantees were provided beyond the four years, but the negotiators hoped and believed black members would be elected on an equitable basis once the experience of a biracial officership was established.

The twenty-member Board of Directors would include twelve white members and eight black members for the first six years. Board members would be elected one from each of the nine geographic districts plus the elected officers. The balance of the members would be at-large members selected by the Board from among nominees made by the Board of the former organization having a deficiency of representatives. For the first year, the Board would include twenty-two members—nine former ASTA members and thirteen former AEA members.

The committee dealing with the protection of the constitutional rights of members—the Committee on Professional Rights and Responsibilities (PR&R) would have equal numbers of AEA and ASTA members. For the six-year interim period, the associate executive secretary would serve as staff consultant to the PR&R committee and direct implementation of the teacher rights program of the association.

The proportion of black members on the committees, as a minimum, would be the same as the proportion of black members in the total membership of the merged organization. Committee chairmanships would be rotated among black and white members.

It was agreed early in the negotiations that the AEA executive secretary would become the executive secretary of the new association. In defining the duties of the executive secretary and associate, it was agreed, in general, that

1. Both the executive secretary and the associate executive secretary would provide coordinated constructive leadership on all matters
2. The associate would direct the PR&R program

3. Both would serve as nonvoting members of the Board of Directors
4. The associate would serve as consultant to local and district associations and related groups

Detailed position descriptions, work schedules, salary schedules, travel policies, and other administrative policies were agreed upon.

The disposition of property and transfer of assets and liabilities to the new organization, a major problem in some mergers, was accomplished with relative ease in Alabama.

The AEA had an office building in Montgomery on the same block as the Martin Luther King Dexter Avenue Baptist Church. It was near the state capitol and could be modified to accommodate the new organization. The ASTA building was sold to Alabama State College. The AEA building was expanded to meet the needs of the merged association.

The selection of a name for the new association became an issue. The black negotiators wanted a completely new name. White members insisted on retaining the name of the white association. They argued that the name was included in the statute governing the state pension plan and thus it would be possible for all staff of the merged association to be covered automatically. If the name were changed, the statute would have to be amended and the Wallace administration was not likely to approve it. They also argued that the name was well established and expressed concern that cooperation with the state government would be weakened if a new name were adopted.

Black negotiators didn't give credence to the arguments but used their concession to win substantive improvements in the agreement to secure a guarantee of a minimum number of minority members on boards and committees beyond the six-year interim period. They also won agreement to a compromise. The AEA name would be followed by a line to read "Formerly the Alabama State Teachers Association and the Alabama Education Association." This would be carried on the letterhead for at least three years. Also, the seal of the organization would carry the initials of the two organizations and the date of the merger.

A merger review committee was agreed upon to evaluate periodically the operation of the merger. The committee of ten members would report to the Board of Directors of the new association and also to the Executive Committee of the NEA on the degree to which the association was achieving the goals of the merger. The committee was also to advise local affiliates on problems related to merger.

The Legal Problems.   All school districts in Alabama since 1967 had been under a federal order to desegregate. In *Lee* v. *Macon*, a three-member federal district court had decreed that the defendants—the Alabama State Board of Education, Governor Lurleen Wallace, the state superintendent of schools, and a hundred school boards and their administrators—be enjoined from discriminating on the basis of race. They were ordered to take specific affirmative action to achieve integration. This order applied to most of the school districts of Alabama. The others were already under specific federal orders to desegregate. Subsequently, the ASTA moved to intervene as plaintiff in these actions to promote enforcement as they affected the integration of teachers. The order provided, among other things, that "teachers and other professional staff members will not be discriminatorily assigned, dismissed, demoted or passed over for retention, promotion or hiring, on the ground of race or color . . . if as a result of desegregation, there is to be a reduction in the total professional staff of a school system, the qualifications of all staff members in the system will be evaluated in selecting the staff member to be released without consideration of race or color."

The ASTA wanted to bring the court's attention to alleged specific violations of the order. It appeared that the merged organization would be permitted to assume the role of the ASTA. At least, there appeared to be no legal barrier.

The problem was not the right, but the will, of the new organization to intervene and accept such a broad obligation.

The ASTA had achieved the status of party plaintiff in *Lee* v. *Macon*, but there were no specific enforcement matters pending before the federal court in which it was involved at the time of our negotiations. However, the attorney for the ASTA was preparing to file with the court more than twenty cases of alleged violations. The ASTA insisted that any cases filed before August 1 (the effective date of merger) be pursued to completion without further review by the new organization.

What concerned the ASTA is that the association might be faced with conditions in which the interests of a black teacher and a white teacher were in conflict, with both looking to the organization for protection.

At the time this question became an issue, the agreement had been approved by the merger committee. It had also been approved by the AEA Executive Committee. The ASTA Executive Committee was withholding action until an understanding could be reached on the continuation of ASTA's interest in the *Lee* v. *Macon* court actions.

The Delegate Assemblies of the two associations were scheduled for May 16, to act on the merger agreement. The deadline for merger by the NEA was July 1. The Alabama legislature was in session and had before it a number of important school measures.

In a move to resolve the matter, the NEA assured the ASTA that if the merged organization declined to pursue any cases pending on August 1, the NEA would continue financial and legal support for the litigation. The ASTA was not satisfied with this offer.

Meanwhile, the AEA announced that unless agreement on merger was achieved by August 1, it would consider the ASTA to have rejected merger and the the whole matter would be subject to renegotiation. Furthermore, the AEA argued, the agreement might have to be resubmitted to the membership, some of whom were having second thoughts about the wisdom of merger.

Finally, two weeks before the August 1 deadline, a resolution of the legal question was achieved. The conditions of settlement were:

1. The NEA would move immediately to intervene as a general party plaintiff under all outstanding federal court orders in Alabama protecting the rights of educators.

2. The NEA agreed to pursue all specific claims of violations of such orders initiated by ASTA prior to August 1, without further screening by the PR&R commission of either the NEA or the merged state association.

3. A procedure was offered for the support of meritorious claims that might arise in the future, allowing cases to go directly from the PR&R commission of the merged organization (on which there would be equal numbers of black and white members) to the NEA Dushane Fund for Teacher Rights.

On July 29, the NEA issued a press release in Montgomery announcing it would file motions by the end of the week substituting the NEA for the ASTA as party plaintiff under existing federal orders.

A written agreement was signed on July 30, resolving the stubborn issue, and on August 21, the three-man federal court granted the NEA request, removing the last obstacle to merger in Alabama.

As an example of the social climate in which negotiations took place, NEA President Irvamae Applegate returned to her hotel room in Birmingham after a meeting to find a message requesting she call a local telephone number. When she dialed the number, she received a recorded message condemning her for supporting the Civil Rights Act, proposing to push children into distant schools not of their parents' choosing, advocating Nazi-style book burning of texts that were not interracial, and "promoting communist socialist propaganda."

Fortunately, teachers' and public school pupils' attitudes were in advance of the attitudes of segments of the general public on matters of race in Alabama. We found this to be true in all southern states.

Mississippi—1976

Throughout the early months of 1969, the white Mississippi Education Association (MEA) and the black Mississippi Teachers Association (MTA), with the help of mediators provided by the NEA, engaged in a last-ditch effort to reach agreement before the July 1 deadline. However, the compromises that made mergers a reality in the other states eluded the mediators in Mississippi. Finally, after an intense but unsuccessful attempt to reach agreement on March 11, it was decided to appoint a fact finder to resolve the disputed issues. Disagreement centered chiefly on matters of representation.

Dr. Fred Hipp, executive secretary of the New Jersey Education Association, was named fact finder after consultation with the officers of both affiliates. The fact-finding hearing was scheduled for March 22 in Jackson. May 3 was set for special meetings of both Delegate Assemblies.

It was understood that, if no agreement was reached by April 15, the NEA Executive Committee would recommend a plan by May 1, based on the recommendations of Dr. Hipp.

Following the hearing at which both affiliates appeared and presented their views, Dr. Hipp prepared a report recommending a merger plan that appeared to give consideration to the views of both groups. The report proposed a three-phase plan with the following general characteristics.

Phase one would create a joint council with equal representation from the MEA and MTA. Its responsibilities would include coordinating the activities of the two organizations, combining committees, drafting a new constitution, and developing a complete merger plan to become effective in one year.

Phase two would cover a six-year period in which the merger plan, including these provisions, would be in effect:

A Board of Directors of twenty-four members would be named, with equal representation of black and white members.

An executive secretary and an associate executive secretary would be named—one from the MEA staff and one from the MTA staff.

A Representative Assembly would be established based on proportional geographical and racial representation and with provision for a two-thirds vote of delegates present and voting for the passage of any measure.

Committees would be created with equal racial representation on five critical committees and proportional representation on all others.

All staff members of both associations would be retained with their present or better rank and with no reduction in pay.

Both associations would dispose of their present properties and a new headquarters would be purchased or rented.

A grievance committee would be named, with equal numbers of black and white members, to resolve problems that could arise from practices of the merged association.

The name of the merged association would be the Mississippi Association of Educators (MAE).

Phase three required the Board of Directors to present to the Delegate Assembly a revised constitution prior to the expiration of the six-year period. At that time, the guarantees, included in the first constitution, would be reconsidered.

The Hipp proposal was reviewed with the MEA and MTA officers on March 29, 1969, and at the conclusion of discussions, a statement was signed by the two presidents and executive secretaries and the NEA state director. The statement said, "This seems to be the best proposal for merger that has come before us in three years and we will recommend it in principle to our respective Boards."

Prospects looked bright for a Mississippi merger following delivery of the report. Both boards had meetings scheduled to consider the proposal.

The NEA Executive Committee reviewed the Hipp report on April 20 and approved it without a dissenting vote. On May 3, the MTA Delegate Assembly approved the Hipp Proposal by a vote of 315 to 4. But the MEA delegates rejected it 468 to 60.

In an analysis of the actions of the two Assemblies, Jim Williams concluded that the difference between the votes of the MEA and MTA was due in large part to the role of the leaders of the two groups. The leaders of the MTA, the president, Dan M. Smith, and members of the merger committee spoke in favor of the plan and urged approval. The MEA, by contrast, voted on the proposal without prior discussion, and its officers did not openly advocate or urge support for the plan.

The Executive Committee, in a special meeting by telephone conference call on May 6, voted to temporarily suspend the MEA until a show-cause hearing could be held later in May.

Following the hearing on May 23, the Executive Committee voted to continue the suspension of the MEA with the understanding that the suspension might become expulsion at any time the Executive Committee concluded that progress toward merger was unsatisfactory. Officers and NEA staff members were instructed to work with the MTA and MEA to accomplish merger before the Philadelphia convention meeting on June 30. If a satisfactory merger could be achieved by that time, the Executive Committee agreed to reconsider the suspension of the MEA.

After an additional unsuccessful try for agreement on June 1, the MEA wired urging the Executive Committee to "keep the door open" to "leave them suspended through the convention."

The Executive Committee continued the MEA suspension until December 31, 1969, but denied delegate credentials to MEA for the Philadelphia meeting.

In October, the Executive Committee allocated funds to permit representatives of the MEA and MTA to hold one more meeting to try to resolve their differences. Both associations, it was reported, had indicated a desire for merger.

At the November 21 meeting, Helen Bain, NEA president-elect, reported that a committee of sixteen (eight each from the MTA and the MEA) had developed a plan for achieving merger and the MEA had agreed to place it on the agenda for action of its Delegate Assembly in March. She also reported that a special meeting of MTA delegates would be required. The Executive Committee agreed to pay the cost of travel and lodging for such a meeting.

In December, Bain again reported that a plan appeared to be developing which could possibly lead to merger. The Executive Committee gave tentative approval to the preliminary report and requested a detailed report for the January 1970 meeting.

At the January meeting, MEA President J. J. Hayden, MEA Executive Secretary Charles A. Johnson, and MTA Executive Secretary C. J. Duckworth, met with the Executive Committee to outline their plan for merger, and the Executive Committee continued the suspension until the March meeting.

On March 18, a hearing was held in Washington, D.C., to give the MEA an opportunity to show cause why it should not be expelled for failure to merge in accord with actions of the NEA Representative Assembly. Five days earlier, the MEA's Representative Assembly turned down the latest merger plan by a vote of 217 to 348. Official action was taken by the Executive Committee to expel the MEA, effective on April 7, 1970. On June 4, NEA President George Fischer reported to the Executive Committee that MEA delegates had failed again to approve merger. This time, the proposal was defeated by only eight votes.

This action left the NEA with a predominantly black Mississippi affiliate with black officers and staff and a headquarters building in the black section of Jackson. The Association was faced with a two-pronged problem: how to make the black MTA attractive to white members who favored a merged organization and still keep the door open for the eventual merger of the two organizations.

On April 12, the MTA was declared to be in good standing and eligible to receive all services of a state affiliate. However, since the object of Resolution 12 was to achieve merger, the MTA was informed it was not in full compliance even though it had voted for the Hipp merger plan. The Executive Committee therefore required that it report, on request, its progress toward achieving full compliance.

Because of the delaying of serious merger action into 1970, it is my considered conclusion that the merger talks became complicated by other events and the NEA's role in them.

On October 29, 1969, the U.S. Supreme Court ordered thirty Mississippi school systems to desegregate their schools immediately. As mentioned earlier, the NEA received a flood of requests for help as a result of the order. The executive secretary on January 8 was directed by the Executive Committee to develop a plan of action to aid in the resolution of problems arising from the order, beginning with an investigation of the situation in Mississippi.

Effects of the Court order on teachers and schools, as revealed in the NEA task force's report referred to earlier, included the wholesale displacement of black educators when schools were combined, the establishment of private schools, discrimination in the assignment of teachers, and testing as a basis for selection of teachers. This development is mentioned here as another example of how external events in the sixties put pressure on the NEA to take actions on several fronts simultaneously, and our actions on one front sometimes adversely effected our progress on another.

In this same period, the NEA's opposition to President Nixon's nomination of Clement F. Haynsworth and Judge G. Harrold Carswell to the Supreme Court won few friends among white leaders in Mississippi.

The feelings of some members on these issues undoubtedly influenced their votes on the merger.

A combination of three factors—problems, effective leadership, and third-party assistance—succeeded in achieving a resumption of talks leading to eventual merger in Mississippi.

While serious obstacles remained, the experience of operating in two separate groups while other related groups were merging, the confusion of two voices for Mississippi teachers, and the exploitation of the division among teachers by those who would limit school improvements helped to bring about the final successful effort for the unification of Mississippi teachers.

In addition to these conditions, Mississippi was fortunate in having two able presidents who could work well together. The leadership of J. D. Williams (MTA) and Bert Thompson (MEA) and the diplomacy of NEA Executive Director Terry Herndon and Regional Director Jim Williams were given much credit by MAE leaders for the successful result.

Initially, the chief problems were not differences on the substantive issues of the merger, but the attitudes and feelings of the participants and their lack of confidence in each other. Since their failure to approve the first merger plan, the MEA had grown in membership and consequently felt self-sufficient. On the other hand, modest progress and feelings of rejection of MTA members created feelings of insecurity.

To those involved in the mergers from the beginning, it became a familiar pattern. Only when the merger committee had met over a long enough period to give members an opportunity to get acquainted with each other as individuals did stereotypes fade, mutual confidence develop, and progress become possible. "The scars of prejudice go deep," said the 1979 MAE president, Helen Moore, "but we are learning to be forgetful."

The toughest substantive problem to solve was that of representation—not only of blacks and whites, but also of teachers and administrators. The differences were ultimately resolved by providing for the following representation for five groups on the sixty-six member Board of Directors.

Thirty-five classroom teachers selected to reflect the racial balance of the membership for the previous year. Five teacher members would represent each of the seven geographic regions of the state.

Fourteen administrators—one elementary and one district administrator from each of the seven districts.

Seven minority members, one from each district to ensure racial balance.

Six elected officers—the president, vice-president, president-elect, secretary treasurer, immediate past president, and NEA director.

Four directors elected to represent the Student Education Association, junior colleges, senior colleges, and the State Department of Education.

Provision was made for the composition of the Board to be proportionate by both race and school position at the end of five years.

An Executive Committee was agreed upon to include the president, vice-president, president-elect, secretary treasurer, and one member from each of the seven districts to serve for a term of one year. It was agreed the committee must reflect the racial composition of the Board of Directors.

The merger agreement provided for delegates to the MAE Representative Assembly to reflect the racial composition of the local associations they represent. Equal representation by race was agreed upon for the Merger Review Committee and the Teacher Rights Committee. All other committees were to be racially balanced, with 40 percent minority representation for three years. Thereafter, representation was to be proportionate to the racial composition of the total membership in the association.

It was agreed that one of the two executive secretaries would be named to that position for the merged organization with the understanding that the one not selected would be the associate executive secretary.

All staff members of the two associations were guaranteed one year's employment.

Merger plans were approved by both Mississippi associations on March 26, 1976, and the merger became effective on September 1, 1976. How was the merger working after three years? An evaluation shows that 90 percent of white members and 85 percent of black members said it was working well or very well. Asked for concrete evidences of success, Henry D. M. Woods, NEA state director, said, "Our Legislative Commission has been able to win salary increases in the past two sessions of the legislature; membership has increased; and our members are better informed about association programs through involvement in them."[36]

Helen Moore said,

> The strengths of both associations have been combined through merger. The two groups can no longer be played against each other, no longer are there two salary schedules, and there is no more competition for credit on measures supported by both groups. We have profited from the mistakes of other states. We initially felt rejected, but we really profited from the delay. Some whites who thought the walls would come tumbling down have lived to see their fears unfounded.
>
> Some of our older blacks said we would be slaves in *their* organization. But our children have been our teachers.
>
> Yes, we got some help from NEA, but when we got down to the nitty-gritty, it was something we had to do for ourselves.[37]

John Ashley, Executive Secretary, said, "The merger is working well. We still have some problems involving the role of Uniserv, the fear of domination by blacks by some members, and the enrollment of 50,000 in private schools. But attitudes are changing. Working together in the classrooms, in athletics, and in other activities means it is no longer a new experience."[38]

Among those giving leadership to the merger effort were J. D. Williams, Helen Moore, Wilma King, Bea Bradley, and Arthur Peyton of the MTA; Bert Thompson, Charles Johnson, L. O. Todd, John Ashley, and Joe Tally of the MEA; and Willard McGuire, Terry Herndon, Jim Williams, Sam Ethridge, Arnold Wolpert, and Joe Fisher of the NEA.

The consummation of the Mississippi merger left only one state, Louisiana, with separate organizations for black and white members.

Louisiana—1977

By February 1969, it was apparent that further mediation sessions were not going to yield an agreement. My March 14 weekly report to the Compliance Committee included this paragraph: "Jim Williams is in Louisiana this week to meet with the two parties. The March 11th meeting did not produce agreement so we have appointed Dr. Dale Kennedy, Executive Secretary, Michigan Education Association, as fact finder. Jim will try to schedule a fact finding hearing for April 1, in Baton Rouge." Before appointment of the fact finder, the officers of both associations were consulted.

The chief issue separating the two organizations was representation. The predominantly white Louisiana Teachers Association (LTA) supported a "one man, one vote" position. The black Louisiana Education Association (LEA) insisted on equal representation on the Board of Directors and certain critical committees, and at least proportional representation on others. In addition, there were other issues not directly connected with merger. One background issue that complicated the situation involved the decision to dismiss five black teachers; one was on the faculty of the school of which the LTA president was the principal.

Dr. Kennedy, after a fact-finding hearing, prepared a report, including a recommended plan for merger. The report was delivered to both associations and reviewed by them.

The report was also reviewed by the NEA Executive Committee, on April 20, 1969. Both affiliates were requested to call meetings of their Delegate Assemblies to act on the fact finder's proposal and report their actions to the Executive Committee by April 30.

A response was received from LTA dated April 28, commenting on each recommendation of the fact finder. No response was received from the LEA within the specified time.

Both associations were advised that if agreement could be reached on amendments to the fact finder's report, the Executive Committee would consider such amendments and approve them if they were consistent with the spirit of Resolution 12.

In the absence of agreement on modifications, the Executive Committee approved the fact finder's report at its meeting in May, but repeated its willingness to consider any agreement the two associations could reach on their own.

On May 24, 1969, the LTA Representative Assembly discussed, but failed to approve, the fact finder's report. However, LTA officers reported the convention was not adjourned. This left open the possibility of reconsidering the action if agreement was reached.

The LEA met in convention on June 16, but did not act on the fact finder's report.

Both the LTA and LEA were suspended by the Executive Committee on June 24, with loss of delegates to the Philadelphia convention. However, the suspension was continued until December 31, 1969, with the understanding that it could be lifted if agreement were reached prior to that date. If, however, the Executive Committee determined that progress was not satisfactory, suspension could be converted to expulsion.

Several attempts were made to resolve the strongly held differences between the two organizations during the summer and fall. However, no agreement could be reached.

In convention meetings held prior to the December 31 deadline, both associations considered the fact finder's proposal. The LEA approved and the LTA rejected it.

At its January meeting, the Executive Committee took two actions. It scheduled a hearing for March 21 to give the LTA an opportunity to show cause why it should not be expelled, and it lifted the suspension of the LEA.

At the February meeting, President George Fischer reported that the LTA might file a law suit against the NEA if it was disaffiliated.

At the show-cause hearing, the LTA raised both procedural and substantive objections to the Executive Committee's action. Procedurally, the LTA argued, its suspension was improper since the Representative Assembly had no established procedures for suspension at the time action was taken in June 1969. Further, the LTA claimed the resolution of the Representative Assembly required the Executive Committee to develop findings showing that continued affiliation of the LTA was prejudicial to the best interests of the NEA. No such findings had been made. The LTA also claimed that its right to due process entitled it to a hearing before an impartial tribunal and the Executive Committee was not impartial.

Substantive objections were twofold: the terms of merger violated the constitutional principal of one man, one vote, and the NEA was requiring of the LTA a condition not required of other state associations, namely, the continued proportional racial representation after an interim period.

At its April meeting, the Executive Committee passed a resolution expelling the LTA effective April 30, 1970. In its decision, the committee held that the LTA's objections were without merit.

With regard to suspension procedures, the committee held that the current procedure related to disaffiliation, and the validity of prior temporary suspension procedures were therefore not relevant.

Concerning the validity of the procedure for terminating the affiliation of the LTA, the committee concluded that Resolution 12 requires only that the Executive Committee make a finding that affiliation is prejudicial to the best interest of the NEA prior to action terminating the affiliation. It does not require that such a finding precede the show-cause hearing.

The committee denied that there was any requirement related to the continued affiliation of a state association for submitting the matter to some wholly disinterested party.

The committee supported the fact finder's recommendation on equal racial representation provisions on the grounds that they apply for an interim period involving two independent sovereign entities and seek the desirable goal that each have an equal voice in the governing of the merged organization. The committee cited provisions of the Georgia and Alabama merger agreements to show that nothing was being required of the LTA that had not been required of other affiliates.

Following its disaffiliation, the LTA did file suit against the NEA, and this had the effect of cutting off further merger talks. However, during the taking of depositions, opportunities arose for me to discuss informally with Horace Robinson, LTA executive secretary, the wisdom of pursuing the legal action as opposed to the resumption of direct communications. It was such a conversation during a luncheon break and the skills of Robert Chanin, NEA general counsel, that eventually led to the resumption of talks, which made possible the completion of the Louisiana merger in 1977.

In 1973, Arvid Anderson, director of the Office of Collective Bargaining, New York City, was appointed by the American Arbitration Association as a neutral to help the two associations reach agreement. His appointment came about as a result of the settlement of the litigation before the U.S. District Court in the Middle District of Louisiana, between the LTA and NEA.

The settlement was approved by Judge West on July 16, 1973, and required that a merger plan be developed with the assistance of a neutral in compliance with the requirements for affiliation with the NEA.

Anderson's efforts spanned a five-year period from 1973 to 1978, with the major effort coming in 1975 and 1976. The final result approved by both organizations in 1977 includes guarantees that go beyond those in the original Kennedy proposal rejected by the LTA. This was a tribute to the leaders of all three associations—the LEA, the LTA, and the NEA— and to the arbitration skills of Arvid Anderson. But the result was not achieved without a great deal of patience, persistence, and expenditure of time and resources by many persons who believed deeply in the benefits to be achieved by merger.

Anderson described the problems and their resolution this way:

> While there were some particular problems of adapting the merger plans to Louisiana, based upon its constituency . . . the real difficulty was not working out the substantive details of merger or a fair allocation between black and white representation. Those factors were important. But the decisive issue was really the attitude of the parties . . . To talk about . . . merger in substantive terms was just not possible. . . . whatever procedural devices could be used to thwart merger and . . . delay the process had been employed over a long period of time.
>
> However, combating those forces and eventually succeeding were persons in . . . the NEA, LEA and LTA that were convinced . . . the days of Apartheid in education in Louisiana were over and . . . the best interests of teachers . . . and the whole education program would be enhanced if . . . teachers could speak with one voice. . . .
>
> There was a sense of religious commitment. I am pursuaded that the basic Christian beliefs of the respective parties did play a role in their commitment that things must change, and there were several instances of very emotional, heart-felt discussions, particularly under the leadership of Mr. Jackson, strongly supported by Ms. Harrison and Mr. Thompson. . . .
>
> As the parties dealt with each other, often on Saturdays, often on evenings over extended periods of time, their knowledge of each other's abilities eventually won the day. . . . They gained respect for each other, which indicated that they probably could work together in one organization. We were then able to establish committees to work on specific proposals for consolidation and this enabled a direct dialogue between the black and white representatives, without the participation of . . . a neutral, even without anyone from NEA at times.[39]

Anderson credited the successful result to the effective leadership of LEA members Basile Miller, president; Jesse Spears, vice-president; Alphonse Jackson, associate executive secretary and member of the state legislature from Shreveport; Arthur Thompson, legal counsel, Shreveport; Gloria Harrison, teacher from Shreveport and LEA president during the most critical period of the merger talks; and Katie Pringle and James Kelley, NEA directors.

From the LTA, Anderson gave credit to Kenneth Payne, president; Horace Robinson, executive secretary, Jim Morris, associate executive secretary; Dr. John H. Mitchell, Alexandria; Dr. Virginia S. Melton, Monroe; James Stafford, Jr.; and NEA staff members Eugene Dryer, Kenneth Kimberlin, and Joe Fisher.

Anderson also had praise for Jim Williams, NEA regional director, and for the full and active support of Executive Director Terry Herndon, and Robert Chanin, deputy director and general counsel.

Both Herndon and Chanin were deeply involved at critical points in the Louisiana merger effort and played key roles. Chanin, working with Horace Robinson and the officers of the LTA, succeeded in negotiating a termination of the lawsuit in favor of an effort to achieve a merger by an out-of-court agreement on a merger plan acceptable to both parties. He also served as continuing adviser to Williams and Anderson during the extended period of negotiation.

Terry Herndon was brought into the process at critical points in the negotiation when Association policy was involved, when his judgment was required, and when the power of his office was needed to initiate discussions, keep them moving, and help avoid breakdowns.

J. K. Haynes, longtime executive secretary of the LEA and an early leader in the civil rights movement, opposed unification of the two associations and, together with a minority who agreed with him, filed a legal action challenging the merger.

THE EFFECT OF MERGERS

What has been the effect of the merging of the black and white affiliates? Some data are available to assist in answering this question. Surveys of member opinion have been made by NEA Research. Evaluation teams have visited the merged associations, talked with members and association leaders, reviewed programs, and reported their findings and recommendations.

I have reviewed the reports of the opinion surveys and the recommendations and observations of the evaluation teams. From these data and my own random observations and interviews with both black and white members and officers, I have formed the following conclusions.

The merged associations are serving all members better than they were served by the separate organizations. The merged organizations are offering broader service programs that provide services to both black and white members not previously enjoyed.

Opinion surveys conducted by NEA Research to determine how members feel about the merger show that seven out of ten members—both white and black—agree that the interests of all members are best served by a single integrated association.

Both black and white members feel their mergers are working well— only about one percent said they were working "poorly." However, a higher percentage of white members than black feel it is working "very well," indicating the need for a sustained effort to improve conditions.

The merged organizations by 1979 had increased their NEA membership over the combined membership of the two separate affiliates at the time of the merger by 197,021.

Total membership for the individual states at the time of merger compared with 1979 membership enrollments show increases ranging from 15 percent in Florida to 148 percent in Texas.

This substantial increase in members has increased the power of the professional organization to achieve its purposes. However, the increase in membership cannot be attributed solely to the mergers. The new NEA constitution, for example, provided for universal unification of membership, which had a significant positive effect on NEA membership.

Obviously, other factors must be considered in interpreting the membership figures for individual states in the accompanying table showing membership growth on a state-by-state basis from the time of merger to 1979. However, it is significant that mergers have not had a negative effect on membership growth, since NEA memberships have increased in all states merged since 1964.

The NEA Executive Committee adopted a wise course of action to achieve mergers of the dual affiliates. Through the entire effort to unite the separate state affiliates, sharp conflict existed between the advocates of "merger now" and the advocates of "go slow and preserve unity". Neither of the two alternatives would have succeeded as well as the one followed by the Executive Committee.

If the liberal forces had prevailed, it is likely the Association would have provoked the withdrawal of up to eleven or more state affiliates. Once they have withdrawn, experience shows, it takes time, patience, effort, and money to bring them back again.

The Representative Assemblies set deadlines for the completion of merger. These deadlines proved to be impractical if strictly observed. They failed to allow for the problems involved in securing favorable actions by large delegate bodies of the two merging parties acting in good faith. Strict construction of the Assembly's action could have resulted in

COMPARISON OF NEA MEMBERSHIP ON MAY 31, 1979, AND AT TIME OF MERGER

State	(1) Date of Merger	(2) At Merger, Membership In Both Affil.	(3) 1979 Membership	(4) Increase (Col. 3 minus col. 2)	(5) Percentage Increase
ALABAMA	1969	19,183	37,256	18,073	94%
ARKANSAS	1969	8,856	15,561	6,705	76
FLORIDA	1966	26,041	29,846	3,805	15
GEORGIA	1969	19,786	36,354	16,568	84
LOUISIANA	1977	11,243[a]	27,659	16,416[b]	146
MISSISSIPPI	1976	5,512[a]	15,915	10,403[b]	189
N. CAROLINA	1970	23,677	48,713	25,036	106
S. CAROLINA	1968	15,967	20,238	4,271	27
TENNESSEE	1967	29,747	44,223	14,476	49
TEXAS	1966	41,535	103,096	61,561	148
VIRGINIA	1967	25,104	44,811	19,707	79
TOTALS		226,651	423,672	197,021	(avg: 87%)

[a]Does not include members of expelled association.   [b]Includes members of two merged associations.

SOURCE: *NEA Handbooks* for 1965–66, 1966–67, 1967–68, 1968–69, 1969–70, 1970–71, 1976–77, 1977–78, and 1979–80.

more suspensions and expulsions. The Executive Committee's decision to continue to work with the leaders of all affiliates acting in good faith was responsible for keeping the number of suspensions to a minimum.

If the conservative forces had prevailed, the talks would probably still be going on, or the mergers, if any, would be very weak.

The Executive Committee, by taking the middle course—interpreting the Assembly's action liberally—was able to avoid a wholesale withdrawal from the Association and emerge with state affiliates that members say are stronger then either of the organizations prior to the merger.

Experience gained from the NEA mergers revealed the need for an external third party. The NEA's criteria and the employment of expert assistance to the merging organizations provided four services to facilitate an equitable result.

First, it gave the leaders of both groups someone else to blame for their discomfort.

Second, it provided the services of neutral persons who were free to propose alternative solutions to problems and possible trade-offs without committing either party.

Third, it kept the pressure on the negotiating teams to reach an agreement within a given time period. It provided the same function the U.S. Supreme Court served in the reapportionment of the state legislatures.

Fourth, perhaps the most important outcome of the merger activity was what happened to the people involved. The activity brought people together who had lived in the same communities for many years but did not know each other. In the process, which began tentatively, friendships were formed. Slowly, feelings of confidence and trust followed. It was this spirit of trust and confidence that made the mergers possible. It is now providing a base of understanding on which to build strong, unified organizations for the future.

The merger of the dual affiliates is another important step toward further democratization of the NEA. Since the NEA took the first step by admitting women to membership in 1866, it has taken a long series of further actions to make the Association more responsive to the needs of its members. These included: the election of the first woman president in 1910; the establishment of the Representative Assembly in 1920; the merger of the ATA and the NEA in 1966; the election of the first black president in 1968; and the adoption of a new constitution. The constitution was written by delegates who represented members in all states and communities in the nation. It is serving to further democratize the Association in a variety of ways. The latest action to further democratize the NEA—completion of the mergers of state affiliates—continues a trend spanning more than a century.

The experience of the NEA in merging its dual affiliates may provide a pattern for other voluntary associations.

When the NEA began the task of merging its separate black and white affiliates, it had no prior experience with the problems it was to face. Officers and staff members learned from their mistakes as well as their successes as they worked with the leaders of the separate state affiliates. The result was that the last mergers were, probably, better mergers than the early ones. Guidelines were revised and improved as experience was gained.

Sooner or later, all organizations must face the same problems that confronted NEA. It is possible the NEA experience may enable them to avoid the pain of the trial-and-error method. While some professional societies have taken the first step of removing racial membership restrictions, most have yet to initiate positive programs of minority involvement. Such programs can provide both opportunities for active involvement by minority members and benefits to the organization through broader participation. Professional societies, especially, have a social responsibility to give leadership for the achievement of racial equality in the nation. If every voluntary membership organization in America were to engage in such a positive program, it could have a powerful impact for the solution of the country's most pressing domestic social problem—racial inequality.

There were many heroes, both black and white, some of whom made substantial personal sacrifices to support their own deeply felt beliefs in the public schools and the principle of equal school opportunity for all children. Among these heroes are the black leaders who suffered the humiliation of being discriminated against and patronized by whites and of being accused of "Uncle Tomism" by their own people for their efforts to achieve equality. Also among them are the white leaders who were snubbed by their neighbors, friends, and even members of their own families for advocating merger and continuing to send their children to the integrated public schools. All these, too numerous to mention by name, were willing to take the personal risks for the principles in which they believed.

CHAPTER SIX

Legislation

The first major national legislative victory of the organized teaching profession came in 1867 when President Andrew Johnson signed a bill creating a Federal Office of Education.

From that time until the present, legislative action in the state and national capitals has been the most effective of all activities for the growth and improvement of the nation's public schools and institutions of higher education.

One of the two men responsible for calling the meeting in Philadelphia that founded the organization later to become the National Education Association, T. W. Valentine, was identified as an alderman, grammar school teacher, and *lobbyist* from Brooklyn.[1]

When the new organization was founded, nineteen state associations were already in existence. The earliest—Rhode Island, New York, and Massachusetts—were all established in 1845. Since education was the responsibility of the state or territorial governments, serving as advocate for the public schools was to become one of the most important activities of the state teachers' organizations. In framing the call for the Philadelphia meeting, the organizers made it clear they wanted to create an organization for all educators in the nation that would speak for teachers in the formulation of national policies in the same way state associations were participating in state policy decisions.

The founders saw the new national association as the collective voice of American educators in the nation's capital, where decisions would be made by the Congress and the president affecting schools and educators.

Through the years, Association leaders have maintained relationships with the White House as well as the Congress. At the 1859 convention in Washington, D.C., President Buchanan held a reception for the delegates and attended one session of the convention.

During those years, the legislative activities of the Association were modest. Membership was small, dues were low, no staff was assigned the special responsibility for following legislation on a full-time basis, and the Association had no Washington headquarters. It was not until 1918—sixty-one years after the NEA was founded—that active membership exceeded 10,000.

Nevertheless, the officers and committee members did give testimony before congressional committees and organized personal contacts with members of Congress by constituents from their home states through the Association's network of state affiliates. This network has been, from the beginning, the greatest source of Association strength in the legislative field. Association leaders soon learned that a request made to a member of Congress by a local constituent was more likely to be acted upon than a plea from a stranger. Moreover, NEA members were articulate, most were active voters, and teachers resided in every congressional district in the nation. These advantages have, through the years, made possible achievements in school legislation beyond the limits of the Association's modest budgets.

In later years, these advantages have been strengthened further by membership growth, establishment of a Washington headquarters, improved methods of information gathering and retrieval, the use of modern communications, and the employment of a permanent staff of specialists. But this did not come about overnight. It happened after experience had demonstrated the need for federal participation in education.

Motivated by the crisis in the public schools caused by World War I, a vigorous movement developed in 1917 to make the Association both more active and more democratic. A National Commission on the Emergency in Education was named to develop a national program for education. The Association established a headquarters in Washington. The following year, the recommendations of the Commission were embodied in the

Smith-Towner Bill. The bill proposed a reorganization of the Federal Office of Education, making it a department of education headed by a secretary in the president's cabinet, and consolidating all education programs within the department.

The bill requested the appropriation of a hundred million dollars for the elimination of illiteracy, Americanization programs, physical education, teacher training, equalization of school opportunity, and partial payment of teacher's salaries. It provided for distribution of money to the states to be used solely for the purpose of encouraging the states in the promotion of education and specified that the federal funds and equal funds provided by each state be administered exclusively by the states.

The Smith-Towner Bill proved to be too large a package for Congress to swallow. Some members of Congress favored one part of the proposal, but not the other. NEA members, too, became divided, advocating splitting the proposal. Typical was Nathan C. Schaeffer, Pennsylvania superintendent of schools, who told the 1918 convention, "Our need for money for school purposes is so great that I am willing to accept federal aid with or without a secretary of education in the president's cabinet."[2]

The Congress did not act on the Smith-Towner Bill. But from 1918 to 1979, it was to be faced intermittently with bills to create a cabinet-level department of education. And proposals to provide federal support were introduced consistently until the achievement of the Elementary and Secondary Education Act of 1965.

When the National Commission on the Emergency in Education made its final report in 1920, a Legislative Commission was appointed to develop and promote legislation within the limits of Association policies. The Commission on the Emergency in Education thus became the forerunner of the Legislative Commission, which advised NEA officers and governing bodies until 1972, when the standing committee on legislation absorbed the duties and functions of the Legislative Commission. In 1977, the Representative Assembly combined the standing committee on legislative matters and the standing committee on educational finance. The new committee was designated the Standing Committee on Legislative and Financial Support for Public Education.

In the 1930s and 1940s, bills sought to equalize school opportunities by formulas designed to distribute federal funds among the states based on relative educational need and ability of the states to pay.

In times of adversity, the need for a collective voice is felt more keenly. The dislocations of World War I and the subsequent period of rebuilding and adapting to peace emphasized that need. Membership increased eighteenfold from 1918 to 1931.

No continuing staff support was provided for the NEA Legislative Commission. Its members and other volunteers, plus staff members who could be released from their other assignments, carried on the national legislative function from 1920 until 1944.

In his report to the 1943 Representative Assembly, H. M. Ivy, chairman of the Legislative Commission, complimented its members and the NEA staff for their efforts in behalf of the legislative program but appealed for adequate resources to support a full-time staff to pursue legislative goals on a full-time basis.

The Executive Committee was directed by the Representative Assembly to study the need for an increase in dues and to present a proposal to the 1944 Representative Assembly.

An increase from three to five dollars in annual dues was approved in 1944, to become effective the following year.

Senator Robert Taft (R., Ohio) opposed the early NEA proposals for federal school support. In 1943, when S-637 was before the Senate, he and Senator William Langer (R., North Dakota) were among the most effective opponents of the bill.

Senator Taft's chief objection to the measure was his fear that federal funds would result in the federal control of schools.

Senator Langer, in the fifth day of debate in the Senate, offered an amendment forbidding discrimination on account of race, creed, or color in the administration of the benefits and funds provided from either the federal government or the supplemental state funds provided for in the act.[3]

The Langer amendment was adopted by a close vote, following which Senator Taft moved to recommit S-637 to the Committee on Education and Labor. The adoption of the Langer amendment had the effect of killing the bill.

Following the Taft motion, Senator Elbert D. Thomas (D., Utah), chairman of the Committee on Education and Labor and sponsor of S-637, said: "I ask about the sincerity of a Senator who argued against the Bill on the score that it gave the Federal Government power to control the use of federal funds in the states, but who actually voted for an amendment which would give the Federal Government such control."[4]

Within a few months, Senator Taft did an about-face and in a subsequent session joined Senator Thomas and Senator Lister Hill in sponsoring an NEA-supported measure to provide federal school aid without federal control. In explaining his new position, he said that after thorough study he had concluded that schools were too important to the nation to permit them to be neglected because of a fear of federal control. It is up to us, he said, to guard against controls, and if Congress doesn't want them, the Congress can see to it they do not occur.

Senator Taft appeared on an NBC radio discussion in February 1948 with Alvin Burger, research director for the National Association of State Chambers of Commerce. Senator Taft, then a sponsor of a school-aid bill in the Senate, spoke for the bill. Burger spoke in opposition. Sterling Fisher of NBC was moderator.

Near the close of the discussion, Burger said, "A senator I admire very much said in 1943, 'once we start, we shall never stop, until the federal government is regulating every detail of the education of our children throughout the forty-eight states.' That senator was you, Senator Taft, and you never spoke truer words. . . . this radio debate should be Senator Robert A. Taft versus Senator Robert A. Taft." To this, Senator Taft replied, "I was against it until I really studied the figures. If you'd really studied the figures, perhaps you'd be converted also."[5]

Opposition to federal school-support proposals took three principal forms: (1) opposition by those who believed that federal support means federal control of schools, (2) opposition by the church-supported schools excluded from the measures, and (3) threatened amendments to withhold federal funds from racially segregated school systems.

The chief spokesman for the control argument was the U.S. Chamber of Commerce. Leading the opposition for the parochial schools was the hierarchy of the Roman Catholic Church and the National Catholic Welfare Conference (NCWC). Racial amendments were offered or threatened by Congressman Adam Clayton Powell of New York so often they came to be known as "Powell amendments."

The Powell amendments were especially difficult for the NEA to deal with. To oppose the amendments could be interpreted by supporters of school desegregation as opposition to desegregation. To fail to oppose the amendment would kill the school bill because it was known that senators and congressmen from states with segregated schools would vote against the amended bill. Moreover, such amendments made it possible for congressmen to cop out by claiming credit for a favorable vote for equality for blacks and avoid the blame for an outright negative vote on the school bill.

The opponents of federal school-support bills, when fearing failure on the merits of the proposals, frequently put pressure on the House Rules Committee to hold bills in the committee to prevent the Congress from voting on them. The Rules Committee became the burial ground for numerous federal school-support bills between 1930 and 1960.

In the early 1950s, bills were before Congress which proposed to use the revenues from oil drilling operations in the tidelands beyond coastal state boundaries. Leader for the proposal was Senator Lister Hill of Mississippi, a consistent supporter of school legislation. A bill passed the Senate in 1953 with the Hill amendment, but the House failed to approve it.

Measures providing federal support for school construction were before the Congress in each session between 1953 and 1957. In 1954, 1955, and 1956, they expired in the House of Representatives.

Several developments in 1957 gave NEA leaders renewed hope for success.

The USSR launched its first sputnik and followed with a second artificial earth satellite a month later. This technological advance by the USSR shocked the American public and set off a new interest in education—especially in mathematics and scientific subjects.

Opinion polls revealed widespread support for federal school-support legislation.

A loosely formed coalition of thirty-six organizations was created in support of a school construction bill. Victory appeared to be imminent.

Vigorous opposition by the U.S. Chamber of Commerce again succeeded in bottling the bill up in the House Rules Committee.

However, some lesser victories were achieved. The National Defense Education Act (NDEA) was passed, providing $115 million for the first year to strengthen defense-related programs in science, mathematics, foreign language, and expanded library services.

The NEA played an active role in expanding and improving the NDEA proposal to bring it into harmony with Association policies.

The NEA-promoted King-Jenkins Bill (HR 4662) to provide equitable tax treatment for teachers received broad support from Congress. The Treasury Department, fearing legislative intrusion into the administration of the tax laws if HR 4662 were approved, issued a ruling, TD 6291, providing for the deduction on income tax returns of teachers' expenses for improving their professional skills and knowledge. This ruling was estimated to save American teachers about $20 million a year, retroactive to 1954. However, in practice, problems of securing uniform administration of the provisions of the regulation and narrow restrictions on deductible activities by the Internal Revenue Service still deny educators equal treatment with other professional groups.

In 1960, the Association made an all-out effort to pass a school construction and teachers' salary bill, leaving the choice of how much should go for each purpose to the states. The bill, S-8, was originally drawn to provide aid for school construction. It was amended in the Senate to include teachers' salaries and passed by a vote of 51 to 34.

The House bill sponsored by Congressman Lee Metcalf (D., Montana) was stalled in the House Rules Committee. All efforts to bring the bill out of the committee failed. In desperation, in March, a seldom-used procedure known as "Calendar Wednesday" was threatened to force consideration of the measure.

On May 18, the Rules Committee, fearing the bill's supporters had the votes to force its release, allowed the bill to be debated on a 7-to-5 vote. During the debate, a freedom-of-choice amendment similar to that approved in the Senate was offered. The presiding officer ruled the amendment out of order, citing a rule adopted in 1822. The rule provided that no subject different from that under consideration would be permitted by amendment. The bill passed the House without the amendment by a vote of 206 to 189.

Senator Lyndon B. Johnson, two weeks later, made a motion in the Senate that the House be requested to give unanimous consent for a conference to resolve the differences in the House and Senate bills. Congressman August Johanson (R., Michigan) objected.

On June 22, 1960, the House Rules Committee voted 7 to 5 not to agree to a conference.

Seldom did a Rules Committee meet in the presence of spectators. However, on this occasion, I was present, along with about a dozen other educators from as many states. I had worked with congressional committees and state legislators for many years but had never witnessed such a callous lack of concern for the democratic process or for the welfare of America's children as the action of the House Rules Committee on that day. Watching twelve congressmen deny the right of their colleagues to complete their work on an important bill that had been approved by majorities in the House and Senate left me and the other educators convinced that congressional reform was long overdue. We made certain that our colleagues in the home states of each committee member received word of how their congressmen voted from someone who was present when the vote was taken.

This is how Congressman Metcalf described the action of the Rules Committee to the 1960 NEA convention in Los Angeles:

> In recent years, there have been indications the Rules Committee has assumed a role that is properly that of the whole House, rather than a group of eight Democrats and four Republicans.
>
> There have been frequent occasions when two of the Democrats voted with the Republicans in order to produce a 6-6 tie—that's equivalent to a traffic light that shows red more or less permanently.

The Chairman of the Rules Committee has been known to delay meetings for weeks or months, especially when confronted with legislation he dislikes. This state of affairs has produced a call for the abolition of the Rules Committee or for changes in procedures so that a handful of willful men cannot block the majority from carrying out the wishes of the people of the country. I do not concur that the Rules Committee should be abolished, but I do believe Congress should evaluate the present situation and provide for more expeditious procedures. . . .

The obstacles and roadblocks the Rules Committee has placed in the path of legislation favored by a majority of the members of the House, and the absolute refusal on the part of a half-dozen men to permit a majority of the House to enact responsible legislation, has made reform of this committee imperative at the beginning of the next Congress. This reform is necessary, not only for the enactment of desirable education legislation, but to permit Congress to carry out its legislative responsibilities in all areas.[6]

The defeat of the Federal Aid Bill after it had received majority votes in both houses was a bitter pill. In the effort, the NEA for the first time was listed by *Congressional Quarterly* as the top spending lobby in the nation. NEA, state, and local leaders testified before congressional committees, met frequently with their representatives in Congress, attended regional workshops to keep up to date on developments, published newsletters to keep members informed, and encouraged members to write individual letters to their senators and congressmen.

The 1960 NEA convention met in Los Angeles while the bill was in the Rules Committee but before the committee had cast its final, lethal vote.

In his report to the delegates, Executive Secretary Carr included a step-by-step history of the measure's progress in the two houses of Congress. He concluded by saying:

We have traced the course of events down to the present moment with regard to the most important legislation the National Education Association has ever sponsored. It is for you to decide whether, in view of the circumstances, the Association shall persevere, or quit, or compromise.

I hope you won't quit. You have a well-equipped headquarters building in Washington. The trustees bought everything necessary for the conduct of your business. . . . There is one thing we did not buy, however, and that is a white flag.[7]

The loss of the bill was due to the traditional opposition based on fear of federal control, separation of church and state, racial issues, and the tight control over the legislative agenda by the powerful House Rules Committee. However, supporters believed the bill could have been passed if President Eisenhower's "good words" had been matched by "good works" with the Congress.

The Association's response to the defeat was to authorize a searching study of the NEA's legislative effort. Leroy Peterson, assistant dean of the

University of Wisconsin, Division of Continuing Education, was employed to direct the study with the assistance of an official of a private marketing research firm.

The Representative Assembly of 1960 amended an already strongly worded resolution on federal school support to back the Legislative Commission's efforts to secure commitments to a broad school-support program in the platforms of both political parties. The amendment also asked delegates and their local and state associations to commit themselves to a positive action program to support the commission "by whatever . . . specific means are deemed advisable."[8]

It had become clear to many that the Association's program of persuading already elected senators and congressmen was not sufficient. Programs must be broadened to include active participation of teachers in the political process, to encourage good candidates to run for office, and to support those who believed the federal government must share the responsibility for school support.

President John F. Kennedy took office on January 20, 1961. Prior to his nomination, NEA leaders had been concerned whether the Catholic senator, if elected, would resist the pressures of the church hierarchy when faced with a decision on federal school legislation. In private and public statements, he assured NEA leaders that while he would follow the cardinal on religious matters, he considered federal school support an educational question. He said that if elected, he would not only support such legislation but would give leadership to the effort. His actions in the initial weeks in the White House dissipated any lingering concerns.

On February 7, two weeks after the inauguration, the president invited NEA officers to the White House to discuss his plans for school legislation. Within sixteen more weeks, the Senate had approved the Morse Bill (S-1021) to provide federal support to the elementary and secondary schools, and on June 25, Congressman Frank Thompson, sponsor of a similar bill in the House, read a personal message from President Kennedy to the Representative Assembly in which he spoke about the bill, its prospects in the House of Representatives, and his goals for American education.

> The most crucial period for this legislation is still ahead, but it is a sound measure. It is a just measure. It is an urgently needed measure—and I have every reason to believe that, with the help of organizations such as yours . . . I will sign into law before the summer is out this nation's first federal aid to education program.
> That will be the end of a 40-year battle. But more than an end, it will be a beginning. . . . Our goal—our objective in obtaining these funds—is not simply to provide an adequate education system—or even a merely good education sys-

tem. Our goal must be an educational system that will permit the maximum development of the talents of every American boy and girl.[9]

But despite clear evidence of public support, able leadership by Senator Morse and Congressman Thompson, the backing of the White House, and a strong commitment in the Democratic party platform, the Morse-Thompson Bill was killed by a single vote margin in the House Rules Committee. The chief cause of the bill's demise was the opposition of the Catholic church. Both Francis Cardinal Spellman and officials of the National Catholic Welfare Conference (NCWC) indicated they considered unjust any measure that did not give Catholic school children a right to participate. In the absence of such a provision in the 1961 legislation, the NCWC did oppose the measure with great vigor.

For the second time in two years, President Kennedy sent a message to Congress, on February 6, 1962, urging broad general support for public schools similar to the Morse Bill passed by the Senate the previous year.

His message contained the following statement on the role of education in a democratic society:

> No task before our nation is more important than expanding and improving the educational opportunities of all our people. The concept that every American deserves the opportunity to attain the highest level of education of which he is capable is not new to this administration—it is a traditional ideal of democracy. But it is time that we moved toward the fulfillment of this ideal with more vigor and less delay.
>
> For education is both the foundation and the unifying force of our democratic way of life—it is the mainspring of our economic and social progress—it is the highest expression of achievement in our society, ennobling and enriching human life. In short, it is at the same time the most profitable investment society can make and the richest reward it can confer.[10]

However, no action was taken on general school support legislation, chiefly because of the reluctance of Congress to again face the emotion-laden issues of race, religion, and federal control in an election year.

President Kennedy on November 19, 1963, met with the executive secretaries of NEA's fifty state affiliates and a few top NEA officers and staff members, in the White House rose garden. On that occasion, he shared his disappointment at the delay in securing legislation that would enable the schools to meet the educational needs of the increased enrollments of children and at the same time construct new schools to accomodate the hundreds of thousands of younger children not yet in school.

The president was in good spirits. After expressing his determination to continue with greater vigor to achieve congressional approval for an acceptable bill, he concluded by saying: "I hope you will continue to prod us and, occasionally, . . . the members of the House and Senate, to see if we can get this job done. I want to thank you. Things don't happen; they are made to happen; and in the field of education they were made to happen by you and your members. So we are very grateful."[11] Following his statement, he visited informally with members in the rose garden for about twenty minutes.

Three days later, on November 22, the president was the victim of an assassin's bullet in Dallas, Texas.

During the 1,000-day administration of President Kennedy, a number of education programs were begun. Others in progress were to be achieved during the Johnson administration that followed. Among the major legislative achievements of the Kennedy administration were:

The establishment of the Peace Corps in 1961

Expanded federal support for vocational education under the Manpower Development and Training Act of 1962

Extension for three years of the benefits of the National Defense Education Act and Public Laws 815 and 874 to aid schools in federally impacted areas

Public Law 88-164, signed on October 31, 1963, providing $329 million over a three-year period for construction of research centers and facilities for the mentally retarded

The initiation of a two-year program for construction of community mental health centers

The initiation of a three-year program for training of teachers for the retarded and handicapped

The authorization of a five-year program of aid to public TV facilities

The initiation of the Civil Rights Bill of 1964 and the Library Bill, providing vastly expanded federal assistance for both library services and construction (both signed by President Johnson after President Kennedy's death)

The Breakthrough

The Elementary and Secondary Education Act (ESEA), signed by President Johnson on April 11, 1965, was the most important single educational event to occur in the first twenty-two years of the NEA's second century.

President Johnson, addressing the NEA Representative Assembly in New York City on July 2, said:

In the last 19 months, your Congress and your President have worked shoulder to shoulder together in the most fruitful partnership for American education in all the history of the American nation.

We passed the $1.2 billion Elementary and Secondary Education Act of 1965, the broadest, most meaningful, and most sweeping federal commitment to education that this nation has ever made.[12]

At the conclusion of the president's address, NEA President Lois Edinger presented an honorary life membership in the Association to President Johnson in recognition of his "dynamic leadership, . . . interest in the advancement of learning and his dedication to the cause of education."[13]

Why did the 1965 effort succeed after almost a half-century of frustration and failure? There is no simple answer. The forces that led to success can be grouped under three general headings: a changed climate in the Congress, a new cast of characters, and a new rationale based on the public concerns of the period.

A New Climate

Several changes took place in the Congress between 1960 and 1965 that had a positive influence on the climate for the passage of ESEA.

In the bitter battle for federal school support in the 87th Congress (1961–1963), 77 percent of the Democrats in the Senate and 66 percent of the Democrats in the House voted for the 1961 bill. Only 27 percent of the Republicans in the Senate and 4 percent in the House voted for it.

The 89th Congress, elected in 1964, increased the number of Democrats in the House by thirty-seven and reduced the number of Republicans by thirty-six.[14] One additional Democrat was added in the Senate, and Republican membership was reduced by one. A great effort was made to promote ESEA as a bipartisan measure. However, federal school-support measures have consistently received greater support from Democrats than Republicans.[15]

The campaign of 1964 offered voters a sharp contrast in philosophies. President Johnson strongly favored federal school support and had a long record of support for such programs, while Senator Barry Goldwater viewed school support as a state and local responsibility.[16]

While party platforms on which candidates are elected do not always foretell how congressmen will vote after the election, the Democrats adopted a strong plank in favor of federal school support.

Three other factors in the Congress were helpful. Adam Clayton Powell replaced Graham A. Barden as chairman of the House Committee on Education and Labor. Barden did not seek reelection in 1960. Congressman Powell, while having authored numerous amendments as leverage against segregated schools, did have a sincere interest in education and indicated he would not offer racial amendments unless he had the support of a majority of the committee. The fact that Powell himself authored a bill re-markably similar to the administration measure made it clear that it would not be killed by a civil rights amendment.

Perhaps the greatest favorable development to improve the climate for ESEA in the Congress was the passage of the Civil Rights Act of 1964, which by force of law denied school funds to segregated school systems, thus obviating the further consideration of Powell amendments.

Another contributing factor to the new climate in the Congress was the effort led by Speaker Sam Rayburn and approved by a majority vote of the House to prevent the House Rules Committee from obstructing the legislative process in 1961. This was accomplished by enlarging the com-mittee from twelve to fifteen members. This gave the speaker an oppor-tunity to change the balance of power on the Committee.

The addition of two school supporters to the Committee—Carl Elliot (D. Alabama) and B. F. Sisk (D., California) made it possible to change an 8-to-7 *negative* vote in the committee in 1961 to an 8-to-7 *positive* vote in 1965. In 1965, eight Democrats voted in favor of advancing the school bill, while two Democrats and five Republicans voted against it.

The New Approach

Support for school bills in previous sessions centered on the need to equalize school opportunities among the states. Generally speaking, be-cause of the heavy reliance on property taxes, the level of support for edu-cation in the nation was being determined by the location of concentra-tions of wealth. Moreover, school-age children were not distributed evenly among the states. For example, in 1977 there were twenty school-age chil-dren per 100 adults in the state with the lowest ratio and twenty-seven per 100 in the highest. It was argued that the federal government was the only level in a position to tax all wealth in the nation and distribute school funds to the states in terms of their relative needs and school responsibili-ties. It was argued further that national unity required a minimum level of education for all children as a basis for responsible citizenship. In the late 1950s and the 1960s, when children born during the baby-boom years following World War II became old enough to go to school, many school systems lacked the local resources to build needed classrooms and operate their schools at acceptable levels.

Furthermore, since the war, the U.S. economy had been constantly ex-panding. The federal income tax had a built-in escalator in tax revenues owing to the increases in personal and corporate earnings and graduated rates, which taxed higher incomes at higher rates. Local governments had no such mechanism, and states with progressive income taxes had been limited in their response to income growth because the federal government had virtually preempted that field. The states and localities were thus left with the more regressive sales, excise, and property taxes to support their government services, including schools. The school crisis of the 1960s came about because new classroom construction could only be financed from the same sources of revenue on which local boards of education relied for operating and maintaining schools. By 1965, these same updated arguments were becoming repetitious to congressmen, and progressive deterioration in schools was not sufficiently apparent to many congressmen to move them to action.

Nineteen sixty-five was a year of anxiety. The Senate Gulf of Tonkin resolution, passed in 1964 in response to reports that U.S. ships had been fired upon by North Vietnamese gunboats, became the basis for expanding the war in Vietnam. Urban poverty and racism were causing tensions in the cities. Malcolm X was shot and killed in New York City. A sheriff's posse and state troopers in Selma, Alabama, injured more than fifty black citizens who organized a march to protest the killing of a black man. A second Selma march, led by the Reverend Dr. Martin Luther King, Jr., began with 3,200 marchers and finished with more than 25,000. Viola Liuzzo was killed by members of the Ku Klux Klan while returning to Selma from Montgomery. Title VII of the Civil Rights Act to end discrimination in private employment went into effect. President Johnson signed the Voting Rights Act to ensure voting rights by federal intervention, if necessary. The Department of Housing and Urban Development was established, and riots erupted in the Watts area of Los Angeles, sparked by the arrest of a black man by white police.

Proponents of the 1965 bill decided to take a new approach by relating their arguments to these problems troubling the nation. The old arithmetic formulas for distributing dollars to the states had become obsolete. They failed to recognize that the education of deprived children required more services and more dollars than that of more fortunate children from middle-class urban families. The new bill proposed to distribute funds to the states on the basis of the numbers of children ages five to seventeen from low-income families. The bill also provided that benefits could be shared by low-income children attending nonpublic schools under certain conditions and including constitutional safeguards.

During the hearings before the House Committee, the point was made by several participants that the current poor families in America were locked in a cycle of poverty and that education held the brightest hope for their escape.

Organizations and Individuals

Following the battles of 1960–1962 on the church-state issue, both public-education and parochial-school spokesmen moderated their views.

There was a good reason for the NEA to moderate its views. The 1962 Representative Assembly amended the Association's policy by limiting its support of federal school aid to those proposals advocating funds only for "tax-supported" public elementary and secondary schools and "publicly controlled and tax supported" higher-education institutions. This action was taken by the delegates over the advice of the Association's professional staff, Legislative Commission, and Resolutions Committee. By so doing, the Association was obligated to oppose those measures which provided aid to private higher-education institutions.

The Kennedy administration proposals that were before the Senate and House included some federal assistance to both public and private institutions of higher education. Both bills were passed but went to a Senate-House conference committee for resolution of the differences.

Executive Secretary Carr has given this account of the events that followed:

> On September 17, 1962, a closed session of the Conference Committee voted out a compromise including student aid, contrary to the House policy, and a program of federal construction grants for engineering, science, and library buildings in *both* public and private institutions. The NEA was obliged by its new resolution to oppose enactment. The House conferees had been instructed by vote of the House not to approve scholarships and a motion to recommit the measure was offered on these grounds. After a bitter debate, during which the NEA's power as a lobby was exaggerated to a most flattering extent, the motion to recommit passed by a vote of 214 to 186.
>
> In the House gallery at the time the vote was taken, I remember vividly my chagrin at being required to rejoice in the defeat of an aid-to-education measure.
>
> The vote evoked much bitterness. The fact that NEA had, in the past, successfully supported much good legislation for higher education was of little help. Many staunch friends of the NEA in Congress were very angry about the vote and the part the NEA played in bringing it about.[17]

The intransigent position taken by the NEA delegates and the equally uncompromising position taken by the National Catholic Welfare Conference account largely for the bitterness and frustration during and immediately following the 87th Congress of 1961–1962.

The NEA and the several higher-education organizations, including many members of the NEA's own Department of Higher Education, were in conflict. The tension between the private and public schools was escalated. And most important, many long-time relationships with supporters of NEA in the Congress and the administration were severely strained. They were earnestly seeking a solution to a difficult public problem and resented the NEA's action.

This public spectacle of the house of education divided caused much regret and internal castigation. As tempers cooled, however, a determination emerged that such a condition would not be repeated.

This incident revealed that the 8,000-member Representative Assembly could make a mistake. It also demonstrated that its mistakes could be corrected.

The next meeting of the Representative Assembly rewrote the Association's policy on aid to public and private schools to provide "that the legislation be consistent with the constitutional provisions respecting an establishment of religion and the tradition of separation of church and state" and "that the legislation contain provision for judicial review as to its constitutionality."[18] This change of policy was sufficiently broad to make it possible for the NEA to support the Elementary and Secondary Education Act the following year.

The New Alliance

One chief factor in the creation of an alliance for school-support legislation was the timing of the effort. Congressmen, public and private education leaders, traditional opponents, and the public had grown weary of the continuing church-state battle. But an equally important positive force was the leadership of President Johnson, whose personal qualities and intimate knowledge of the legislative process made it possible to capitalize on the favorable potential of the moment. He had strong convictions about the need for federal school support from his experience as a teacher and principal, an administrator of the National Youth Administration, and a participant in the House and Senate in the consideration of several federal school-support measures. He gave a high priority to the ESEA proposals, was impatient with delays, and did not hesitate to use the powers of his office to achieve support. He was skilled in the art of compromise and politician enough to sense the desirability of weakening the opposing forces while strengthening existing support.

With the able assistance of Commissioner Keppel, President Johnson became the chief catalyst who, through the power of his office, made possible the development of an alliance in support of the ESEA, which had appeared impossible a few short months before the bill was considered by the House Committee on Education and Labor.

On March 1, 1965, President Johnson invited 225 local, state, and national school leaders to the White House. The meeting was held in the East Room in the late afternoon. The president arrived looking weary but warmed to the task as he delivered a short prepared statement revealing both the depth of his commitment to the principle of federal participation in education and his rationale for ESEA. He received spontaneous applause as he addressed the group as "fellow educators." Then he said:

> Human historian H. G. Wells once wrote: "It becomes more and more a race between education and catastrophe." You and I cannot be indifferent to the outcome of that race. We care deeply about the winner, and because we do care so deeply about the winner, that is why we are all in the East Room of the White House today.
>
> I don't think that I need to tell you how important to the outcome of that race is the education legislation that is now before the Congress. I hope that it is important enough that most of you have studied it in detail. I hope that you understand that it represents the very best thinking that the leading educators of this country can produce. Way back last summer I asked some of the most outstanding educational minds to tackle this problem. I gave them a single instruction: find out how we can best invest each education dollar so it can do the most good.
>
> Your support and the support of every leading education group proves that they did their job better than I had hoped, because for the first time we have succeeded in finding goals which unite us rather than divide us. The experts spent a great deal of time and study working out a formula which would be fair to every state and fair to every county and fair to every child and would put the education dollar where that dollar is needed most *now*.
>
> We decided that our first job was to help the schools serving the children from the very lowest income groups. Those families constitute the number one burden in this nation on the school systems.
>
> We know that they cannot bear their share of the taxes to help pay for their education. And unless those children get a good education we know that they become dropouts and they become delinquents and they become tax eaters instead of tax payers.
>
> We know that they will join the unemployed and that is why we put top priority on breaking the vicious cycle that today threatens the future of five million children in this great land of opportunity which we talk about so much.
>
> The Johnson administration's continuing concern is for the improved educational opportunity for all children in this land.
>
> You can keep your blood pressure down if you want to. You can sit in your rocking chair and talk about the days that have gone by if you choose. But as far as I am concerned, I am going to use every rostrum and every forum and every searchlight that I can to tell the people of this country and their elected representatives that we can no longer avoid overcrowded classrooms and half-day sessions.[19]

The president delivered his prepared statement in about fifteen minutes. Then he rolled it up and reminisced about his teaching experiences, reinforcing the points made in his opening remarks with conviction and by citing personal examples. This went on for about forty minutes.

Attendance at the conference was one of my most memorable Washington experiences. I had attended conferences in which educators had expressed such faith in education. But I had never heard such unrestrained commitments from a president of the United States.

The shift of the National Catholic Welfare Conference from opponent to supporter was largely the result of compromises for the inclusion of benefits to children enrolled in private schools by the efforts of the president, Secretary of HEW Celebrezze, and Commissioner of Education Keppel.

Robert E. McKay, chairman of the Legislative Commission, was the chief spokesman for the NEA. During the entire period that HR 2362 was before the Congress, the NEA shuttled hundreds of state and local leaders in and out of Washington to work with their congressmen to furnish information, write speeches, and produce other materials as needed. The NEA Legislative Commission staff was increased by borrowing staff from affiliates and other NEA units.

Chairman McKay, in a taped memorandum to me in September 1979, said:

> At the risk of sounding terribly immodest, I have concluded that the NEA was responsible for the passage of ESEA. Not solely responsible—but without the action and the leadership of the National Education Association, I am sure that the bill would not have passed, or at least . . . not have passed in the form it was finally in, or without a major devastating battle within the educational ranks.
>
> Although the records will not show this, I believe that the fast action of the Legislative Commission in immediately endorsing the president's proposal on behalf of NEA was the catalyst that brought other organizations into line and made possible the presentation of an almost unanimous educational front in support of the proposals in Congress.
>
> Behind the scenes, preceding the December 1964 meeting of the Legislative Commission in Washington, it was quietly agreed that if we were to let the NEA machinery take its normal course of having a formal study and declaration by the Board of Directors, some educational organizations, probably, would have raised serious objections to the president's proposal—particularly those involving the religious question—and would have influenced other organizations to raise objections or to . . . oppose the legislation.
>
> To prevent this, the key members of the NEA legislative staff—Jim McCaskill and John Lumley—arranged for a representative of the U.S. Office of Education—Sam Halperin—to meet privately with members of the Legislative Commission in advance of the president's public announcement of his plans, to

permit us to make a detailed analysis and study of the proposal. We went down the line title by title and concluded that the proposal as it was then drafted met the guidelines which had been established by the NEA's official policymaking bodies. On the basis of that, I drafted a press release . . . stating the unequivocal support of the National Education Association for the president's educational program.

This action, which, as I look back on it, may have been viewed by some of the traditionalists in the organization as being precipitous, nevertheless gave the educational community the basis for moving swiftly to obtain one of the greatest gains in school finance history.

The decision of the Legislative Commission to support the legislation, subject to some amendments which were subsequently written into the bill, was based on an interpretation of the NEA policy, which . . . had been and still is strictly in support of constitutional separation of church and state. We reasoned that the various aspects of the program which made it more appealing and eventually acceptable to the Catholic church hierarchy did not violate the separation of church and state. We had been told in advance that the attorney general, Mr. Katzenbach, had researched the question on behalf of the president and had made that same conclusion. For example, we concluded that the loaning of library books or textbooks to students who happened to be in private or parochial schools . . . did not constitute public support of parochial schools inasmuch as there was written into the bill a guarantee that the title to and control of those textbooks and other instructional materials remained in the hands of a public agency. By the same token, we concluded that the provision which permitted students of parochial schools to attend some of the classes operated by public schools, particularly in vocational training and in the use of laboratories and in participation in the proposed new community education centers, did not . . . constitute the use of public funds for the support of private education.

There was written into the act specific prohibitions against the allocation of any funds by the states . . . for direct support of private or parochial schools and the use of any of the money from the act to finance or enhance or to promote in any way religious instruction.

Concerning the role of NEA staff members, McKay continued:

I can't say enough for the exceptionally skillful and effective work done by members of the NEA legislative staff in bringing about the enactment of this bill. Jim McCaskill and John Lumley were the principal operators on Capitol Hill who knew their way around so well that they were able to accomplish seeming miracles. This is best illustrated by the fact that after the bill passed and the committee was in Executive Session meeting behind closed doors, John Lumley was on the inside of the meeting room assisting the members of the committee in "marking up" or putting together the final version of the bill. I think this the most eloquent testimony to the confidence and stature of anyone who works in the legislative field . . . to be invited in . . . as a trusted consultant to the committee.[20]

By far the greatest change in the NEA legislative area has been the achievement of federal school support, an Association goal of forty-six years. Now that the principle has been established, the Association must continue to secure adequate funding for the act, evaluate results, and be alert to changes in society that could signal the need for adjustments in the program to enable it to best serve the national interest.

A National Department of Education with Cabinet Status

The NEA's Legislative program for the 96th Congress (1979–80) included as its first priority the establishment of a federal cabinet-level Department of Education.

The proposal had the backing of President Carter, who said in his State of the Union message to Congress, "In my view, education issues deserve more attention and better, more accountable management than they can receive in a department as large and complex as HEW."

Administration bills were introduced in both the House and Senate early in the session. The Senate bill, S-210, was sponsored by Senator Abraham Ribicoff (D., Connecticut), a former secretary of the Department of Health, Education, and Welfare, who guided a similar measure through the Senate in the 95th Congress. However, the House did not act on the bill, requiring that new legislation be introduced again in both bodies.

Senator Ribicoff in the 96th Congress was joined by forty-six of his Senate colleagues as sponsors of the bill—thirty-four Democrats and twelve Republicans—including Senate minority leader Howard Baker (R., Tennessee) and majority leader Robert Byrd (D., West Virginia).

The House bill, HR 2444, was introduced in the House of Representatives by Representative Jack Brooks (D., Texas), with seventy-two cosponsors.

The Senate passed its bill on April 30, 1979, by an impressive vote of 72 to 21. A month later, on May 2, the House Committee on Government Operations voted to send the measure to the House by a razor-thin majority of 20 to 19.

Debate began in July. In the course of the discussion, four extraneous amendments were adopted; all were highly controversial. One provided that no individual be denied educational opportunities by rules, regulations, standards, guidelines, and orders that utilize any ratios, quotas, or other numerical requirements related to race, creed, color, national origin, or sex. The other three dealt with abortion, school prayers, and busing. It would be difficult to identify four current topics that would create a greater split among supporters of the bill or generate more emotional controversy.

On July 17, the House passed two motions. A motion by the principal sponsor, Congressman Brooks, "that the House insist on its amendments to the Senate Bill (S-210) to establsh a Department of Education and request a conference with the Senate," passed by a vote of 263 to 156.[21] A second motion, by Representative Robert S. Walker (R., Pennsylvania), provided that the House conferees be instructed to insist on the provisions contained in section 101(2) of the House version of the bill.[22]

Many educators saw the controversial amendments to be a repeat of the familiar strategy to defeat the bill by confusing the issues and dividing the measures supporters. But in this case the tactic was frustrated by the bill's supporters. The amendments were deleted by the Senate-House Conference Committee and the conference committee's report was approved by both houses.

If the NEA has become more aggressive in recent years, it has been because it has been necessary to be more assertive. The Congress—especially the House—has for years played games with important educational bills. Its methods were by no means models of democratic procedures. The tactic of attaching one or more controversial amendments is an old one. It has been used to defeat education bills since 1943, when Senator Langer of North Carolina offered a racial amendment to defeat the Thomas-Hill Federal Aid Bill S-637.

Since that time, it has been used frequently in the House. It is a cunning way to kill a bill without a record vote on its merits.

Why is a separate cabinet-level Department of Education needed? The case rests on four general arguments.

I. *Education did not get the attention it deserved as a part of the Department of Health, Education, and Welfare.*

    A. Standing between the U.S. commissioner of education and the president are two superiors—the secretary of HEW and an assistant secretary—either of whom may have little interest or experience in education. This inhibiting arrangement has been an important reason the Office of Education has had thirteen commissioners in twelve years.[23]

    B. This situation is not only a frustration to the commissioner but a disservice to the president, who needs and deserves to receive advice and counsel direct from the nation's top education officer.

    C. Moreover, Congress would profit from having one central source of information on education matters.

II. *Conditions have changed; new administrative machinery is required.*

    A. In 1954, when President Eisenhower created the Department of HEW, expenditures were $2 billion and education expenditures were $235 million. In 1978, HEW expenditures (exclusive of education) were $160 billion and education expenditures were $8.1 billion.

B. Furthermore, 90 percent of health and welfare expenditures are fixed by statute and are not subject to administrative control. But education expenditures are controllable administratively. As a result, when budgets are cut, the economy ax often falls on the education budget.

III. *Federal education programs should be coordinated.*

A. More than forty federal agencies and bureaus are now involved in approximately two hundred educational programs. For example, Indian schools are administered by the Bureau of Indian Affairs in the Department of the Interior; schools for dependents of servicemen overseas are administered by the Department of Defense; and the school lunch program is administered by the Department of Agriculture.

B. Efforts at coordination under the present arrangement have met with limited success largely because of the stature of the Office of Education and the natural bureaucratic efforts of separate departments to "defend their turf."

C. The present variety of uncoordinated and overlapping educational programs with no uniform standards is confusing, inefficient, and indefensible.

IV. *Education is sufficiently important to the nation to justify a cabinet-level Department of Education.*

A. A Department of Education, headed by a secretary in the president's cabinet, would have both the status and the freedom of action to give leadership to the schools of the nation.

B. The new status would be more likely to attract able and talented leaders.

C. Cabinet status would enable the president to hold the secretary accountable for administering and coordinating all federal education programs.

D. Such status would be symbolic of the importance of education to the health, strength, and prosperity of the nation.

The bill to create a separate Department of Education was opposed by the American Federation of Teachers. Writing in the April 1979 issue of *The American Teacher*, AFT president Albert Shanker said supporters claim that a separate department would accomplish two major objectives. "First, it would give greater prestige to education. Second, it would consolidate and coordinate various education programs which are paid for by

the United States government but administered by different departments
. . . giving 'prestige' to education is not a good reason to create a department. Who can say in advance such a department would enjoy high or
low prestige?" With regard to the coordination of education programs
now spread through different departments, Shanker said, "When the bill
was first introduced, the constituent groups in these other departments
were outraged."

If the programs in other departments were to be coordinated in the new
department, Shanker claimed, the bill could not pass the Congress. So, he
said, the president submitted a new bill that excluded most of the programs that were to be coordinated. Shanker advocated defeat of the Bill.[24]

Some congressmen used the conflict between the two organizations as
an excuse to cast a negative vote on the measure.

The AFT's opposition was probably interpreted correctly by Eliot Marshall. He wrote in the *New Republic* that "plans for the Education Department could conceivably include sections of the Labor Department,
saying: 'It would be particularly irritating to let an independent union
like NEA—which surely would dominate the new department—get its
hands on pieces of the labor machinery.' And, reported Marshall, Congress is equally aware of AFT's attitude, noting that 'one Senate aide said
the AFT is against having a department because NEA is for it.' "[25]

Some Comments on the NEA's Legislation Program

Many persons not well acquainted with the NEA's wide variety of programs tend to regard the Association chiefly as a Washington lobby. Actually, only 7.5 percent of the NEA budget is devoted to lobbying. The
total number of staff of the Washington legislative support office is seventeen. Nine consultants are stationed in regional offices, making a total legislative staff of twenty-six, including professionals and clerical personnel.

NEA annual expenditures for lobbying activities since 1957 have varied
from a low of $41,600 in 1962 to a high of $321,000 in 1977. In one year
(1959), the NEA was listed as the top spender in the nation among the
professional societies, and in the five-year period from 1965 to 1969, it
was among the top twenty-four. Since 1969, however, the NEA has not
been included on the list of top spenders among the federal lobbies.

The Washington office has the backing of a modern electronic data-
gathering and -retrieval system and is connected to the offices of NEA's
fifty-two state affiliates by a Telex network for instant communication.

Not all of the NEA's legislative activity takes place in Washington. Its
state affiliates were engaged in legislative activity in the states before the
NEA was established. And today, most of the NEA legislative action takes

place in the state capitols. In recent years, because of inflation, the more favorable tax position of the federal government, and the recognition of the importance of education to the national welfare, more and more activity has taken place in Washington. But the large reservoir of legislative talent residing in its nationwide network of state affiliates is one of the Association's greatest strengths in the legislative field.

Not all of the NEA's legislative activity is involved in supporting its own proposals. Each session of Congress—each meeting of the state legislatures—brings a new crop of proposals affecting the schools for better or worse. A recent example is the proposed tuition tax credit, which posed a serious threat to the public schools; and its defeat consumed a great deal of time and effort of the legislative staff.

Another aspect of legislation is securing the funding once a piece of legislation is approved by Congress. After its initial funding, it must be renewed for subsequent years. Consequently, a portion of the time of the legislative staff is required just to maintain the fruits of previous legislative victories.

Legislative activity is not a solo performance. To pass a bill in the Congress usually requires an external group to serve as advocate—to communicate the need for action, organize external support, secure sponsors, and help the lawmakers understand and support the proposal. Furthermore, most school proposals effect a number of groups—teachers, parents, school administrators, school board members, other school employees, and many voluntary nonschool organizations. Usually, coalitions are formed of all major groups with an interest in a legislative proposal. An organization such as the NEA has the resources to bring such groups together for the purpose of developing a consensus on the content of the proposals and to plan and organize the support activities.

At the time of the Nixon veto of the HEW appropriations in 1969–70, the NEA took the initiative in forming the Committee for Full Funding. So successful was the initial effort that the coalition, involving some seventy different organizations, is still in existence in substantially its original form. The director of the NEA legislative program, Stan McFarland, was named the first chairman, and the treasurer of the National School Boards Association served as treasurer.

Educators who are devoting their lives to education have learned they can't afford to be indifferent to legislative activity. For it is the process by which America's public policies are fashioned. It is the process by which the schools are nourished.

The chief changes in the legislative activity of the NEA in the first twenty-two years of its second century include the approval of the Elementary and Secondary Education Act, which established federal responsibility for education, easily the most significant educational development of the past half-century.

The other longstanding major objective of the NEA, the creation of the cabinet-level Department of Education, was achieved in the 97th Congress. On September 27, 1979, when the House approved the legislation to elevate education to cabinet status, NEA President Willard H. McGuire declared it "one of education's finest hours" and an action from which "all Americans will benefit."

The legislation brought 152 education programs scattered throughout the federal bureaucracy into one administrative unit with direct access to the White House.

The measure passed the Senate handily by a vote of 69 to 2. The margin in the House was much narrower, 215 to 201.

The new department includes education programs formerly lodged in the Departments of Defense, Justice, Housing and Urban Development, Labor, and Agriculture, and the National Science Foundation.

A third objective, discussed in a previous chapter, a national collective-bargaining statute covering teachers and other public employees, will continue on the NEA legislative agenda.

A major development in the general area of legislation is the active entry of the NEA into the national arena of political action, to be discussed in the pages that follow.

CHAPTER SEVEN

Political Action

No change in the NEA in recent years has provoked as much concern among conservative groups as the Association's entry into political activity by forming a national political action organization, NEA-PAC.

One magazine, *Reader's Digest*, headlined a story about the action: "The NEA: A Washington Lobby Run Rampant." The story concluded that the NEA's support of a separate Department of Education with a cabinet-level administrator "would deliver a mortal blow to our traditional system of grass-roots control of education."[1]

Both the *Reader's Digest* article and a news magazine story titled "When Educators Put the Arm on Congress" quoted a congressman and outspoken critic of a separate Office of Education, John Ashbrook (R., Ohio), as saying, "I think there's a growing concern that the NEA's priorities these days break down like this—power first, politics second, education third."[2]

Responding to the *Reader's Digest* article, NEA Executive Secretary Terry Herndon said:

> The . . . article is not so much a report on NEA's political effort but rather a statement of disagreement with the substance of the effort. We seek an expanded federal responsibility for the support of state and local efforts to provide educational opportunities. *Reader's Digest* opposes this effort and strives to

identify its position with the public interest. We obviously disagree and find our effort to be in the public interest.

Our efforts to achieve a Department and more financial aid are joint efforts with the School Boards Association, the administrators associations, the PTA, many civil rights organizations and much of the labor movement.[3]

Concerning the congressman's charges, Herndon declared, "Mr. Ashbrook has opposed the 18 year old vote, postcard voter registration, ERA, appropriations to education, labor law reform, the Department of Education. . . . It is little wonder that the activism of NEA and other popular groups make him nervous."[4]

Rationale for Entering into Political Activity

The NEA was drawn into active participation in the political process in the same manner it embraced collective bargaining and leaped into an active role in school desegregation. Changes in society required it.

The NEA lagged behind its state affiliates in concluding it must take an active role in the election process. The success or failure of the state associations has been measured largely by how effective they have been in winning increases in state school budgets. A substantial portion of that responsibility now resides in Washington with NEA.

State legislators, congressmen, and senators all have their own set of personal interests and values. Generally speaking, they are supported by contributions and other forms of help by citizens and organizations sharing those interests, philosophies, and values. Few educators or organizations of educators can match the money contributions of those individuals and organizations who customarily oppose state, federal, and local school appropriations. But teachers' organizations learned that as radio and television time, newspaper ads, and campaign materials became more and more expensive, few prospective candidates with an altruistic concern for education, but without a personal fortune, could afford to seek election. The state associations realized they could not compete with the conservative groups and the taxpayers' organizations in terms of monetary contributions. But by organizing a political action committee they could, through modest contributions by individual members, assist candidates to the extent of covering filing fees and other initial expenses. However, the greatest support the teachers' groups found they could offer was volunteer services by Association members residing in the local election districts.

In the early stages, all contributions were through volunteer services as well as through providing forums for candidates and using the Association's publications networks to inform members of the positions of candidates on questions of special interest to teachers.

As the federal income tax bite began to limit the fiscal response of states to the explosion in school population in the 1950s and 1960s and to reduction in the purchasing power of school budgets, it became apparent that the federal government must play a stronger role in financing schools. It had a tax source in the federal income tax that was self-adjusting to inflation. At the same time, it reduced the ability of the states to use their only progressive tax source—the state income tax.

While federal school-support bills had been before Congress constantly since 1918, NEA leaders began in earnest to push them in the mid-1950s. As they did so, they soon found they must adopt on the national scene some methods found to be successful in the states.

Also, in the period from 1955 to 1960, significant progress was made toward achieving a federal support bill. In the 84th Congress (1955–56), the Kelley Bill was debated in the House but defeated with the adoption of a Powell amendment. In the 85th Congress, the Kelley Bill was defeated in the House, but the Murray-Metcalf Bill was passed there. It was the first time in history for a school-support bill to receive such a favorable vote in the House. However, the Rules Committee's failure to permit a resolution of Senate and House differences killed the measure. The treatment of the school bill in the House heightened the resolve of NEA leaders to pursue the battle with greater vigor.

In the following 87th and 88th Congresses, the articulate leadership of President Kennedy and the overwhelming public support indicated by the opinion polls sustained supporters, although support was not strong enough to prevail over the bitter opposition of parochial school forces.

All of this activity involving alternate periods of elation and depression was highly educational for the large numbers of local, state, and national leaders involved. Coming close to victory only to see it slip from their grasp because of the cunning methods of conservative interests was highly motivating. It is not surprising that pressures on the NEA increased during this period to more nearly match the strength of the opposition by adopting a more aggressive and sophisticated political action program.

While there was a wide divergence in the interests of the 435 members of the U.S. House of Representatives, they all had one major interest in common: getting reelected every two years.

One popular method of accumulating election funds was to hold testimonial dinners and to invite friends to attend at from fifty dollars a plate upward. Obviously, all those legislative advocates who had been seeking votes from a congressman were numbered among the "friends" to receive invitations.

Contributions by the Association were ruled to be illegal. So, initially, NEA staff members were solicited personally to make individual contributions to enable one or two associates to put in an appearance. This soon became an inequitable burden on those staff members. Furthermore, it was not possible to treat fairly all candidates to whom an obligation was felt.

How NEA-PAC Developed

The first contributions of cash for political action were authorized by the Representative Assembly in 1973. But pressures for a more aggressive role in national politics by teachers had been building for more than a decade.

In 1956, the Representative Assembly adopted a resolution urging every teacher to exercise the right and obligation to be an active, informed citizen, with an intelligent concern for the issues, for the public policy decisions, and for the selection of competent public officials.

That resolution has become a continuing resolution that has been strengthened and made more specific in recent years. It was proposed originally by the Citizenship Committee, one of the first committees established by the NEA. Its original mission was to study and report what the times and conditions demanded of the schools in terms of preparing pupils to accept the responsibilities of active citizenship. It later became involved in the induction into citizenship of new voters. Also, it cooperated for many years with the U.S. Department of Justice in sponsoring an annual National Conference on Citizenship involving a thousand organizations and agencies concerned with the rights and duties of citizens.

Through publications, film strips, and conferences, the committee promoted programs designed to encourage teachers to take an active role in politics by registering, voting, participating in the political process, and supporting candidates.

In 1963, the Citizenship Committee, in cooperation with several other NEA units, began a series of regional political clinics. The first, held in Cleveland, featured urban problems and the ways in which political action could enable teacher's organizations to have an impact on their solution. Members of Congress and state and local political leaders advised participants on the most effective ways of solving school and community problems by working through the political system. These clinics continued until 1970.

In 1968, an ad hoc committee of the Board of Directors was appointed, to include the chairman of the Citizenship Committee, to explore the possibility of establishing a national political action committee. The committee reported its findings to the Board on February 15, 1969. Following the report, the Board voted to name a task force to develop plans for forming an organization under NEA sponsorship to enable educators to participate legally in political action, including supporting candidates. The Board urged the task force to complete a plan as quickly as possible to permit it to become operational without undue delay.[5]

The following year, 1970, the task force recommended to the Board that a political action committee be created and the budget of the Citizenship Committee be increased to permit it to stimulate the organization of political action arms in those states where they did not exist and to strengthen those already in existence.

The recommendations were defeated after the Legislative Commission submitted a statement indicating it was a good idea but opposing the creation of a national Political Action Committee (PAC) at that time. The opposition was based on five points: (1) The proposal was premature because financing was not assured. (2) Congressional elections would occur in 1970. The announcement of the organization would bring many requests from congressional candidates that could not be met. (3) Adequate plans to coordinate the activities of a national PAC with the several state organizations were lacking. (4) Information concerning the effect a PAC would have on the NEA's federal tax status was lacking. (5) If the plan were to falter in the initial stages, the Association's image would be damaged.[6]

Later, in the meeting, a motion was made and approved that the president of NEA appoint a committee from the Board to prepare a minority report regarding the creation of a PAC, to be referred to the Representative Assembly. The Assembly would be in session later in that week in Philadelphia.[7]

The following day, June 29, 1970, a motion was made and carried to reconsider the matter of creating a national PAC. The committee named by the president the previous day then recommended that the task force be continued for one additional year to continue to study the feasibility and advisability of the formation of a PAC for education and that it initiate a pilot program with one volunteer state desiring assistance in organizing a state PAC. The funding of the pilot project was to be negotiated with the pilot state organization. This compromise proposal by the committee was adopted by the Board.[8]

Meanwhile, the NEA president and Executive Committee had been involved in some political activity. On November 4, 1969, President George Fischer organized a meeting of the Executive Committee by telephone conference call to discuss the question of whether the Association should take a public position on the nomination of Clement F. Haynsworth to the

U.S. Supreme Court. The Executive Committee concurred with President Fischer that the nomination should be opposed and approved copy for the following telegram to go to members of the U.S. Senate and with minor amendments to President Nixon:

> The National Education Association, representing more than two million professional educators in 9,000 state and local affiliates, vigorously opposes the confirmation of Clement F. Haynsworth to fill the vacant seat on the U.S. Supreme Court. Judge Haynsworth's record on civil rights renders him unfit to hold this high position. The rights of every school child could be abridged by his confirmation. NEA urges you to vote against confirmation of Judge Haynsworth, in the interest of equal opportunity for all American citizens.[9]

About two months later, on February 11, 1970, the Executive Committee took a similar action to recommend to the Board of Directors that the NEA oppose the nomination of Judge G. Harrold Carswell. The basis of the action was "Judge Carswell's record . . . on civil and human rights and his questionable competency as a judge."[10]

The nominations of both Haynsworth and Carswell were withdrawn. These actions marked the first time the NEA had taken a position on a nominee to the U.S. Supreme Court.

Although the Executive Committee action on Judge Carswell's nomination met with resistance from some Board members, at a meeting the next day, the Board supported the Executive Committee's action by voting to oppose the nomination, with eleven of the ninety-seven Board members requesting their votes be recorded in the negative.

The NEA was involved in political action. All that remained was the task of setting up the machinery to comply with the Federal Corrupt Practices Act and the Internal Revenue Code, and to provide for coordination with the PACs already in existence in the states. This, however, was not a simple task. Procedures had to be developed that involved state political action groups in decisions on the endorsement of candidates. An integrated system of handling the collection of state and national contributions had to be designed. The NEA's tax status as a nonprofit organization had to be protected.

President-elect Catherine Barrett chose the responsibility for doing the groundwork necessary to launch the new activity. By February 1972, she reported to the Board of Directors that a meeting of presidents, executive secretaries, and chairmen of state political action groups had reached a consensus on the general purpose of a national NEA-PAC and procedures for coordinated funding. Other problems, such as the endorsement procedures for national candidates, remained for a second conference scheduled later that month.

By mid-March, the Board of Directors had received reports from independent consultants containing specific recommendations for organizing NEA-PAC based on the experiences of other groups operating successful PAC arms.

By the end of April, guidelines were in preparation. Board members and staff had made personal contributions of $2,225 to get the fund started, and a fund-raising reception to be held in a Washington Hotel in June had been planned, to publicly launch the NEA-PAC.

Guidelines for NEA-PAC were considered and approved by the Board of Directors in June, and in July the Representative Assembly adopted a motion directing the president of the Association to take the necessary steps to recommend a procedure for endorsing a candidate for president of the United States to the 1974 meeting of the Representative Assembly. The Assembly also authorized a one-dollar contribution each year in addition to Association membership dues. The one-dollar contributions would go to NEA-PAC to support political action unless the member requested that it be refunded. The Assembly also directed the Board, in cooperation with NEA-PAC, to perfect a system of funding conforming to state and federal laws and proceed to perfect the organization of a fully functioning national political action committee for education.

By September, NEA-PAC had adopted a strategy for the 1972 national election which was outlined in a Telex statement to the state affiliates. The statement said the NEA would elect candidates for national offices who would support education; urge members to elect Senate and House candidates who were strong supporters of education; and step up its campaign activities, including financial and other assistance, in an intensive grass-roots effort to achieve this goal.[11]

The Telex message said the Association would not support a presidential candidate in 1972. However, NEA President Barrett reported that representatives of the state PACs supported an Executive Committee statement charging the Nixon administration with "callous disregard for education."[12]

Reporting to the 1973 Representative Assembly, President Barrett declared: "In 1972, teacher political activity reached its highest level . . . teachers played an active role in electing 30 percent of the House of Representatives, and 40 percent of the 33 candidates elected in the Senate. NEA-PAC became a reality last September. It supported 32 candidates. Twenty-six of them won." She also reported that forty-four states had functioning PACs.[13]

In his first report to the Representative Assembly, and just two months after his appointment as the NEA's seventh executive secretary, Terry

Herndon outlined some goals and strategies for the profession. On political action, he stressed the importance of active participation in the political process; outlined the coordinated roles of the local, state, and national components of the profession; and recognized one of the chief problems that had slowed the Association's progress toward fully effective political action—permitting individual differences to obscure professional agreement on goals. Elaborating on the latter point, he said: "We are slowed dramatically because half are Republican and half are Democrat, and each half frequently forgets that the other half is also comprised of teachers. I hope we have arrived at a level of understanding that permits us all to know and to commit ourselves to the premise that political difference is sufferable, but political indifference is absolutely intolerable."[14]

At the conclusion of the 1973 Representative Assembly, according to custom, the new president was given an opportunity to address the delegates. One of the most forceful statements of the future direction of the NEA was delivered by the newly elected president, Helen Wise, who brought the delegates to their feet with her candid outline of problems and her projected plans to attack them. It was a heady period in the Association's history. For a decade, the Association had undergone a period of introspection. It wrestled with the internal pain of change and the division of power among the governance units and the change of program emphasis among the NEA and its state and local affiliates.

This was a new beginning. The new constitution had been adopted. A new, young leadership team was at the helm, and a spirit of unity and confidence permeated the organization despite the presence of a number of lingering divisive problems. There was a general feeling of rebirth and confidence in the ability of the Association to cope with the problems as they came.

"NEA has indeed awakened and we are on our way," Helen Wise exclaimed.

> Our first major objective, politically and legislatively, will be to reverse the national leadership in Washington and put a friend of education in the White House and more friends of education in Congress.
>
> We will initiate a grass roots campaign that will bring about the victories that we must have in 1976, and if that means building a war chest to get friends of education elected—then we need to keep the old lid open and continue to plunk in the money.
>
> One thing is certain—the NEA will never again sit out a national election.
>
> In fact, we will build NEA's political force over the next two years to the point where the Presidential candidates will seek NEA endorsement.[15]

In her report to the Representative Assembly the following year (1974), President Wise asked the delegates to approve the guidelines for endorsement of candidates and pledge to elect friends of education in 1976 not only to the House and Senate but to the White House as well. The decision of the president not to veto the bill to increase funds for education came about for the first time in five years for one reason only—because the NEA had the votes to override that veto and the president knew it.[16]

Procedure for Endorsing Presidential Candidates

Some organizations endorse political candidates based on the judgment of their national officers. Not the NEA. The decision is made by an elaborate procedure involving members from all states, and the Association is bound by their decisions. The NEA procedure includes a number of options to cover variable circumstances.

An Incumbent President. The endorsement of an incumbent president may be accomplished by a vote of the delegates to the NEA Representative Assembly in its annual meeting or by mailed ballot before the annual meeting. In either event, a 58 percent majority of those voting is required for endorsement.

Three Options. If three options are included on the ballot—including the names of two candidates and "no endorsement"—endorsement would require a simple majority vote. The vote would be by mailed ballot.

Ballots are mailed to delegates, elected by NEA members in each state, within two weeks of the last major political party nominating convention.

Within a week of the identification of all party nominees, a ballot is prepared by NEA-PAC. Recommendation of a candidate may be made by NEA-PAC, but it must be made at least three days before ballots are mailed.

Two Options. If only two options appear on the ballot, the same procedure would be followed as outlined for three options, but endorsement would require a 58 percent majority of those voting.

Endorsement before the Representative Assembly. A presidential candidate may be endorsed by a mail ballot prior to the annual NEA Representative Assembly and/or the political party nominating conventions by 58 percent majority vote of the delegates to the Assembly.

Primary Election. Endorsement of a candidate for president may be made by the 123-person NEA Board of Directors prior to the party nominating conventions by a 58 percent majority of the Board. However, the endorsement may not be implemented in a state without concurrence of the NEA state affiliate. Subsequent endorsement would require use of the appropriate foregoing procedures.

Other Provisions.   The screening of candidates, preparation of ballots, and development of operating procedures are the responsibility of NEA-PAC. These duties are carried out with consultation and the participation of NEA state and local affiliates.

The actions of President Richard M. Nixon did a great deal to motivate NEA leaders and members to enter into political action in an aggressive way. He made it necessary. Otherwise, the executive could nullify all of the Association's efforts to secure school funds from the Congress. Consistently, between 1968 and the time he resigned in 1973, Nixon attempted to influence Congress to limit school funds to the amounts he proposed in his budgets by threatening to veto them if the amounts were increased. If appropriations exceeding his proposals were passed, he attempted to prevent their expenditure by impounding the funds.

On one occasion, after a bitter battle in which the president used the full power of his office to influence Congress to sustain his veto of school funds, he invited those who voted to sustain his veto to the White House for a victory celebration. Such actions had the same effects on school supporters as the games played by the House Rules Committee to defeat school support bills: it increased their determination to overcome the obstacle by increased legislative and political activity.

Some Thoughts on Legislation and Political Action

Teachers' attitudes toward political activity by members of the NEA have changed dramatically in the years since the celebration of NEA's centennial in 1957.

Periodic opinion polls conducted by the NEA revealed that in 1960, a bare majority of teachers felt they should participate actively in national politics. By 1968, four-fifths of male teachers and two-thirds of female teachers believed they should be active participants. By 1972, a substantial majority of both sexes supported the establishment of local, state, and national PACs.

As one who has followed closely the actions of members of Congress and the White House, and the concurrent actions of the teaching profession, I must conclude that American teachers working in the NEA have sought to solve school and teacher problems by recognizing the realities of political life in the United States and attempting to adapt to them in a logical way. The use of the resources available to them to influence the system in the direction of their values has naturally been of concern to those with a different set of values. Congress must deal with the clash of values and make decisions that in its judgment reflect the will of a majority of Americans.

It is natural that conservative groups with a major interst in controlling public spending would be alarmed at the growing power of the NEA. But the test of whether the NEA's new power is good or bad for the nation will depend not upon how much power the NEA has but upon how it is used. Obviously, a majority of NEA members believe it is being used to further the public interest.

A review of a few of the major legislative proposals approved by Congress with support by NEA since 1957 will give the general direction of NEA's interests.

1958. Congress enacted an NEA-backed law to aid in the education of mentally retarded children.

The National Defense Education Act (NDEA) was approved. It provided federal loans to students in institutions of higher education; financial help to strengthen elementary and secondary science, mathematics, and modern foreign language instruction; national defense fellowships; guidance, counseling, and testing, and identification and encouragement, of able students; and other programs. The NEA was instrumental in amending the act to provide safeguards against federal controls.

1961. Funds were provided to train teachers of deaf children. The Peace Corps Act established a permanent organization to supply U.S. teachers and technicians to underdeveloped nations.

1962. The Manpower Development and Training Act provided for occupational training and retraining of the nation's labor force. The Educational TV Act authorized federal grants to educational institutions or nonprofit groups to assist in building educational television stations.

1963. The Health Professions Assistance Act authorized $236.4 million to construct and rehabilitate teaching facilities for physicians, dentists, and others and for loans to students in medical professions.

The Mental Retardation Facilities and Community Mental Health Centers Construction Act provided for matching grants to build mental retardation facilities, community mental health centers, and training of teachers for retarded children.

The Higher Education Facilities Act authorized $1.2 billion for a three-year program of grants and loans for construction at colleges and universities.

The Vocational Education Act authorized $1.5 billion to enlarge vocational education programs, expand and extend the National Defense Education Act, and continue aid to schools in federally impacted areas.

The Manpower Development and Training Amendments expanded youth training programs and provided basic education courses for jobless illiterates seeking training.

1964. The Aid to Public Libraries Act amended the 1956 act to extend federal public library assistance to urban as well as rural areas.

Amendments were approved to extend and expand both the NDEA and the aid to areas impacted due to federal activities.

The NDEA institutes for the advanced training of teachers was broadened to include teachers of English, reading, history, and geography, teachers of "disadvantaged youth," librarians, and educational media specialists.

The NDEA provided loans for college and university students, fellowships to prepare for careers in colleges and university teaching, loans and grants to schools for teaching materials, and the teacher training institutes.

Loans and matching grants were made available to states for the purchase of equipment and were broadened to include materials for the teaching of English, reading, history, geography, and civics.

1965. Public Law 89-10, the Elementary and Secondary Education Act, passed by Congress with major support from the NEA, provided $1.2 billion for elementary and high schools the first year.

1966. The Veterans' Readjustment Benefits Act of 1966 was enacted by Congress with NEA support.

1970. The Drug Abuse Education Act passed by Congress with NEA support.

1971. The NEA strongly supported the Voting Rights Amendment giving eighteen- to twenty-year-olds the right to vote in congressional and presidential elections. The NEA prompted the House Ways and Means Committee to include a provision for hospital insurance for teachers and other public employees not covered by Social Security.

1972. The NEA gave active support to the Equal Rights Amendment and to strengthening of the enforcement powers of the Equal Opportunities Commission. A $20 million omnibus higher-education bill was supported by the Association.

1974. The NEA achieved the release of $1.1 billion in formerly impounded federal funds for health and education programs.

1975. NEA efforts secured a $25 billion authorization extending for four years the Elementary and Secondary Education Act. The chairman of the House Education and Labor Committee gave credit to the NEA for its passage.

1976. The president's veto of the 1976 Education Appropriation Bill providing $7.5 billion for education was overridden. Also overridden was the presidential veto of $475 million for Head Start, Delinquent Youth Programs, and Remediation of Child Abuse. An additional administrative veto of the $2.6 billion appropriation for the school lunch program was also overridden.

The NEA and allied organizations lobbied successfully for $945 million in supplemental funds for higher education, aid to the handicapped, improvement of services to handicapped children, and the Voting Rights Extension Act, extending the 1965 act to correct historical disenfranchisement.

1977. The NEA proposed and succeeded in securing the approval of Congress for an initial appropriation of $75 million to establish centers for teachers to develop in-service programs related to their needs, the centers to be designed and controlled by teachers. The Association and allied organizations won an increase of $500 million in federal funds for higher education; $450 million for ESEA, including increases for vocational education; aid to the handicapped; and an $800 million appropriation for impacted areas—an increase of $7 million over the previous year.

1979. The NEA's long-term goal—the establishment of a separate National Department of Education administered by a secretary of education in the president's cabinet—was achieved.

How Successful Has NEA Been in Political Action?

The NEA's record in its first year of publicly endorsing candidates for the House and Senate seems to have established a pattern for subsequent years. In that year, 1972, NEA-PAC endorsed thirty-two candidates. Twenty-six were elected—80 percent of those endorsed.

In 1974, 229 candidates for the House were elected of 282 endorsed, and 21 Senatorial candidates were elected from 28 endorsed—another 80 percent record.

NEA-PAC endorsed 323 House candidates and 26 candidates for the Senate in 1976. Winning seats in the House were 272, and 19 candidates won Senate seats—an 83 percent record.

The 1978 elections produced a 77 percent success ratio, with 197 out of 247 candidates endorsed winning election to the House and 13 out of 24 winning their Senate races.

The NEA's endorsement of President Carter and its active participation in the national convention and campaign were given generous credit by the president and his staff as an important factor in his election.

After comparing the views of candidate Carter and President Ford in 1976, the delegates votes 85 to 15 percent to endorse Mr. Carter. Because President Carter kept his promises to the NEA, the Board of Directors in 1979 endorsed him in the primary elections.

One of the gratifying developments of the more aggressive political action policy, according to NEA leaders, is that more and more candidates are consulting with them prior to the election on the Association's legislative goals and priorities.

Political Action Committees have grown rapidly in the last half of the decade of the 1970s. In that period, the number of PACs is estimated to have increased from less than 100 to more than 2,000. What are the organizations that contribute to PACs? Some are professional and trade associations. Some of these, and the amounts they contributed to the 1978 elections, are: The American Medical Association PAC ($1,644,795), National Association of Realtors PAC ($1,122,378), National Automobile Dealers Association PAC ($975,675), American Dental Association PAC ($510,050), National Association of Life Underwriters PAC ($380,638), and National Rifle Association PAC ($369,412).

Some are labor organizations: The United Auto Worker PAC ($964,465), AFL-CIO PAC ($920,841), United Steel Worker PAC ($594,930), United Transportation Union PAC ($557,603), Machinists and Aerospace Workers PAC ($536,538), and Communications Workers of America PAC ($474,633).

Some are private corporations: International Paper Co. PAC ($173,056), Standard Oil of Indiana PAC ($154,800), Dart Industries, Inc. PAC ($119,300), American Family Corporation PAC ($113,650), Winn-Dixie Stores, Inc. PAC ($112,942), and General Electric Co. PAC ($112,020).[17]

By comparison, NEA-PAC in 1978 elections spent $335,347. Teachers should not overemphasize monetary contributions, important as they are. The greatest resource possessed by teachers is the sum total of personal resources of almost two million members residing in every congressional district in the United States. Their collective influence as active local citizens in their own communities, coordinated by a national strategy, can add up to a tremendous political force beyond the limits of what money can buy.

The NEA had 302 delegates and 162 alternates at the 1980 Democratic National Convention—more than the total number of delegates from any state except California, and California's delegation included 24 NEA delegates. The Association also had 11 delegates and 11 alternates at the Republican National Convention in Detroit.

Vice President Walter Mondale told a caucus meeting at the New York Democratic Convention, "I've learned that if you want to go somewhere in national politics these days, you better get the NEA behind you."[18]

Some have cautioned that the all-out support for one candidate carries with it the risk of political punishment should the opposing candidate be elected. This is possible. However, my experience in politics leads me to believe that the risk is minimal. Elected public officials respect power. Once elected they are concerned about being re-elected. They are, therefore, more likely to court than punish groups they know to have the power to exert significant influence in the next election.

The *Wall Street Journal* declared at the close of the 1980 political party conventions that "the National Education Association's political clout reflects a new brand of sophisticated special interest politics. . . . It's clear," said the Journal, "that the NEA has become a force to be reckoned with in the era of 'reform' politics."[19]

CHAPTER EIGHT

Improvement of Instruction

The greatest recent change in the NEA's program for the improvement of instruction occurred in 1974 when the Congress approved authorization for the establishment of teacher centers. The act, drafted by NEA personnel, was based on a concept evolved from the Association's experience helping local teachers' groups to influence in-service programs. Teachers have long complained that in-service programs were unrelated to the real problems in the classroom. They have also complained about their inability to influence district programs.

In at least one instance, with the backing of a cash grant from the NEA, a local teachers' group was able to persuade the school board to negotiate a program that gave them a voice in determining the content of the in-service program.

The teacher centers are based on the concept that teachers know best what their problems are and in-service programs should be organized to help them find solutions. This is in contrast to the usual college credit program offered by teacher training institutions. The content typically must be acceptable to the graduate dean but may have little or no relationship to the needs perceived by teachers. The teacher centers, on the other hand, exist to provide solutions to the problems teachers themselves iden-

tify. The responsibility of the center staff is to assist the teacher to find solutions in an atmosphere free from administrative pressures.

John Ryor, NEA president, writing in *Today's Education*, said:

> It is . . . in both the public interest and the interest of the teaching profession
> that teachers be heavily involved in developing programs for improving their
> own practice. In my view, this isn't a lofty ideal but a practical imperative.
> There must be a process that guarantees to teachers their participation in the
> design of such programs, so that they can be confident that their wishes and
> needs for improvement will be served. There must, also, be places where
> teachers can go to put such programs into action. Teacher centers meet both
> these objectives. With enactment of the teacher center program, we have for
> the first time a federal law that makes it possible to place some professional de-
> velopment activities in the hands of local teachers—an unquestionably historic
> event.[1]

Sixty-one centers were funded for the first year with a federal appropriation of $8.25 million. Federal regulations governing the operation of the
centers were issued by HEW in January 1978, and the centers began operating the following autumn.

Center programs are initiated by a teacher center policy board usually
organized by the teachers' collective-bargaining agent or, if bargaining
does not exist, by the organization to which a majority of a district's
teachers belong.

The policy board develops and approves a plan for presentation to the
school board or institution of higher education. The school board or other
institution submits the plan to the state department of education. After
review by the state school agency, plans go to the secretary of education,
who will award grants to those judged to be worthy of funding.

Regulations require that full-time classroom teachers make up a majority of the teacher center policy board. Funding is based on the creativity
and general merit of the proposals.

The plans are intended not to replace but to supplement present programs, and local groups are warned that federal funds must not be substi-
tuted for existing in-service programs.

The program has not operated long enough to prove its value, but the
concept is a sound one and early evaluations should be used to ensure that
continued funding goes only to those plans which live up to the teacher
center promise.

There is a substantial body of opinion both within and outside the NEA
membership that the program for the improvement of instruction has fal-
tered in the past few years, since collective bargaining has claimed so
much of the Association's energies. Critics point to the past influential

commissions—such as the Commission on the Reorganization of Secondary Education, which produced the seven cardinal principals, and the reports of the Educational Policies Commission—and ask what the Association is doing of comparable quality and with comparable impact.

Part of this feeling stems from an illusion. Until the early 1970s, the NEA had thirty departments. Each produced journals, bulletins, books, reports, and newsletters published by the NEA. If they were of high quality, the NEA received the credit. If they were not, the NEA took the blame. Neither was deserved in most cases.

Moreover, the age of the supermen is passed. Pronouncements of prestigious bodies no longer have the influence they once enjoyed. And the foundations and research organizations have increased in both numbers and financial support.

I told NEA leaders that I had encountered the feeling among some members that NEA leadership in instruction was declining and inquired how they responded to the critics.

President Willard McGuire denied it was true and said the NEA was now working in different and more effective ways. For example, he said, the Association not only played a leading role in getting the teacher center legislation passed by Congress and the White House but also, through its close relationship with the U.S. Office of Education, participated actively in the drafting of the rules and regulations for administration of the act.

> That program is controlled by those who are in direct contact with students every day—it is quite a move from any kind of in-service training that has previously been part of our education process. While it is very new and still expanding, it certainly is a way in which the improvement of instruction is a part of the national program. . . . I think it is through these kinds of activities we are able as a national organization to impact on instruction. . . while the methods are different than they were a decade ago, . . . I think they are now even more meaningful because a national organization can't directly interact with some sixteen or seventeen thousand school districts.[2]

Executive Director Terry Herndon also disputed the charge. Asked how he answers those who say the NEA has shifted the emphasis away from instruction, he said:

> I tell them first that there has been a shift in emphasis. I don't deny that inasmuch as ten years ago—fifteen years ago—the point in time they reference—NEA was engaged in very little trade-union-type activity and now it is a major focus of all that we do—mutual benefit activity of one kind or another, politics, and collective bargaining. However, I think the characterization is often unfair because they suggest that we have significantly reduced what we were doing in terms of professional development and instructional services. That is not correct. Emphasis has shifted, but it is not as quantitative as they would like. We

still spend five million dollars a year on instruction and professional development activities, and my guess is that that doesn't depart very far from what NEA spent at the time these people see as the high water mark. The shift in emphasis has come about through the dedication of the new resources. We are doing something more than we did before.

Secondly, I try to focus them on process. I raise questions about the efficacy of what we did before, as compared with the efficacy of what we do now. I think we have a more realistic appraisal of what NEA can do and should do. And NEA and its members generally lack the legal authority to implement their own objectives. That authority is vested by law in boards of education, state legislatures, state departments of education, whatever. We now admit that honestly. Our strategy is to develop the position and then move that objective into the legislative arena, into the political arena, to the bargaining table, into a public information program. I believe we have more effect on public policy in regard to education and instruction than we ever did, even though the strategies are not as tidy as they once were.[3]

The NEA program budget is organized around the priorities reviewed and established annually by the Representative Assembly. Currently the NEA has six broad goals. Those six goals and the percentage of the total 1979–80 budget for programs appropriated to each are as follows: economic and professional security for all educators (9.52%), significant legislative support for public education (7.45%), human and civil rights in education (9.84%), leadership in solving social problems (1.16%), an independent, united teaching organization (12.99%), and professional excellence (8.33%). Professional excellence is the goal area encompassing instructional improvement activities.

Analysis of Association budgets for the 1970s shows that, while the percentage of the total budgets devoted to professional excellence has exceeded that for 1979–80 in some years, the dollar appropriation to instruction activities in 1979–80 exceeds any other year. In fact, it exceeded the year in which instruction received the highest percentage of the budget—1971–72—by $2.5 million, and exceeded the year with the second highest appropriation—1978–79—by $800,000.

The National Foundation

The NEA had, for many years, been able to attract tax-free grants from individuals and corporations to support research projects on education problems of current interest. For example, during the period following the launching of the first Russian sputnik, when there was great interest in the education of academically talented pupils, the NEA received a grant from a private corporation for a project to develop programs for the gifted. During the late 1970s, when there was increased public concern about handicapped students, the NEA received a grant to develop and market instructional materials for deaf children.

When the NEA was classified by the Internal Revenue Service as a nonprofit charitable organization, under Section 501C(3) of the Internal Revenue Code, such grants by private donors were tax-deductible.

When the NEA's more aggressive participation in collective bargaining, legislation, and political action became visible in the early 1960s, the IRS proposed a change in its classification. The new classification would not permit donors to take tax deductions for grants to the NEA.

The NEA's legal counsel was asked to recommend alternative courses open to the Association that would permit it to continue to serve the economic legislative and political needs of its members and still permit it to accept tax-free research grants.

Two alternatives were suggested. One would separate the organization into two parts. The lobbying, collective bargaining, and field activities would be organized as a business league under Section 501C(6) of the Internal Revenue Code, and the purely educational activities would retain the tax-exempt status under Section 501C(3).

The second option would be to establish a separate foundation to accept and administer research grants for purely educational activities which could retain the NEA's tax-exempt status under Section 501C(3). All other activities of the NEA could then accept the business league status under Section 501C(6).

The National Foundation for the Improvement of Education (NFIE) was incorporated as an educational and charitable organization under Section 501C(3) on July 7, 1969.

One of the great strengths of the NFIE is that it has ready access to the NEA's network of 10,000 local and 53 state affiliates through which the results of research can be implemented. Also, the research being a product of the teachers' own organization should give it credibility and increase the likelihood of its acceptance and use in the classroom.

Grants received to support education research in the decade from NFIE's organization to January 1980 total over $3.5 million. In addition, the NEA has contributed about $750,000 to the NFIE and provided office space at a reduced rate. Other contributions from individuals and organizations amount to about $25,000.

In its brief history, the NFIE has not achieved a fraction of its potential. It is surprising that it has attracted the funds it has received. But given the unique promise of the foundation to secure the implementation of its reserach findings, the annual volume of research grants to special projects should approach the total volume for the first decade with a reasonable promotional program.

The chief sources of grants for special-purpose projects in the first decade came from federal agencies and private foundations. These two sources together have accounted for about 80 percent of the NFIE's total grant income to date.

In addition, the new manager of the foundation plans to launch a campaign for the accumulation of funds that will permit it to operate as a true foundation. The possibilities of such a program are exciting. The foundation could make grants to teacher-initiated innovative projects of special value to NEA members and affiliates. It could encourage innovation through mini-grants to individual teachers with imaginative plans for the improvement of teaching.

In the eighteen years from 1958–59 to 1976–77, the NEA received over $12 million in grants. These grants were received with minimal effort. It is my impression that more were received because an NEA officer or staff member had an idea for a promising project and outside sources of funding were sought either because Association funds were not available or because the project did not come within the limits of current Association priorities.

Some projects came to the NEA without any effort on its part. They came because a government agency lacked the talent, or felt a nonofficial agency could provide the service better, and so contracted with the NEA to do it for them.

It will be interesting to see what the NFIE can become if a sincere effort is made to promote it. There are many private corporations and individuals who will always be looking for worthy tax-deductible opportunities. With a good presentation of its possibilities, I think many would consider making an investment in the improvement of public education by attacking the problem where education takes place—in the classroom.

With new leadership at the helm of both the Foundation and the NEA instruction units and with a close relationship existing between them the prospects are bright for a strong influence by NEA for the improvement of instruction in the 1980s.

Publications

Since 1913 the National Education Association has published a professional journal, a subscription to which is purchased by payment of the annual membership dues in the organization. The first journal was the *NEA*

Bulletin. The name was changed to the *NEA Journal* in 1921, and since 1973 the name of the official organ of the Association has been *Today's Education*.

The name change in 1973 was a part of a reorganization of the whole NEA communications program, and since that time the journal has served a more specialized function.

Until 1973 the *NEA Journal* was the major publication of the Association. While it had always devoted most of its content to problems of instruction encountered by the classroom teacher, it had gradually become an interpreter of the total program of the NEA. Legislation, political action, collective bargaining, and internal organization issues began crowding the instructional content. So in 1972 the Association, with the aid of a New York consulting firm, reviewed the entire communications program.

To that time the *NEA Journal* had been published monthly except for June, July, and August. A tabloid newspaper, *NEA Reporter* began publishing in 1962 to provide members with fresh news that could not be delayed for inclusion in the next *NEA Journal*.

Results of the 1972–73 evaluation were the following decisions: to change the name of the journal to *Today's Education*; to increase both the circulation and the number of issues of the *NEA Reporter*; and to reduce the publication of *Today's Education* to four times a year and devote its content exclusively to current issues and trends in education and practical, helpful ideas for teachers.

Beginning with the February-March 1980 issue of *Today's Education*, the Association offered each member a choice of one of three editions: a general edition (as in the past), an elementary edition, and a social studies edition. This was an experimental effort to serve the specialized needs of the various segments of the NEA membership. If it is successful, the options will be extended to other levels and subject matter areas.

For many years, the *NEA Journal* was one tangible evidence of membership in the NEA. In 1980, because of the need for news of current developments, it is supplemented by the *Reporter* and other special communications. The *NEA Reporter* is published eight times a year.

Special Publications

The problems in education change as the problems in society change. A recent Gallop survey of public opinion showed that Americans considered discipline to be the school problem of most concern to teachers, parents, and the public at large.

The NEA's response was an attractively packaged kit made available to teachers through their state and local affiliates. The kit included a section on classroom techniques, including tips for organizing and maintaining a well-disciplined classroom. Another section included tips for parents and suggested ways to involve parents in the solution to discipline problems. A bibliography of articles, books, and other resource materials was included, with advice on using the materials as resources for activities developed by local community groups. This is only one example of an NEA service in the instructional field.

Efforts are made by the Association to keep abreast of current concerns and develop background materials as a basis for policy decisions. Information is communicated to members in special publications and through the Association's regular publications. Some recent subjects include violence in the schools, competency-based education, the overreliance on testing, class size, child abuse, migrant education, children's TV programs, accountability, in-service education, and sexism in education.

In the late 1950s and early 1960s, the NEA's programs for the improvement of instruction were implemented through the thirty NEA departments or through special projects.

In his report to the 1959 Representative Assembly, the executive secretary reported on three projects financed from the previous year's budget. The subjects of the three projects were juvenile delinquency, school finance, and working conditions of teachers and school administrators.

The 1963–64 *NEA Handbook* lists six projects funded by special allocations from the Association budget, by grants from outside agencies or cooperatively by the NEA and independent organizations or agencies. The projects were established for specific periods of time and for specific purposes. They included the Urban Project; projects for the deaf, school dropouts, and the academically talented; and projects related to the educational implications of automation and to English composition.

The Urban Project was funded completely by the Association. Others were supported cooperatively by the NEA and grants from The U.S. Office of Education, the Ford Foundation, the Carnegie Corporation, IBM, and the Dean Langmuir Foundation.

The 1959 Representative Assembly established a Special Project on Instruction, which deserves mention. In his report to the 1960 Assembly, Dr. Carr outlined its purpose.

New forces ranging from the splitting of the atom to the exploration of space, play upon education with great intensity. Thorough appraisal is needed to meet problems created by the critical world situation, the explosion of knowledge, cleavages in educational philosophy, and attendant criticism of the schools. Many voices are heard with varying definitions of a sound program of elementary and secondary education. Some call for a return of the so-called solid subjects. Some would dictate the same program for all pupils, regardless of individual differences. Some ignore what we know about the learning process. *It is time for the teaching profession itself to examine current changes in school programs and to recommend curriculum and organization of subject matter* [emphasis added].[4]

The mission of the project was "to make thoughtful and creative recommendations to serve as a guide to the profession and the public in their combined efforts to study and improve the quality of the instructional program in the schools."[5]

Two years later, President Hazel Blanchard devoted a substantial part of her report to the 1962 Denver meeting of the Representative Assembly to the report of the Special Project on Instruction.

Schools for the Sixties was an overview volume comprising the official report of the Project on Instruction. President Blanchard told the delegates it did not provide easy answers to complex problems but provided sound guidelines as a basis for determining what to teach and how to organize the schools. She told the delegates that the Michigan Education Association already had a statewide program under way based on the recommendations of the project, and the Roanoke, Virginia, public schools were using some of its findings in their program. She said the report was directed to school board members, other interested citizens who influence school decisions, and members of the teaching profession.

The following year, 1963, three supporting volumes were published, all directed to the teaching profession. The titles were *Deciding What to Teach, Education in a Changing Society,* and *Planning and Organizing for Teaching.*

Three auxiliary reports were published earlier. They were *The Scholars Look at the Schools, The Principals Look at the Schools,* and *Current Curriculum Studies in Academic Subjects.*

Following completion of the project, the Center for the Study of Instruction was established within the NEA, with Dr. Ole Sand as its director. The function of the center was to build upon the work of the project through continuing studies of educational issues, develop new ideas, initiate and assist in educational innovations, serve as a clearing house, and encourage the implementation of the project's findings.

Eleven consultant teams were organized to help selected schools, colleges, state school agencies, and state and local NEA affiliates to apply the findings of the project.

The other functions of the center continue to assist NEA members and affiliates to improve the quality of instruction in the schools.

The NEA and Teacher Education

The Representative Assembly, at its 1946 meeting in Buffalo, established the National Commission on Teacher Education and Professional Standards (TEPS). The delegates were concerned about the employment of large numbers of teachers who had not met professional standards. Only 60 percent of the nation's teachers held bachelor's or higher degrees. Others were holders of emergency credentials due to the loss of certificated teachers to the armed services and war industries during World War II. The Assembly charged the Commission with developing a continuing program of teacher recruitment, selection, preparation, certification, and the advancement of professional standards, including standards for institutions that prepare teachers.

The Commission encouraged affiliates to organize counterpart committees in each state to implement the programs developed at an annual national conference. The national conferences brought together teacher association leaders, professors and administrators of teacher education, state directors of teacher personnel, representatives of the various academic disciplines, students preparing to become teachers, school administrators, and school board members.

The Commission encouraged the organization of high school clubs and chapters of student NEA organizations on college and university campuses, published newsletters, reports of studies, and conference reports. A constant stream of recommendations for action was channeled to affiliates to help them secure the enactment of state legislation governing professional standards and practices.

The TEPS Commission program continued until a 1971 reorganization consolidated four units into one Division of Instruction and Professional Development headed by an assistant executive secretary. The new organization did not de-emphasize the TEPS program. It combined it with other NEA instructional activities for a more unified program. The substance of the TEPS program has continued with shifts in emphasis to meet new conditions.

The mission of the new unit, Executive Secretary Lambert told the 1971 Representative Assembly, was "to provide instructional services to state and local education associations, to monitor and evaluate all the new developments in education, to lend leadership and assistance in negotiating for instructional improvement, to force the upgrading of teacher education programs, and finally to provide the leadership the teaching profession so badly needs to get control of its own destiny. And what I am talking about is the control of licensing, the control of admission to the profession, the control of standards of practice and standards of elimination of malpractice. This new unit will give us what we need to move ahead in the control of things the profession should control."[6]

In the period from its creation in 1946 to the reorganization of the NEA's instruction program in 1971, the TEPS Commission and its network of state and local TEPS committees had a great impact. Certification standards were improved, substandard credentials were virtually eliminated, participation in the Association programs by student members was greatly increased, and a national accrediting agency for teacher education programs was established.

Accreditation

In 1954, largely through the efforts of the TEPS Commission, an independent national accrediting agency for teacher education was established—the National Council for Accreditation of Teacher Education (NCATE).

While NCATE grew out of the deliberations of the TEPS Commission and the director of the NEA's TEPS Commission took a leave of absence from his position to develop the preliminary documents, NCATE was created under the joint parentage of five national organizations. They were: the American Association of Colleges for Teacher Education (AACTE), the NEA, the National Association of State Directors of Teacher Education and Certification (NASDTEC), the Council of Chief State School Officers (CCSSO), and the National School Boards Association (NSBA).

The general purpose of NCATE was to improve teacher education in the United States. Its constitution outlined three ways it would seek to improve teacher education: (1) by developing standards, policies, and procedures for the accreditation of programs for the education of teachers; (2) by accrediting programs and publishing annually a list of those institutions whose programs have been accredited by the Council; and, (3) by encouraging its constituent organizations to perform well their respective roles in the improvement of teacher education.

The composition of the twenty-one-member governing council of NCATE originally included representation from the NEA, the teacher education institutions, the state school agencies, school boards, and representatives of the learned societies. Representation has been adjusted twice since the council was created—in 1965 and 1974.

The 1974 change was initiated when the NEA withdrew its support from the NCATE and threatened to withdraw from further participation. The reason for the NEA's action was that the Association was making major financial contributions to support the NCATE but the NEA members (teacher members particularly) were playing a minor role in the operation of the NCATE. This NEA action was a reflection of the growing aspiration of teachers to have a greater voice in the determination of policies affecting them.

After the recommendations of a series of work conferences were received and considered by the Council and a coordinating board, a new constitution was adopted. It provided for more equitable representation between the NEA and AACTE, transferred the authority for standards from the AACTE to the NCATE, and provided for the addition of new constituent members.

Equally important new policies and procedures were adopted providing a new balance for site-visiting teams, which gave greater representation to students, minority representation on each team, and limited higher education representation to no more than 50 percent.

Standards were also revised to include a new component on multicultural education.

By 1979, 545 institutions had been accredited by the NCATE. While this number represents only 40 percent of the 1,367 institutions preparing teachers, it includes those graduating 85 percent of the nation's teachers.

The services of the NCATE are voluntary. No institution is accredited unless it volunteers to go through the procedure. However, the time is approaching when NCATE accreditation will become virtually mandatory since those institutions not accredited will find it increasingly difficult to attract students as more and more school systems require candidates for teaching positions to be graduates of NCATE-accredited institutions.

CHAPTER NINE

From Stress to Unity

Previous chapters have dealt with social changes and their effects on the National Education Association. In this chapter a different aspect of change will be considered: the impact of social changes on Association leadership and the influence of leadership in the process of adapting to new conditions.

THE CARR ADMINISTRATION

Dr. William G. Carr was named executive secretary on the retirement of Dr. Willard E. Givens in August 1952. He had been a member of the NEA staff since 1929, first as an assistant director of the Research Division. He became director of the division two years later, and in 1936 he became secretary of the newly created Educational Policies Commission while retaining the directorship of the Research Division. He became associate executive secretary in 1941 and served in that capacity until his appointment to succeed Dr. Givens as the NEA's fifth executive secretary.

In 1945, Dr. Carr had served as consultant to the American delegation to the United Nations Conference on International Organization in San Francisco. At the conference, Dr. Carr and other NEA representatives gave leadership for a voice for education in the achievement of the peace. The result was the founding of the United Nations Educational, Scientific, and Cultural Organization (UNESCO).

At the time of his appointment, Dr. Carr said, he "felt incapable of supplying leadership to the staff as it was then organized—or more accurately, as it was disbursed. Sixty-seven units reporting directly to the Executive Secretary meant that, under the tyranny of the clock and of the calendar, most of the staff units would report to no one."[1]

So he proposed to the Board of Directors that a reorganization plan be authorized to enable the staff to serve the membership more efficiently. His plan, approved by the Board in 1955, provided for seven assistant executive secretaries, each to be responsible for administering a service area. The seven areas were field operations, education services, professional development and welfare, lay relations, business management, information services, and legislation. The executive secretary and his seven assistant executive secretaries met together weekly from eleven to twelve o'clock. This management group came to be known as the Cabinet. Cabinet meetings under Dr. Carr were not models of shared decisionmaking. We did not always reach a consensus on agenda questions prepared by Dr. Carr. The purpose of the meeting was to advise the executive secretary. Sometimes the discussion would consist of going around the table in rapid succession, each participant giving his response to a question, after which Dr. Carr would thank the group for their assistance and say their views would be considered in formulating his decision.

Dr. Carr was a strong administrator. He made decisions promptly and with seeming ease. He was formal even with those with whom he worked intimately, though his formality was tempered by a sly sense of humor.

Fred Hipp, executive secretary of the New Jersey state affiliate, who had worked intimately with Dr. Carr for many years, told me that for several years he addressed his letters to Dr. Carr "Dear Bill." The reply always came back "Dear Dr. Hipp." Finally, Dr. Hipp said, he gave up and went back to the formal "Dear Dr. Carr."

Dr. Richard Carpenter, NEA business manager, referred to Dr. Carr as "Father Carr." The relationship between the executive secretary and his assistant secretaries was somewhat similar to the father-son relationship in a patriarchal family.

In his verbal communications, Dr. Carr was fluent but economical with words. Frequently he would return a memo requesting a decision with his handwritten response in the margin. He was conscientious in responding to such requests. During pressure periods when other duties prevented him from answering the dozens of memos and letters on his desk, he would take them home and not return to the office until all had been answered.

He had strong feelings about some administration prerogatives he considered basic. For example, on one occasion a budget director position was proposed. His response: "In an organization as defused as NEA, one of the few ways [the executive secretary] can influence program is to have a clear voice as to the budget to be recommended. If this is muted, it would deprive the Executive Secretary of an instrument he needs to discharge the duties assigned to him by the bylaws."[2]

Dr. Carr had a lightning-quick mind and could be impatient with those less well endowed. Arthur Corey, in a tribute to Dr. Carr on his retirement, referred to him as a scholar and an intellectual who gave "academic respectability to teacher association leadership."[3]

It would be a mistake to describe the Carr administration without including the valuable contributions of Lyle Ashby, deputy executive secretary from 1958 to 1970. The two men—different in temperament, style, and background—complemented each other in a way that multiplied the value of both. Where Dr. Carr was quick to reach a decision, Dr. Ashby was sensitive and contemplative. To some, Dr. Carr was cool and aloof. Dr. Ashby was approachable, warm, and understanding. It would be difficult to find a better combination of talent for the period in which the two men served.

While Dr. Carr's staff reorganizations in the 1950s improved the administrability of the NEA somewhat, many problems remained. The task of changing the course of an organization is not a simple one under the best of conditions. Changing the NEA was complicated by two characteristics: its complex governance structure and its ambiguous nature.

The governance responsibilities of the NEA in 1957 were divided among four bodies: a Representative Assembly of thousands of delegates; a seventy-eight-member Board of Directors; an eleven-member Executive Committee; and a five-member Board of Trustees.

In addition, the Association had thirty departments, most of which had separate staffs, budgets, and elected officers. All but two had separate membership dues—the Department of Classroom Teachers and the Association for Higher Education. The requirements for departments, while minimal, had not been enforced. It was not uncommon for a department to adopt and announce education policies in conflict with those of the NEA.

The NEA was both the national voice of fifty state and local affiliates and the parent organization of a loosely organized family of national organizations in Washington. Sometimes the lobbying activities of the departments with the administration, Board, and Executive Committee influenced decisions outside of the formal decisionmaking machinery, and this kept the Association from changing as rapidly as it should have done.

As the Association moved into collective bargaining in the early 1960s, teachers began urging enforcement of the NEA membership requirement for departments. Administrator groups complained about the large sums of money budgeted for legal services and collective-bargaining elections. Such activities, they said, were pulling the Association apart. The money could be used for "more important purposes" without disturbing the unity of the education profession.

Between 1960 and 1967, questions of NEA department relations were raised with increasing frequency. They were both a concern and an irritant. But it remained for the Constitutional Convention in 1972 to establish standards for departments and other nongovernance national affiliates. The standards provided for at least 75 percent of the membership of the affiliates to also be members of the NEA.

By 1975–76 only four departments and affiliates remained.

Both Dr. Carr and Dr. Ashby felt keenly that the departments and the national affiliated organizations should remain a part of the NEA. They felt commitments had been made to the organizations that the NEA had a moral obligation to honor.

Having had the responsibility, as deputy executive secretary, for coordinating the groups, I reached the conclusion in 1972 that cooperation would probably be facilitated if the administrators' organizations were to withdraw. However, I felt then, and still feel, that some mechanism should exist to join the efforts of all education groups in a united front for the promotion of education in all areas of mutual concern. Such an arrangement should include organizations such as the National Congress of Parents and Teachers and the National School Board Association as well as the present and former NEA affiliated groups and public groups with a deep commitment to education but with no direct responsibility for schools.

Civil Rights

Dr. Carr has related that just before becoming executive secretary in 1952 he was asked to make a prediction of future events affecting education.

He predicted that the courts would rule on the question of school desegregation within five years. Then came the 1954 decision of the Supreme Court, followed by other events, including the bus boycott and the Civil

Rights Act, which greatly changed the nation. "In one aspect or another," Dr. Carr said, "the NEA position on civil rights profoundly concerned me almost every day during the remainder of my term of office. During these troubled fourteen years I clung to two major principles; first, that in the conduct of its own affairs the NEA itself would avoid and repudiate every form of racial discrimination; second, that the unity of the teaching profession should be preserved."[4]

Dr. Carr's views on the NEA's role in the integration of schools were presented to the Executive Committee in 1960. The occasion was the consideration of a resolution on the subject by the Representative Assembly. Dr. Carr said that "the integration controversy is a legal, political, and judicial question on which teachers are entitled to their personal opinions, just as other citizens—no more and no less. It is not up to the NEA to settle these issues. The National Education Association is opposed to the closing of schools and the improper treatment of teachers."[5] This position, with which Dr. Carr felt comfortable, caused some discomfort to staff members working in the field in representation elections, mergers, and personnel cases.

I remember one incident vividly. It occurred in the mid-1960s while I was assistant executive secretary for Field and Urban Services. The national field staff of approximately sixty members assembled in the Horace Mann Room in the NEA headquarters to begin the second day of our meetings. I was presiding. While I was making some preliminary announcements before introducing the morning program, non-field staff members began entering the room and standing near the walls. The usual practice at field staff meetings was to arrange tables in a rectangle and seat staff members on the outside of the tables so that all could face each other. An audience at such meetings was a new experience. I was curious to know what was happening.

As soon as the meeting was opened for discussion, a field staff member from California asked to present a resolution that several staff members had framed after the adjournment of the previous evening's meeting. This was a departure from the traditional informal conduct of such meetings. I inquired about the subject of the proposed resolution. He responded, "NEA's position on civil rights." I then asked him to present the proposal and I would let the staff decide what they wanted to do with it. He began to read the resolution, which asked that the NEA be a more aggressive advocate in the civil rights area, and was citing some problems encountered in the field in which the present policy put staff members at a disadvantage. At that moment, Dr. Carr strode into the room and asked whether the field staff thought it was a policymaking body.

I informed Dr. Carr that a group of staff members had proposed a resolution and were presenting it to the full field staff. He asked to whom the resolution would be directed. I said it would be submitted to him, if adopted, to convey to him the judgment of the field staff. He left the room, and the field staff passed the resolution, which was communicated to Dr. Carr the following day. But it had no immediate impact on NEA policy.

This incident revealed Dr. Carr's concern for the civil rights problem and his apparent complete faith in the soundness of his guiding principles. It also revealed the efficiency of the NEA "grapevine" during that difficult period.

The year 1964 was a landmark year for the NEA. It was the year the Representative Assembly passed Resolution 12 requiring the NEA's dual state affiliates to form a single merged organization, providing a time table, and placing the responsibility for compliance with the Executive Committee. The Civil Rights Act was enacted by Congress. The joint committee of the NEA and the ATA took the initial steps that led to a merger two years later. Three state affiliates in Florida, North Carolina, and Texas removed racial membership restrictions, and in Prince Edward County, Virginia, where schools had been closed since 1959, the Prince Edward Free School Association operated schools for black children and some white children with the NEA's active support.

In Dr. Carr's annual report to the Representative Assembly, he advised the delegates "against any attempt by the NEA to coerce or threaten its affiliates. Such an attempt would retard or halt voluntary processes such as I have just reported to you. I can assure you now—as I assured the 1963 Delegate Assembly—that without added pressure or new resolutions your officers will continue to work diligently in this area."[6] The delegates responded by passing Resolution 12. At that time, eleven state affiliates remained unmerged.

Resolution 12 was the basic document, modified as the process of merger progressed, that guided NEA efforts to complete the merger of all but seven state affiliates and spurred the unification of the NEA and ATA by the time Dr. Carr retired in July 1967.

Relationships

During the Carr administration it was the policy of the Association that the salary of the elected president be continued by his/her school employer. The NEA then reimbursed the employer for the full amount of the actual school salary plus regular school benefits.

The President, in that period, spent almost full time in the field speaking at state conventions and institutes and attending meetings of the NEA and related organizations, except for short periods in Washington to preside at meetings of the Board of Directors and Executive Committee or to testify before congressional committees.

The role of president began to change in the middle and late 1960s.

From 1964 to 1979, the presidents were either former officers of urban associations or candidates acceptable to the coalition of urban, northern, and western liberals and blacks. Most were young and eager to play a stronger leadership role than their predecessors. They wanted to keep in close touch with the ongoing programs of the Association. They pushed for more frequent meetings of the Board and Executive Committee.

In 1957, the Board of Directors met three times. The three meetings covered seven days. The Executive Committee also met three times, for a total of eleven days. A decade later, in 1967, the Board of Directors met three times on eleven days and the Executive Committee met fourteen times on twenty-two days.

This more aggressive posture of the presidents was in part a reflection of the increased demands for Association services and the intensity of concern of members. It was also, in part, a conviction of the younger Classroom Teacher presidents that the Association must be more responsive to membership needs.

More and more, the presidents began to make decisions and take action on matters they considered urgent without waiting for consultation and actions by the executive secretary and the governing bodies.

Such actions caused tensions between the president and executive secretary, and beginning in 1964, pressure began to build for a Constitutional Convention to revise the organization structure to make the decisionmaking machinery more efficient and more responsive to members' needs. The first mention of the need for a Constitutional Convention, to my knowledge, was made at the meeting of the National Council of Urban Education Associations held in Tucson in 1964.

A group of urban leaders invited Braulio Alonso, a member of the Executive Committee, and me to meet with them after an evening session. They were concerned that the complex structure of the Association was preventing it from adapting to changing conditions.

Braulio Alonso was to be a candidate for the office of president-elect of the Association in 1966, and the urban leaders sought to impress upon him the urgent need for the NEA to streamline the structure to reduce the influence of conservative school administrators and to adopt a more aggressive posture. Alonso, in an address to the urban leaders, made no specific commitment for a Constitutional Convention, but demonstrated an understanding of urban problems, and a respect for their proposals, and acknowledged the need for structural changes.

The 1964 Representative Assembly adopted an item of New Business directing the Board of Directors, the Executive Committee, and the executive secretary to take the necessary steps to initiate a complete study of the structure of the Association.[7]

The Board of Trustees

The Board of Trustees had been the center of controversy on two previous occasions in NEA history and was to become an issue again in the mid-1960s. The charter gave the Trustees responsibility for the safekeeping and investment of the Permanent Fund, the election of the executive secretary and the determination of his salary.

The Board of Trustees had elected Dr. Carr to a four-year term expiring on July 31, 1964. On April 17, 1964, the Board of Trustees adopted a motion to reelect Dr. Carr for a four-year term effective August 1, 1964.

The Association had a policy for retirement of staff at age sixty-five. The four-year term would run to 1968, and Dr. Carr would be sixty-five in 1966. The motion to reappoint received four favorable votes and one negative vote. Trustee Lester Bufford explained his negative vote by saying he did not support the four-year term because, in his judgment, it was inconsistent with current NEA policy.[8]

The leaders of the politically active urban education associations, black associations, and northern and western liberals had been looking at the calendar and anticipating the naming of a successor to Dr. Carr in 1966. When word of the Trustees' action leaked out, reaction varied from disappointment to anger. Dr. Carr had had a long, distinguished, and successful career. Their respect for his ability and long service to the Association restrained them from making any move for change prior to the normal retirement date. But, they said, the action of the Trustees appeared to be another case of protecting the Association from the will of the members.

At the 1966 meeting of the Representative Assembly, a motion was adopted by a vote of 1,548 to 1,403, instructing the Board of Trustees to name a five-member screening committee to seek out and interview candidates for the position of executive secretary and to recommend three to the body responsible for appointing the NEA executive secretary. The committee chairman and one member were to be educators who belonged to the NEA but held no position of responsibility in it, and three members were to be selected from the NEA Executive Committee.

Following the 1966 Representative Assembly, Dr. Carr requested that the Board of Trustees proceed to set the machinery in motion to select a successor and relieve him of the position at the earliest time possible. The Representative Assembly accepted a resolution (No. 66-26) directing that a proposal be submitted to Congress to amend the NEA charter to authorize the appointment of the executive secretary by the Executive Committee rather than by the Trustees. The Committee on Bylaws and Rules was also asked to give notice to the 1966 convention of a proposed change in the bylaws to occur at the 1967 meeting to bring them into conformity with the charter.

The bylaws were amended the following year (1967) to remove the appointment of the executive secretary from the Trustees and to make it the responsibility of the Executive Committee.

The appointment of Dr. Sam M. Lambert to succeed Dr. Carr was announced to the NEA staff at a special meeting in the NEA building on March 2, 1967; he was to take office the following August.

THE LAMBERT YEARS: 1967–1972

Dr. Lambert's succession in August 1967 occurred in the same month NEA honored the enrollment of its one-millionth member. Dr. Lambert had joined the staff of the NEA Research Division at age thirty-seven in 1950. Previously, he had been a teacher of mathematics in West Virginia, a staff member of the West Virginia state school agency, and director of research for the NEA's West Virginia state affiliate—the West Virginia Education Association.

He was named to head the NEA Research Division in 1956. In that position, he gave leadership for the modernization of the Association's data processing system and perfected a program for sampling public and membership opinions on education issues. At the time of his appointment to the chief administrative position, he was assistant executive secretary for Information Services, an assignment he had held for two years.

Dr. Lambert's appointment was well received by the urban group, the liberals, classroom teachers, the educators for human rights, and also the conservatives, state association leaders, administrators, and national affiliates. In his work in the Research Division and Information Services, he was a supplier of needed services unidentified with the divisive issues in the organization. He had written an article published in the *NEA Journal*, in 1963, titled "Angry Young Men in Teaching." It was a graphic description of the plight of young men teachers in the early 1960s, told in the actual words of teachers' responses to an NEA survey. He concluded the article with this paragraph:

> The typical man teaching in today's schools is both angry and impatient. He thinks he is entitled to a better break in this era of two-car families and electric can openers, and he is. He is fed up with working nights, weekends, and holidays trying to make ends meet on a teacher's salary. He is tired of sacrificing his family for his profession. While many people are sympathetic, the exodus of talented men from teaching goes on . . . and on . . . and on.[9]

The views expressed in the article, which received wide circulation, and the sympathetic response of the Research Division to the needs of urban leaders and minorities, identified Dr. Lambert with the forces for change in the Association.

In his first address to the Representative Assembly, shortly before assuming his new duties, Dr. Lambert left no doubt in the minds of the delegates as to his position on the issues of collective bargaining for teachers and active participation to solve the problems of urbanization and minorities.

"The teaching profession," he declared, "is going to have a far greater impact on education than ever before." He called upon the Association to be a more imaginative force in solving the problems of big cities, and characterized the growing militancy of teachers as evidence of an intense desire for something better for both students and teachers.

He proposed to simplify the NEA structure, strengthen and revitalize local associations, increase dues, intensify Association efforts to achieve a greater share of funding for schools from the federal government, and make membership in the Association both professionally necessary and economically desirable for all educators.

President-elect Braulio Alonso followed with a call for the Association to become an active participant in the political arena. "As long as we depend upon government for funds, we must be active in politics," he said.

Vice-President Hubert H. Humphrey supported the president-elect. "Our teachers were led to believe," he said, "that they should be aloof from political life. The elected officials looked upon the teacher . . . either with disdain or with the spirit of charity, or would try to get him out of their hair by offering him a little something. That day is over. It's been over for a lot longer than you know."

The Lambert term thus began with a solid identity with the forces of change—change to improve the efficiency and power of the Association, but also a commitment to use that power to be a positive influence to give direction to the changes in society.

The Lambert years were both a period of action on Association programs and a period of introspection and renewal. The two activities were not always compatible, but both were necessary. The old structure was not capable of responding promptly to the new problems of teachers and schools.

When the Lambert administration took over, several problems had been before the Association on which both members and staff were eager and impatient for solutions.

The Association's organization structure was outmoded and inefficient. Discussions by two committees on reorganization had been going on for almost three years. A preliminary report had been given to the Executive Committee, Board of Directors, and Representative Assembly. An organizational development committee had been named. But few visible changes had taken place.

The NEA staff had been pressing unsuccessfully for an orderly procedure for negotiating with the Association management similar to procedures advocated by the Association for teachers.

The proponents of change looked forward to a more agressive Association posture on civil rights.

The officers and Executive Committee were calling for more frequent meetings and a more active and responsible leadership role.

A more vigorous legislative program was advocated, backed by an aggressive entry into politics.

An expansion of the services of the Dushane Fund for Teacher Rights was being advocated to protect minority members whose continued employment was threatened as desegregation took place; to protect all members from the growing number of dismissals for exercising their constitutional rights; and to protect local officers threatened with dismissal for activities related to their duties as Association leaders.

Dr. Irvamae Applegate concluded her term of office at the close of the 1967 Representative Assembly. During her year as president, she had given special attention to the problems involved in merging the separate affiliates in the South. She had one more year to serve on the Executive Committee as immediate past president. To permit her to pursue her interest in the mergers, incoming president Braulio Alonso appointed her to the Compliance Committee. Alonso, a Florida school principal, had been a supporter of the urban movement and an enthusiastic supporter of the new thrust for collective bargaining for teachers, a more active role in political action, school desegregation, and merger of the dual affiliates. He was also an advocate for extending to NEA staff members the opportunity to negotiate with the Association on terms and conditions of work under procedures similar to those advocated by the Association for teachers.

Collective Bargaining for Staff

Proposals had been made by the NEA staff organization (NEASO) to the Executive Committee during the Carr administration.

NEASO had met with the Executive Committee early in 1966 and proposed a bargaining procedure. The Executive Committee agreed to study the proposal and requested that a survey be made of the departments housed in the NEA building to determine their attitude toward it.

It had been the practice of the Association to name an advisory personnel committee of ten—five members of NEASO, three NEA representatives named by the NEA executive secretary, and two representatives of NEA departments named by the executive secretaries of the thirty departments as a group.

Dr. Carr felt that collective bargaining was neither appropriate for the NEA nor feasible because of the departmental structure of the Association. Also, I believe he interpreted the move as an expression of lack of confidence in his administration. I think he found this very difficult to accept, believing that the staff had been treated fairly, even generously, during his administration.

I remember getting a telephone call from Dr. Carr after the NEASO proposal was received. I was then assistant executive secretary for Field Services. He asked that I call a meeting of members of the field staff to give him an opportunity to talk with them about the NEASO proposal. He said he was making the same request of the other assistant executive secretaries. I advised him against going ahead with the meeting. Field staff members were working daily with affiliates, helping them to win the right to bargain with their school boards. I told him that in my judgment, they would not respond kindly to an appeal to repudiate the efforts of officers of their staff organization who were asking for the same rights the NEA was promoting for teachers. He was not dissuaded, so the meeting was called. After about a one-hour discussion, it adjourned and he departed. Within minutes, the phone rang. It was Dr. Carr. He said, "You were right. I shouldn't have done it."

The survey requested by the Executive Committee was initiated. But before the results were reported, the Representative Assembly acted to adopt a resolution recommending that the right to negotiate advocated by the Association for teachers be extended to staff members of the NEA and its affiliates.

Following the mandate of the Representative Assembly, President Alonso recommended, and the Executive Committee approved, the appointment of a committee composed of equal representation from the Executive Committee, the administration, and NEASO to develop a set of principles as a framework for a bargaining procedure.

In early 1967, a drafting committee was named to put together an agreement that could be submitted to NEASO and the Executive Committee. On the committee were E. H. Mellon, Director from Illinois; George D. Fischer, Executive Committee; Robert Eaves, Department of Elementary School Principals. Sam M. Lambert and I, represented the administration. The procedure was approved on May 20, 1967. Sam Lambert became executive secretary on August 1. Since he had participated in drafting the procedure, NEASO members knew he favored a formal negotiating procedure for determining policies on working conditions. Shortly after Dr. Lambert's appointment, NEASO hosted a party in his honor on a chartered cruise on the Potomac. The Lambert administration had begun with a feeling of unity among staff, officers, and administration. NEASO had achieved an organizational objective and assurance from the new administration that the procedure would be administered by an executive officer who was committed to the process.

Staff Officer Relationships

The first black president of the NEA was elected and took office as president-elect at the same time as the Lambert administration. Elizabeth Duncan Koontz would become president the following year at the close of the 1968 meeting of the Representative Assembly.

Mrs. Koontz, a teacher of mentally retarded children in Salisbury, North Carolina, was a member of a distinguished family of educators. She had been president of the local, district, state, and national Departments of Classroom Teachers, as well as the recipient of numerous honors for her contributions to civic activities.

Her election to the presidency of NEA boosted the morale of minority members and served as concrete evidence of the Association's sincerity in its commitment to the principle of racial equality.

The Alonso year, while one of action on problems related to collective bargaining, desegregation, and merger of dual affiliates, had been a year of unified effort. The first half of Mrs. Koontz's term continued the close working relationship. However, as stated earlier, there was a growing feeling on the part of presidents going back to the early 1960s that they should play a stronger leadership role in the Association.

Early in January 1969, Mrs. Koontz was offered an appointment by President Nixon, to head the Women's Bureau of the U.S. Department of Labor. In a meeting by telephone conference, the Executive Committee was told of the offer. Their reaction was a combination of reluctance to have her leave the NEA presidency, pride, and support for her decision if she decided to accept the federal post.

She did accept the position. Her resignation was accepted at the January meeting of the Executive Committee, and President-elect George D. Fischer succeeded to the position of president six months early.

Fischer, an Iowa teacher, had been president of the Des Moines NEA affiliate, a member of the Board of Directors of the Iowa State Education Association, and an active participant in the National Council of Urban Education Associations.

In January, Fischer was interviewed in his home city of Des Moines about his plans for the NEA. The interview was punctuated with expletives and included statements such as the following which appeared to be calculated to offend the public and segments of the NEA membership: "I don't give a damn about administrators and superintendents. If they really were leaders in education, we wouldn't need the NEA. All I care about is teachers."

Asked if he had made any deals in order to become head of the NEA, he said: "I certainly did—fourteen deals. I had fourteen appointments to make, so I made fourteen deals."

Asked if he thought the public would support his views, he replied, "I don't care if they do or not. The public doesn't always support the right things, you know."[10]

The interview, which appeared first in the *Omaha World Herald* on January 23, was reprinted in newspapers across the nation. Thousands of copies were distributed on the boardwalk in Atlantic City the next month at the annual meeting of the American Association of School Administrators, then a department of the NEA.

The Board of Directors held its February meeting in Atlanta, with George Fischer presiding. Many Board members were incensed about the interview. When the matter was raised at the meeting, Fischer explained "that in many ways the articles represented his thinking, but he had understood that they would be informal personality pieces and that the reporter failed to protect him and took advantage of the situation."[11]

Following his explanation, a vote of confidence motion was made, seconded, then tabled. While the matter dominated the out-of-meeting discussions, the subject remained on the table. No procedures existed in the NEA bylaws for censure or impeachment. No further action was taken. However, this matter did cause tension in the Association for weeks afterward.[12]

Fischer became the advocate for a stronger role for the president. He advocated two- or three-year terms, a higher salary, a more prestigious office, a reorganization of the staff of the president's office, less travel, and greater direct involvement in the ongoing programs of the Association.

Fischer felt strongly that the NEA's presence as a national power must be felt in Washington if the Association's legislative proposals were to receive the attention they deserved. He had strong support for this objective by a substantial segment of the membership.

George Fischer told me on one occasion that his method of operation was to meet head-on a problem that needed to be solved and then be prepared to "take the flack." This approach did serve to dramatize some of the problems of the NEA during his term of office. It remained for the Bain, Morrison, and Wise terms to pick up the pieces.

Following Fischer as president was Helen Bain. She had been president of the Nashville–Davidson County, Tennessee, affiliate and came to prominence in the NEA as an early leader in the urban movement. Her views of the role of the NEA president were in general agreement with those of Fischer. She was one of the early presidents of the National Council of Urban Education Associations.

President Don Morrison expressed his opinion on the relationship of the president and executive secretary to the 1972 Representative Assembly in Atlantic City:

> We have to make a decision—either you structure the organization so that the staff is running it, or you want your wishes and your aspirations reflected through the elected leadership. In my opinion, you cannot leave the Presidents in one or two years and then change them and throw them out each time. People in government and other agencies have very little confidence in dealing with a President who is gone in a few months. . . . Once the NEA has chosen the new President-elect, the current President becomes a lame duck. . . . Also, the media deals with organizations . . . through personalities . . . when personalities change, they are not able to get acquainted with them, to know them, and to really build the NEA as a powerful image in this country.[13]

Restructuring the Association

There had been earnest discussion of the need to restructure the NEA since the Seattle meeting in 1964 when the Representative Assembly directed that a study be made. There was general agreement on the need for restructuring. There were widely divergent views on the best way to achieve it.

Urban leaders advocated a Constitutional Convention. Conservatives pointed to numerous bylaw changes in recent years, insisting that the present structure permits change without the risks and expense of a convention if the Representative Assembly could agree on the changes it wanted to make.

Between 1964 and 1971, four committees were involved in the effort.

An ad hoc staff committee was created to recommend a procedure. It proposed a self-study plan with the assistance of consultants with expertise in managing organizational change.

This led to the establishment of the NEA Development Project (NEADP) in the spring of 1965. One of its first recommendations was for the creation of a planning office within the NEA to consider what school conditions were likely to be five, ten, or more years in the future and what programs would likely be required. This planning unit became the Committee on Planning and Organizational Development (CPOD), appointed in 1967.

The fourth committee was appointed as a result of an action of the 1969 Representative Assembly meeting in Philadelphia.

A plan was presented to the Representative Assembly by a California delegate, which was debated at two sessions, the debate covering twenty-nine pages in the *Proceedings*.[14]

Because delegates felt the need for more information concerning the cost of a Constitutional Convention and the feasibility of such a convention's achieving its intended purpose, they did not approve the proposal. However, they did approve the concept of a Constitutional Convention and directed the Board of Directors to have a study made of the feasibility of holding such a convention. A report including projected cost, objectives, and representation was requested, to be furnished to delegates thirty days before the 1970 meeting in San Francisco.

A committee of seventeen members headed by Catharine Barrett, New York, presented a plan to the 1970 Representative Assembly. The report held that a Constitutional Convention involving 500 delegates was feasible and could be held for approximately $280,000.

The plan was reproduced in the *NEA Reporter* and mailed to the delegates a month in advance of the San Francisco meeting. Hearings were also held in San Francisco before the plan was presented to the Assembly for action.

The committee proposal was amended and passed by the delegates after a long and intense debate. The decision to restructure the NEA by a representative Constitutional Convention had been made. The convention was scheduled to meet for two weeks in Fort Collins, Colorado, on the campus of Colorado State University on July 17, 1971.

The Constitutional Convention became the central point at which the several political forces within the organization converged. The delegates were carefully balanced to provide representation for all segments of the membership. Major points of view were represented by the minority caucuses; classroom teachers; administrators; local, state and national leaders; urban and rural leaders; and representatives of national departments and affiliates.

The chief issues with which the delegates contended were membership; roles of the president and other executive officers; representation of rural, urban, state, and local affiliates; and minority representation.

Membership

Of the four issues, membership was the single most difficult to resolve. In fact, it had the convention deadlocked for more than a week. The question to be resolved was: Shall the membership be composed of classroom teachers only, or should it be all-inclusive as it had been in the past (composed of classroom teachers and administrators)?

A compromise broke up the logjam. It provided for determination of the composition of membership by vote of the individual affiliates.

Within the NEA, provision was made for the composition of the Board of Directors and the Representative Assembly, classroom teachers and administrators to be included on the basis of proportional representation.

Assurance was given in convention documents that teachers would be dominant on all elected and appointed bodies.

The compromise enabled the convention to achieve its purpose without expelling the school administrators. But it did assure teachers that administrators would occupy a minority position in the Association in the future.

Role of Executive Officers

The convention provided for three salaried full-time executive officers: a president, vice-president, and secretary-treasurer.

The role of the president was sharpened to make that officer the chief policy spokesman for the Association. The term of the president was extended from one to two years, with eligibility for reelection to one additional two-year term. The rationale for the longer term was the delegates' belief that a one-year term did not give the president enough time to develop a program, provide for its support in the budget, and be held accountable before facing election again.

The title of executive secretary was changed to executive director, and that position and that of deputy director were not continued as executive officers of the Association.

The duties of the executive director, as redefined by the convention, included the employment and supervision of the staff; serving as consultant and adviser to the officers and governing bodies, being spokesman on matters of established policy (at the discretion of the president), administering the budgets authorized by the governing bodies, and, other duties usually associated with the position of administrator of the staff.

The responsibilities of supervising and coordinating the administrative, financial, and professional activities of the Association, heretofore the responsibility of the executive director, were now to be shared with the executive officers.

Representation

The original plan recommended by the Constitutional Convention would have provided for representation according to membership on a straight numerical basis. That plan provided for ratification by an affirmative vote of a majority of state affiliates. The majority had to include at least 50 percent of the NEA membership on May 31, 1972.

Before submitting the proposal for ratification, Catharine Barrett, in an action exhibiting great insight, appointed a committee to consider possible amendments, in the event the original plan failed to be ratified. The Committee of Twelve included six urban leaders who were strong supporters of the plan and six conservatives who opposed the original plan.

The ratification vote did fail, receiving only 163,592 affirmative and 230,446 negative votes, and only seventeen states showed a majority of positive votes. Positive votes from twenty-seven states were required for ratification.

The 1973 Representative Assembly voted to accept a compromise proposal of the Committee of Twelve, and the Assembly amended the plan to implement its recommendations. This effected the election of the Board of Directors by a procedure similar to that used in the past, restoring the Executive Committee; the election of the Executive Committee by the Representative Assembly; a change in the basis of representation of the states in the Assembly; and the limitation of the service of executive officers to two two-year terms.

Other changes accomplished by the Constitutional Convention and the 1973 Representative Assembly included:

Adoption of a procedure for the impeachment of an officer

Creation of a judiciary body or review board

Redefinition of membership categories to include seven classes of members; active, staff, paraprofessional, educational secretary, student, retired, and associate

Setting of standards for the representation of ethnic minorities

Redefinition of standards for affiliating national organizations and elimination of all departments

Provision for recall of an NEA state director and a procedure for recalling an incumbent director

Provision for the election of members of the Board of Directors by secret ballot and open nominations

Strengthening of standards for the affiliation of local and state affiliates

Provision for the appointment of the executive director by the Executive Committee and deletion of references to the Board of Trustees from the governing documents

Discontinuation of the acceptance of life membership in the Association

Requirement that all affiliates, local and state, require members to belong to the local, state, and national associations, by September 1972.

Minority Guarantees

Minority groups have formed caucuses to formulate positions on candidates or other matters before the Representative Assembly, or to develop their own proposals for the consideration of the Assembly, Board of Directors, and Executive Comittee.

Under the governing documents approved by the 1973 Assembly, minimum guarantees of representation for ethnic minorities were approved. Minority representation on the Board of Directors, Executive Committee, and Association committees was set at 20 percent. Representation in the Assembly was based on the proportion of the identified ethnic minority populations within each state. Each state affiliate was given the responsibility, in cooperation with its local affiliates, to elect minority delegates at least equal to the proportion of ethnic minority population of the state.

The delegates to the 1973 Assembly voted 5,613 to 2,749 to approve the new constitution and bylaws, with amendments. A plan for transition to the new governing documents was adopted to bring them into full effect by September 1, 1975.

Except for the press, radio, and TV staff, who maintained the convention press office, only three NEA staff members were present at the Constitutional Convention. All three were deeply involved in the preparation for and organization of the convention—John Cox, special assistant to the president; Irma Kramer, special assistant to the executive director in charge of governance relations; and Jack Kleinman, staff contact for the Committee on Planning and Organizational Development.

Except for invited presentations by President Don Morrison, Executive Secretary Sam Lambert, General Counsel Bob Chanin, Irma Kramer, and Jack Kleinmann, the delegates developed the constitution from data collected by NEA study committees and their own resources. Having participated directly in the creation of the new NEA, thousands of members now shared a proprietary interest and pride in the organization. If they continue to maintain that interest and recognize that renewal is a constant process, it can be an effective assurance of organizational strength and vigor. The selection of the Constitutional Convention as a means of renewal of the NEA was a rare expression of faith and confidence by the officers of the organization in the ability and integrity of the members.

No such fundamental change in an organization could take place without creating anxiety and feelings of insecurity among those staff members whose livelihood depended on continued employment by the Association. Those feelings of insecurity were enhanced for those whose responsibilities frequently placed them in the cross-fire of the many divisive issues considered over long months of debate while responding to the insistent demands of the ongoing service programs in a critical period in the life of the Association.

Staff Strike

The NEA's employees' organization called a strike in the spring of 1971 when agreement could not be reached within the limits set by the Executive Committee. The strike was called at a time when the Association was preparing for the Representative Assembly to be held in July in Detroit. Rumors reached the management that staff members planned to enlist the support of the Detroit unions and, with their support, could threaten to prevent the opening of the annual meeting.

The strike lasted nine days before a settlement was reached—a settlement that was not a clear victory for either party. In those nine days, 325 employees continued to report for work, and 450 were either on the picket line or remained at home. Living through a strike is always difficult. For the NEA, it was especially hard, even traumatic, for some of the management personnel. They had been leaders in winning the right to bargain for teachers, had walked the picket lines and encouraged members to take the risks involved in aggressive action to achieve better school conditions.

But striking against an employee organization was different. That organization had demonstrated publicly its sensitivity to the needs of employees. Why didn't the employees trust them? Why did they fail to recognize that there were reasonable limits beyond which we could not go? These were some of the questions that troubled management personnel who believed they were employee-oriented managers.

The NEA's General Counsel Robert Chanin played a central role in bringing about a resolution of the issues involved in the strike. Neither management nor staff had experienced a strike before. Both had to find their roles. Chanin's knowledge and experience with labor law and labor relations was a key factor in reaching a settlement.

In his message to the Representative Assembly, Sam Lambert acknowledged both the right of employees to strike and management's responsibility to protect the financial health of the Association. He also reported the settlement was fair and equitable; the employees were back at work and getting along surprisingly well.[15]

Merger of AFT and NEA

The National Education Association and the American Federation of Teachers together enrolled only a small fraction of potential members at the close of World War I. In 1918, NEA had an enrollment of 10,000 to AFT's 1,500 members.

As the two organizations began to grow in the postwar period, they took separate paths. The NEA based its organization on strong state affiliates. The rationale for this approach was twofold: (1) the constitutions of the states placed the legal responsibility for the public schools on the state government, and (2) the state legislatures adopted the state budgets and determined what sources should provide the tax support for the public schools. Since decisions on these important functions were to be made at the state level, a strong advocate at the state capitols was necessary to the schools' prosperity.

In contrast, the AFT built its structure on the local community level. The rationale for that approach was that a strong voice was needed where the members lived and worked and where decisions were made by local school boards. If the involvement of higher levels of government were necessary, sufficient pressure applied to the local decisionmakers would cause them to seek relief from the higher levels of government.

As a result of the dominance of the state legislatures in the four or five decades after World War I, NEA membership grew rapidly from 10,000 in 1918 to 714,000 in 1960. In that same period, AFT membership rose from 1,500 to 59,000 in 1960.

However, with the movement to consolidate schools and school districts into larger and larger units, more and more of the problems that affected school personnel required solution in the local school system.

This development caused the NEA's activities to shift to the local level. Concurrently, the growing need for funds beyond the ability of the local community caused the AFT to be more and more concerned with what went on in the state legislatures.

It is not surprising that beginning in 1968, proposals began to surface for the merger of the two national organizations. The first formal proposal came in a letter from Charles Cogen, the 1968 president of the AFT, to the president of the NEA Department of Classroom Teachers.

At that time, the two greatest obstacles to merger appeared to be membership eligibility and the AFL-CIO affiliation of the AFT.

NEA membership included all professional school personnel, and AFT membership was almost exclusively classroom teachers.

The NEA had a long tradition of independence and freedom to cooperate with all groups having an interest in the welfare of schools. Affiliation with the AFL-CIO had two serious handicaps: (1) it could alienate other groups that had given strong support to NEA programs in the past, and (2) education legislative proposals, not always compatible with AFL-CIO priorities, would have to take their place among the prioritized objectives of organized labor. Moreover, such affiliation would also carry with it obligations related to noneducation issues that many educators were unwilling to assume. And since public schools were attended by all children, teachers felt an obligation to remain independent of any one segment of society.

Accordingly, President Koontz responded to the Cogen letter rejecting the proposal and inviting the AFT to terminate its AFL-CIO connection and join the NEA and its state and local affiliates. Periodically thereafter until the mid-1970s, proposals arose both from within and between the two organizations.

The most recent effort, in 1973–74, failed after the conventions of both organizations had approved entering into talks to explore the possibility of uniting to form one organization for the teachers of the nation. Talks began on October 2, 1973, and were terminated the following February. Later the AFT asked that the NEA resume talks. However, President

Helen Wise reported to the Board of Directors on May 3, 1974, that she had sent the following letter to David Selden, president of the AFT:

> We see little purpose to a resumption of NEA-AFT talks. One of the reasons why we terminated the prior talks was the AFT's insistence on AFL-CIO affiliation, a position which is contrary to the mandate of the NEA's Representative Assembly. Unless and until the AFT is willing to change its position on the affiliation question and on such other critical items as minority guarantees and secret ballot elections, agreement is not possible and a resumption of talks would be futile.[16]

Although each group blamed the other for failure of the talks, I think they were doomed to fail from the start. The conventions of both organizations had locked the parties into rigid positions with little latitude for movement.

Association Finances

Through the first three years of the Lambert administration, the demand for expanded services continued to outrun Association resources. The 1967 Representative Assembly had increased membership dues from ten to fifteen dollars effective in 1968–69. However, in March 1968, a crisis developed in Florida, and in response to an urgent request from the Florida Education Association (FEA), the Board of Directors approved a two-million-dollar loan to the FEA. That same month the Executive Committee authorized the executive secretary to borrow five million dollars from the bank.

State affiliates were faced with financing election campaigns for the selection of an organization to represent school personnel in collective bargaining. Lawsuits involving the protection of members and Association leaders burgeoned. These expenses, added to those required to finance the ongoing programs, left the state affiliates short of funds. Some, having exhausted their borrowing limits, spent NEA dues revenue to meet local crises instead of transmitting it to the NEA.

As a result, the NEA ended the 1969 year with a deficit of $180,000.

The Executive Secretary reported on June 25, 1969, that the FEA was over its charter limit on debt and unable to begin to repay the NEA loan.

In September, Dr. Lambert told the Executive Committee that $1,742,000 was still unpaid on membership dues for the previous year. At the October meeting, he reported one state affiliate was holding $400,000 of NEA dues, and at the October meeting the following year, he said almost four million dollars in NEA dues revenue was outstanding.

Two actions were taken by the Association to improve its financial condition. Dues were increased for a second time in two years, from fifteen to twenty-five dollars, by the 1969 Representative Assembly, effective in 1970–71, and a staff member was assigned to negotiate promissory notes for the payment of NEA dues revenue untransmitted from previous years. A transmittal schedule was also adopted, with penalties for those affiliates failing to observe its conditions. But despite these actions, financial problems continued to plague the Association throughout the Lambert administration. They were caused by three principal developments: inflation, the demands of unbudgeted crisis situations, and the one-year delay in securing increases in membership dues after their authorization by the governing bodies.

Two additional actions were initiated in 1969 and 1970 to ease the Association's financial problems. The funding of the Dushane Fund for Teacher Rights was increased, and a crisis fund was established, enabling the state affiliates to increase their borrowing power by combining the lines of credit of NEA and the participating state affiliates.

Change of Tax Status

For many years, the NEA and its departments had accepted grants from private persons, corporations, foundations, and public agencies for research projects, surveys, studies, or other activities designed to improve the quality of education.

The Association was able to attract such grants because of its nonprofit classification under Section 501C(3) of the Internal Revenue Code, making it eligible to receive tax-free grants. However, as the Association became more assertive in its legislative and political activity, the Internal Revenue Service began to raise questions about the need to reassign the Association to a classification more appropriate to the new activities. These talks continued from 1963 to 1968, when the IRS proposed that the NEA accept a reduction in its status to that of a business league.

Desiring to continue to be able to attract tax-free grants for education research projects and still be responsive to the economic needs of the members, the NEA requested its legal counsel to explore possible alternative courses of action.

The Executive Committee, after considering the options, agreed to accept the designation of business league if certain safeguards to the Association and its staff were ensured. To retain the ability to attract research grants, a separate foundation was created retaining the NEA's previous tax-exempt status.

The organization of the National Foundation for the Improvement of Education was authorized on December 8, 1968, and an interim board was named to complete the work necessary to make the foundation operational.

Achievements of the Lambert Administration

The five-year Lambert administration was one of turmoil and change. It was also a period of significant achievement. Sharing the credit for leadership in the Lambert years were six presidents: Braulio Alonso (1967–68), Elizabeth Koontz (1968–69), George D. Fischer (1968–70), Helen Bain (1970–71), Donald E. Morrison (1971–72), and Catharine Barrett (1972–73).

These are some of the major achievements of the Lambert years.

Unification of membership was achieved in twenty-nine states, bringing the total number of states with unified membership to thirty-eight.

Merger of separate state affiliates was accomplished in five states, leaving only two states remaining unmerged.

State laws were enacted in twenty-two states authorizing collective bargaining and defining procedures covering 1.4 million school instructional employees.

Membership dues increased from ten dollars in 1967 to twenty-five dollars in 1972.

Membership in the Association was increased by 137,747 members—from 1,028,456 in 1967 to 1,166,203 in 1972.

A cooperative plan known as Uniserv, adopted in 1970, provided full-time salaried professional personnel to strengthen the programs and services of local affiliates. In 1972 there were 600 Uniserv personnel at work with local associations.

Resources were increased substantially for the Dushane Fund for Teacher Rights.

A crisis fund was established to extend the borrowing capacity of state affiliates to assist them to survive crisis periods.

An NEA staff academy was created to train Association leaders at all levels.

A coalition of American Public Employees was organized to permit educators and other public employees to work together cooperatively on matters of mutual interest. The coalition represents approximately four million public employees.

A National Foundation for the Improvement of Education was created to permit the NEA to continue to attract private and other tax-deductible grants to support research projects for the improvement of education.

The NEA was in the final stage of being transformed from a "national holding company" for the several state affiliates to an aggressive national organization with the power to set its own program related to the needs of its 1.2 million members in all states of the nation.

These achievements, made during a period fraught with divisive problems, must be considered to get a balanced view of a critical period in the life of the National Education Association.

Unfinished Business

Unfinished business included the completion of the work of the Constitutional Convention. Its recommendations had been approved by the 1972 Representative Assembly but were to be rejected by a vote of the membership four months later.

Another major piece of unfinished business was the implementation of the action of the 1972 Assembly that changed Association bylaws to require all state affiliates to adopt either a policy of unified professional membership or a plan for its implementation by the beginning of the 1972–73 membership year.

The Last Lambert Report

Sam Lambert surprised the delegates and even his staff colleagues in Atlantic City with a dramatic speech unlike any he or any other executive secretary, to my knowledge, had made to a meeting of the Representative Assembly.

He began by saying, "This may be the last report I'll ever make to an NEA Representative Assembly. After I have said what I *must* say, I may be unemployed.

"But, come what may, the things I am going to say here today are going to be the real gut feelings of Sam Lambert, and I don't really care what the personal consequences are."

Then the executive secretary, who had for five years identified himself with the forces of change in the Association, attacked as a "debacle" the Association's action in supporting the Florida Teachers' strike—a strike he had described to the Dallas meeting of the Representative Assembly four years earlier as a victory that "reversed a ten-year trend of educational neglect and decay," and "one of the biggest 'show and tell' demonstrations in the history of education."[17]

He lectured state affiliates for their lax fiscal policies then saddling the NEA with the results. "If this sounds like an angry speech," he declared "I can only say I have a lot to be angry about."[18]

He attacked the recent merger of the New York State Teachers Association and the American Federation of Teachers. Pointing out that the action was in conflict with a goal adopted by the Assembly the previous year, he asked, "Will unity in New York . . . mean disunity in NEA? If so, how much and with what consequences?"[19]

He expressed serious reservations about four provisions in the Constitutional Convention documents:

1. "A very powerful President and an Executive Director, substantially reduced in status, prestige and authority," he said, will require the executive director "to support the politicians or his tenure will be very short."
2. "The patchwork arrangement for who can be a member," he said, was inconsistent and illogical.
3. "If these documents are adopted as they stand . . . our 17 national affiliates and 11 associated organizations will depart the scene for good."
4. "There appears to be a thread of thought running throughout the documents to the effect that national-to-local relationships are all-important, that national-to-state relationships are of no importance at all."[20]

I asked Dr. Lambert, in an interview in Washington in the summer of 1979, what had motivated him to make the speech. He said it was no single issue but a series of developments coming one after the other until he felt he must speak out.

In the past, the executive secretary's report to the Representative Assembly was somewhat of a team effort. The deputy and assistant executive secretaries were asked to contribute, and all participated in the decision on the major points to be given emphasis. In 1972, I was not consulted, nor to my knowledge was any other member of the top executive staff. I asked Dr. Lambert about this afterward. He said it was deliberate; he didn't want anyone else to feel they had to share the responsibility.

At the next regular meeting of the Executive Committee, I walked to the board room entrance at the announced time for the meeting to begin and found a note on the door. It said that a special executive session was in progress. This puzzled me because as the deputy executive secretary, I had been included in executive sessions.

I returned to my office. In about thirty minutes Dr. Lambert appeared and told me he had accepted a leave of absence until he would qualify for retirement the following year. The Executive Committee had asked him to inquire if I would take over the duties of the executive secretary for the balance of the meeting. I did take over as deputy executive secretary on August 29, 1972. At the September meeting I was named acting executive secretary, a position I held until my retirement on May 1, 1973. Terry E. Herndon became the executive director on May 1, 1973.

In reflecting on the Lambert years, I feel that at the time of his appointment Dr. Lambert believed in the need for the NEA to adopt collective bargaining, an active role in civil rights, and the changes perceived to be necessary to accommodate them. As the cleavage between teachers and administrators became more imminent, however, his internal conflict, plus the stress of living with continued uncertainty, led him to identify with the position of the leaders of the administrator groups with whom he had had a long and cordial relationship.

In some respects Sam Lambert was a contrast to his predecessor, Dr. Carr. Dr. Carr made decisions quickly and seemingly with ease, whereas decisions were difficult for Dr. Lambert. He worried about them both before and after they were made.

The result was an accumulation of worries during critical periods that threatened his health. He was a heavy smoker and his consumption of cigarettes increased in periods of stress. One colleague observed that he could always determine the level of stress in the executive office by the number of stubbs in the king-size ashtray on the executive secretary's desk.

While Dr. Carr was reserved, urbane, precise in his use of language, and impeccable in dress and grooming, Dr. Lambert was casual and enjoyed referring to himself as a country boy from West Virginia. Dr. Carr was a member of the prestigious Cosmos Club. Dr. Lambert's favorite place for lunch was the drugstore on the corner of Fourteenth and "L" Street.

Dr. Carr enjoyed the exercise of power. Dr. Lambert neither sought power nor enjoyed using it. Yet both men, in different ways, influenced the course of the Association in a critical period of its life.

THE WEST INTERIM ADMINISTRATION: 1972-1973

My eight-month service as deputy and acting executive secretary was not the most satisfying period of my career. It was a period of searching for a satisfactory solution to the structure problem that had caused the membership to reject the original Constitutional Convention document. The relation of elected and staff officers was unclear. The Executive Committee was divided on the merger with the American Federation of

Teachers. The New York State Teachers Association, NEA's New York state affiliate, merged with the AFT without the NEA's participation. Both officers and staff were weary of the uncertainty and eager to put an end to the structure question, and the title of "acting" executive secretary limited my ability to do some of the things I knew should be done.

I elected not to be a candidate for the permanent position. I was less than two years from mandatory retirement. It was a logical time for a new management team to take over the new NEA. I am glad I had the experience but would have no desire to repeat it. However, I appreciated the support given to me by my staff colleagues, Association officers, and governance bodies in our common effort to preserve the stability of the Association until action could be taken by the Representative Assembly to complete the reorganization.

The Compromise Proposal

One of the chief activities of the period between the Lambert retirement and the Herndon appointment was the development of the compromise restructure proposal of the Committee of Twelve, for presentation to the 1973 Representative Assembly.

Each of the major power groups in the organization was asked to prepare position papers setting forth their views on the issues. The statements were published in the *NEA Reporter* for January 1972. The following excerpts reveal the divergence of positions of three groups on the membership issue—the Association of Classroom Teachers, School Administrators, and the National Council of Urban Education Associations.

> Classroom teachers believe that regardless of what provisions are included in the final document, one principle is essential: that classroom teachers must be accorded peer status among all segments of the education profession. [From a statement by the Association of Classroom Teachers]

> To remain all-inclusive, NEA must overhaul the proposed constitution and bylaws so that special interest groups may exist as an integral part of the inclusive structure but may retain its identity as autonomous entities without subservience. . . . [The proposals] . . . would demolish the concept of professional unity through the National Education Association. [From a statement by the American Association of School Administrators, the National Association of Elementary School Principals, and the National Association of Secondary School Principals]

> NCUEA believes it is time to tell it like it is. Neither ACT nor AASA is happy with the compromise. ACT wants an autonomous classroom teachers organiza-

tion. AASA wants to maintain the status quo. That is what makes the con con compromise so right. It represents the only vehicle for changing the status quo without ripping us apart.

NCUEA believes con con has achieved a true compromise between classroom teachers and administrators. While guaranteeing that control of the organized teaching profession will rightfully be in the hands of classroom teachers, the document also provides for proportional representation of administrators. [From a statement by the National Council of Urban Education Associations]

John Ryor, chairman of the committee, summarized for the Board of Directors changes in the plan approved by the Constitutional Convention but rejected by the membership. Ryor expressed the belief that the committee's proposals would reduce conflict in the Association and improve its governance machinery.

The committee proposal reinstated the Board of Directors and Executive Committee and clarified the functions of each body; increased the minimum guarantees for delegate representation in the Representative Assembly; eliminated the offices of past president and president-elect; extended the terms of the president, vice-president and secretary-treasurer; provided for local determination of membership; and clarified the role of the executive director.

The Board voted to approve the committee's recommendations at its June 1973 meeting prior to the Portland meeting of the Representative Assembly.

The Committee's compromise proposal opened the way for the Portland 1973 Assembly to attract enough delegate support to salvage the work of the Constitutional Convention. It put together an Association structure that could be supported by all major power groups in the NEA.

The capable leadership demonstrated by committee chairman Ryor was recognized by the delegates to the 1975 Representative Assembly, who elected him the first president to serve under the new constitution. He was reelected in 1977 for a second term.

The Missouri Disaffiliation

The NEA Executive Committee, in the spring of 1973, voted to disaffiliate the Missouri State Teachers Association (MSTA). The MSTA had not complied with the provisions of the NEA's revised bylaws requiring that all state affiliates shall have adopted a policy of unified membership or a plan for implementing of such a policy beginning with the 1972–73 membership year.

A hearing had been held to give MSTA an opportunity to present its case.

The action by the Executive Committee marked the transition of the NEA from a service agency for its affiliates to a national organization with the power to set the direction of the teaching profession and to enforce its national policies.

The Association acted promptly to recognize a new state affiliate—the Missouri NEA—to replace MSTA, which had been organized a year before the NEA was founded and recognized as an NEA state affiliate for more than a century.

It was a wrenching experience for me, as acting executive secretary, to bring charges against a state affiliate headed by officers who had held responsible positions in the NEA and with whom I had worked intimately for many years.

Significant gains were made in organizing higher-education faculties. In February 1973, the NEA had 106 affiliates on college and university campuses representing 46,600 members in collective bargaining out of a potential of 933,000 members in higher education. At that time, 82,452 were organized for bargaining. Of that number, the NEA represented 56 percent, compared with 36 percent for the AFT and 8 percent for the American Association of University Professors (AAUP).

By January 1973, all but three state affiliates were in compliance with the NEA's bylaw requirements of unified membership. Only two states with separate affiliates for black and white members remained unmerged, and over 1.4 million instructional personnel were covered by bargaining agreements.

THE HERNDON ADMINISTRATION: 1973-

The 1973 Portland, Oregon, meeting of the Representative Assembly was a landmark in the life of the NEA. It was significant for several reasons.

It marked the end of a nine-year period of renewal of the Association. The compromise offered by the Committee of Twelve brought together all of the power groups in the Association under the new constitution. It was the beginning of a new life for the NEA. The Association was headed by a new team of young and dynamic leaders—President Helen Wise, Vice-President Jim Harris, the NEA's second black president-elect, and Executive Director Terry Herndon, then in his early thirties.

One cannot read the verbatim proceedings of the Portland meeting without being struck by the impatience of the delegates. For almost nine years they had struggled to fashion a set of governing documents that could be supported by all segments of the profession. They had grown weary of their preoccupation with the machinery of the organization. They were eager to end the struggle and focus on the tasks of serving the members and improving the schools.

The compromise proposal was the vehicle that brought them together. They felt a sense of pride in the product and in having been active participants in the process.

It was a euphoric period, an ideal time for the beginning of a new administration, despite the unfinished business that had to be dealt with.

The long period of uncertainty that had taken its toll in staff morale was over. It was a new beginning.

Interview with Terry Herndon

Six years after the Portland meeting, I met with Terry Herndon in his Washington office. In a taped interview, I asked him a series of questions about his experiences in those six years. Here are my questions and his responses.

WEST: "What do you consider your major achievements in your first six years?"

HERNDON: "At the time I was appointed, we were in the throws of the debate on the new constitution. That constitution was adopted at the NEA convention shortly after I arrived. At that time we had a large number of states that had complied by filing a plan but were not yet unified. Many . . . predicted that they wouldn't. We dedicated most of our energy for the first year or year and a half to that problem. We were able to achieve total unification."

Legislation and Political Action. "I believe that our legislative program is NEA's basic reason for being. Professional programs and support services for state and local affiliates are important, but it is the federal program that creates a unique need to be filled by a national organization. The importance that I attribute to this program creates frustration with the rate of progress but our achievements are substantial.

"During the Nixon-Ford era we played defense. Much of our energy was invested in overriding vetoes and trying to hold our own. We were very successful but, in the area of federal aid to education, we still lost ground to inflation. With the help of the Carter administration, we have increased federal aid even beyond those losses.

"Three years ago I would have said that our greatest achievement was the imminent passage of a collective bargaining statute; but, the Supreme Court eviscerated that effort and the victory was lost. Therefore, I am a bit apprehensive but nevertheless say that the imminent passage of a bill to create a Department of Education is our most significant achievement. I think that two or three months from now I will be able to claim it for certain." (The proposed establishment of the Department of Education, headed by a cabinet level Secretary, was signed by President Carter on September 27, 1979—four months after this interview was taped.)

"We have won unemployment compensation for teachers. This was a significant breakthrough. In the area of school program, NEA's role in passing a new authorization for federal money to educate handicapped children, Title IX to fight discrimination against women and girls. And the creation of federally funded teacher centers are sources of pride.

"There is persistent Congressional effort to create federal funding for private schools and to mandate universal Social Security. We have been central to the regular defeat of both.

"Much of this record is directly attributable to my greatest pleasure— the development of teachers as a political force. In 1976, NEA members entered presidential politics in a very heavy way. We were the largest organized delegation at both the Republican and Democratic national conventions.

"NEA members played a critical role in the election of the present [Carter-Mondale] administration. Even though one is always ambivalent about an incumbent, I am absolutely certain that we were right and am proud of our role. The Carter budgets have proposed the greatest increases in federal spending for schools ever. He has fought hard for the Department and just as hard against tuition tax credits for private school tuition.

"Reservations about Carter's presidency notwithstanding, the other choice was the election of Gerald Ford. Ford was admittedly hostile to collective bargaining for public employees and other labor needs. He openly opposed the Department of Education and increased federal aid to education. In fact, he appeared sympathetic to the Republican platform's call for reduced federal aid. Comparing where we are now to where we would have been with a continuation of the Ford presidency, I have to say that that election was a turning point. It was a close election and that made our role more significant than it might have been.

"In addition, it is important to observe that all of these gains were voted by the Congress. Therefore, our aggressive efforts to elect friends of education to Congress have been equally important.

"My greatest disappointments are also in this area of program. We have not broken through with general federal aid and we have not gained the federal bargaining bill. These issues will dominate the future."

Legal Services. "We have added several new programs. Probably the most significant of those was the total revision of our approach to legal services in a way that completely integrated our Dushane Fund operation with the legal services program in the states. It has cost NEA significantly more money in states where we used to spend none and in the states that were most aggressive in legal defense work. At the same time, it has caused many other states to perform better for teachers than they had heretofore. We can safely say that we protect our members better than does any trade union or professional society in the country."

Special Services. "I think we have effectively resolved the very divisive conflicts we used to have around the insurance programs and other special services programs. We are presently into a totally unified approach to special services."

Electronic Systems. "The use of the computer as a support service for NEA and the affiliates has been, I think, a rather striking development. Next year we will have about half of the states on the NEA regional membership processing system where they process their membership directly into the NEA electronic membership file and computer.

"Related to that we have also developed a research program that we refer to as BSSN—Bargaining Support System Network—that allows the states to have direct access to the NEA computer and to receive most of their research support from NEA now electronically rather than in print. Next year all of the states will be a part of this system. It is my guess that within five years, electronic linkage will be one of the most important relationships between the NEA and the affiliates. It will very likely have profound implications for all service delivery systems."

[In some sixteen states a procedure had been in use by the NEA called the reverse check-off. This procedure provided for the deduction from member's salaries of contributions to the NEA's political action organization (NEA-PAC) unless a member expressly asked that such deductions not be made. Recently the Federal Elections Commission ruled that such deductions must be discontinued and refunds must be made to any members requesting them.]

WEST: "Do you consider the loss of the reverse check-off a serious handicap to NEA's political action program?"

HERNDON: "No, I don't. I will have to cite a couple of historical reasons for that. It is my strong belief that our greatest resource is our human resource. That is what makes us an extraordinary organization. We have ex-

traordinary people. We are ubiquitous. We are capable and we are interested. Our time and energy should be focused on mobilizing our people.
In this regard the reverse check-off was really counterproductive. It
raised a lot of money, but for many people did not constitute commitment
to anything beyond an abstract idea of political action because there was
nobody from the leadership of the organization going to that member and
saying, 'Here's what we want to do—here's why it's important—make a
commitment.' Now, as a result of losing the reverse check-off, we have
had every member in some sixteen states contacted by representatives.
Many of them have chosen to sign. Many of them have chosen not to sign.
But we will have an adequate financial base for our political program.
And, I believe, be free of the easy-money syndrome. So I think it will have
a wholesome effect—all things considered."

Merger and Unification.   "I played a very direct personal role in concluding the process of merging the black and white organizations in the
South. I was deeply involved in Mississippi and Louisiana.

"I suppose if I were to look at the most difficult things I have done—
and therefore, I take great satisfaction from them—it would be the mergers in Mississippi and Louisiana and the unification of states like Texas,
Arkansas, Georgia and others which were difficult."

Florida Disaffiliation.   "In a sense it's negative, but I think that in a
very real way, the disaffiliation of the Florida Education Association was
a signficant milestone for NEA. It really was, to my knowledge anyway,
the first time in NEA's history when it stood up to the test of policy confrontation with a large state affiliate. The affiliate was blatantly violating
the policy of the convention, and we saw that through. I think that had a
very significant effect on the . . . psychology of the organization. The
Board and the Delegate Assembly came to see themselves as the stewards
of a significant national organization not to be ignored. We became something more than a loose confederation of sovereign state affiliates.

"It would be unfair to my many predecessors in NEA to ignore what
NEA did in terms of the merger mandate and the mandate that ultimately
led to the collision with Missouri State Teachers Association. But I think
the Florida situation, in a sense, was special in that it was simply an organizational policy that was involved. There were not profound moral
overtones in terms of social need and social conscience. It was just NEA
acting like a national organization.

"This was tested again by the New York United Teachers. Only there
NEA was not the prime decisionmaker. The decision was made in New
York. That was an affiliate with over 200,000 members. It came to the

Board of Directors and simply laid down an ultimatum. It was essentially this: if it is your intent now, or ever to enforce the policies of NEA, we will disaffiliate and we must have asurance that you won't enforce those policies. The Board said, so be it, we are an organization. We have standards, policies, and rules. If you have no commitment to those, go your way."

WEST: "Do you have any regrets?"

HERNDON: "I have many disappointments. I am disappointed with the status of collective bargaining. I continue to believe . . . it is our most important challenge. With the exception of a relatively modest law in Tennessee and some revisions in the laws in states that already had the best laws, we really have made no progress on the matter of statutory collective-bargaining rights for our members in several years. We continue to have people going to jail. We continue to have people paying confiscatory fines. I think we have to press for that effort even though it is not a very promising one at the moment."

WEST: "I find some members feel that cooperation with other education groups on matters of mutual concern is not continuing. Is that true?"

HERNDON: "Those people are right. I don't think we relate as effectively to the other professional societies as we ought to. As a result, I expect there is a waste of resources both here and in their houses. That is not a result of malice or ill will. We continue to have friendly relationships with all of those organizations, but since they have left this building and are no longer located here, they get involved in what they are doing and we get involved in what we are doing and the interchange doesn't flow naturally. My guess is it won't unless it is structured."

WEST: "What is the prospect of merger with AFT?"

HERNDON: "I think that in the foreseeable future there is virtually none. It is my belief that if somebody simply strolled in and laid a proposition before the deliberative bodies of NEA right now, we would again have instant polarization. So I just don't think it is possible. Now, if NEA were to sustain some serious losses, or if the AFT were to sustain some serious losses, that might make it possible for one or the other of us to make concessions. But at the present time both are either growing or holding their own, are big enough to function and are relatively comfortable. I don't think very many of the leaders perceive the existence of two organizations to be really counterproductive.

"If you check my incoming interview six years ago, you will find that I believed merger was inevitable. It was a question of when, not whether—a question of the terms. I don't see it that way after six years."[21]

The Current Administration

Terry Herndon lost no time in making his leadership felt in the Association.

Fewer than three months after becoming executive director, he outlined a strategy for the teaching profession in his address to the Representative Assembly. He called on the delegates to put aside their personal agendas and conflicts of the past and to build a new solidarity based on a five-point offensive:

> "First, the acquisition and consolidation of a power base for this profession; second, the expansion and extension of an effective intervention mechanism such as bargaining and lobbying; third, the vigilant protection of the professional and human rights of every teacher; fourth, the substantive development of our profession; and, . . . finally, the selling of that profession."

"The path to teacher power," he declared, "is the concentration of teacher energy behind a goal and a single, organized offensive."

Three days later, Helen Wise, in her first address to the delegates as the president of the Association, put an end to the conflict over the roles and relationships of the president and executive director.

> "There is now a very clear understanding of the respective roles of the president and executive director. . . . NEA is a single organization that speaks for teachers. And while the president's role is one of establishing and guiding policy, the executive [director] is responsible for the implementation of that policy and the direction of staff. Terry and I are in complete agreement on that philosophy and will work together to assure its effective operation, and neither of us is suspicious of the other's motives or positions, the NEA will prosper and grow under this form of governance."

True to President Wise's prediction, the Association has prospered. Terry Herndon's strategy for the profession has been accepted and pursued methodically through the terms of four presidents. By 1980 many tangible results were evident.

The Association played a key role in electing the President of the United States in 1976. And that support was not forgotten by President Carter after the election. NEA's legislative goal of establishing a separate federal department of education became a goal of the administration. And the goal became a reality largely because it had the active support of the White House.

Appropriations for continuing school programs were increased with the support of the administration.

Teacher centers were authorized and established with federal funding. And tuition tax credit proposals that would weaken the public schools were defeated.

These and other legislative achievements, already mentioned, did not happen solely as a result of White House support. They happened as a result of favorable action by the Congress and a carefully developed plan by NEA to mobilize the energies of teachers and other citizens with an active concern for education.

Philip Shabecoff, in an article in the *New York Times* on the 1980 campaign, wrote:

> Walter Moore, who coordinates the labor activities for the Carter-Mondale Presidential Committee, waxed particularly enthusiastic about the National Education Association, the 1.8 million member union of teachers and school administrators.
>
> "The NEA is a full partner in our campaign," Mr. Moore said. "They have a full field organization everywhere we go. We just plug them in wherever we are weak and they do a job."
>
> The educators union, which sent 172 of its own members as delegates to the 1976 Democratic convention and hopes to exceed that total this year, has members in . . . every state and in communities of all sizes. They are especially well represented in the suburbs, an area where most unions have limited influence.[22]

David S. Broder and Kathy Sawyer, reporters for the *Washington Post*, devoted an entire article to the NEA's activity in the 1980 Iowa presidential primary which said in part:

> In its transformation from prim professional organization into a hard nosed labor union, the 124-year-old NEA has been able to marshal remarkable natural resources that set it apart from other trade unions.
>
> With 1.8 million members in 12,000 affiliates nationwide, it reaches into virtually every American Community.
>
> It has an average of 6,000 members in every congressional district—members who are educated and who know and are known by a lot of people.
>
> "They can get you into any community in a campaign, and no other union can do that," said William Romjue, the Carter-Mondale coordinator in Iowa. "In small towns especially, the teachers know everyone."[23]

"NEA's new offensive is opening doors for us which will further increase the Association's political influence," President Willard McGuire said. "The doors to the White House are open to NEA leaders and more and more frequently candidates for Congress and other political offices are consulting with us in advance about our legislative priorities."

Upon the completion of his second two-year term as NEA president, John Ryor accepted a position on the White House staff working with organized interest groups on programs of special concern to the President.

How has the NEA achieved the gains of the past seven years of the Herndon administration?

Five developments, in my opinion, account for the NEA's success and its new image.

1. The association is unified. The achievement of unified membership and the accompanying unification of programs has tied the three levels of the organization together. It has eliminated the internal conflicts resulting from duplication of services. Each level—local, state and national —now provides by agreement those services it is best equipped to provide. The NEA and all of its affiliates are now committed to a single program pursued nationwide and involving work with the centers of power at all levels.

2. The goals of the organization are clearly defined, programs and strategies are understood, and there is broad participation by members in program implementation. Throughout the seven years the goals, objectives, and strategies have been consistent and methodically pursued.

3. The Association's decisionmaking machinery and the service delivery system have been made more efficient. Much was accomplished to simplify decisionmaking by the adoption of the new constitution. With that action the NEA shed its ambiguous nature and became a single organization that carries out its purposes through a network of fifty-three state and ten thousand local affiliates. A staff reorganization in 1979–80 provided for the delivery of a coordinated program of services through six regional NEA offices located in Washington, Boston, Atlanta, St. Paul, Denver, and Burlingame. Each office serves from eight to ten states.

4. The problems and needs of teachers and education make the services of a strong united organization of the teaching profession more evident to prospective members than in more tranquil periods. Over the years the greatest growth in the organization has occurred in times of adversity. In the past teachers have been exploited. They have been deprived of constitutional rights because they lacked the resources to defend themselves. In the past decade Association services for the protection of its members, students, and schools has increased greatly. Membership has increased and with the increased numbers the power of the Association has grown. Moreover, members who are secure in the knowledge that their oganization will support them are willing to take the risks inherent in social actions to improve school conditions.

5. Finally, one of the most important factors accounting for the NEA's success in the Herndon administration is the high quality of both the elected and staff leadership. The leadership team has provided for the in-

fusion of fresh ideas from the rotating terms of the elected presidents. At the same time the Association has benefited from the continuity of the appointed executive director by giving the security necessary to recruit and retain competent staff members and manage the Association resources.

Each of the four presidents taking office since 1973 has brought to the position different points of view and new ideas which had been tested in the election campaigns at the Representative Assemblies. All had their own views as to program areas that should be given special emphasis and all found they also had to adapt to deal with issues that arose during their terms.

Helen Wise (1973–74) had a deep interest in strengthening the organization and program of the NEA's fledgling Political Action Committee which became operational in the term of her predecessor, Catharine Barrett, but her interest covered the broad span of services provided by the Association. Dr. Wise and Terry Herndon made an ideal team to launch a new era under the NEA's new constitution. Both had been leaders of NEA state affiliates. This common experience gave credibility to their efforts in working with the states to erase the scars of the past and unite the organization.

James E. Harris (1974–75), the NEA's second black president, had a special interest in providing improved school opportunities for those suffering from neglect: the children of migrant workers, the poor, the handicapped, and the victims of racial discrimination. To call the attention of the public to the plight of those penalized by neglect and to mobilize support to correct the situation, President Harris established the NEA Project Educational Neglect. Surveys were made to determine the dimensions of the problem. Reports were made. Corrective recommendations were developed and reported to a national conference on educational neglect, to congressional committees, and to the public.

John Ryor (1975–79), a Michigan teacher and former president of the Michigan Education Association, was the first NEA president to be elected for a two-year term under the new constitution. He had served as chairman of the NEA committee that developed the compromise proposal and broke the impasse leading to the adoption of the new constitution by the 1973 Representative Assembly. His presidency of the NEA's Michigan affiliate was distinguished by his successful leadership for ratification of the Equal Rights Amendment and constructive efforts to deal with the special educational needs of minority and disadvantaged children.

A youthful, attractive, photogenic, outspoken leader, Ryor quickly became a symbol of the NEA's new power. He was sought after by reporters for the press and TV who found they could rely on him for a news story that was always timely and frequently provocative. He was an effective spokesman for such NEA objectives as a separate federal department of education, the passage of the Equal Rights Amendment, and human rights, and against the overreliance on testing in the schools and tuition tax credits.

In 1977, at the conclusion of his two-year term, Ryor was re-elected without oppositon for a second term.

Willard McGuire (1979-   ) served two terms as vice president during John Ryor's presidency, and was then elected president in 1979. He came to prominence in the NEA in 1972 when the chairman of the Minneapolis meeting of the Constitutional Convention, Eugene Duckworth, was unable to chair the meeting due to injuries sustained in an automobile accident. Willard McGuire was drafted to step into the breach, which he did with great skill and even-handed judgment. His priorities as president followed closely those of his predecessor, John Ryor, with emphasis on legislation and political action. Based on his four years service as vice president and the initial year of his term as president, it appears safe to predict the continuation of a unified leadership team at the helm in the NEA for the foreseeable future.

Terry Herndon (1973-   )

In its first seven years, Terry Herndon's administration has been successful in forming a new and close working relationship with the NEA's state affiliates. He has moved with skill to define, with participation by state association leaders, the roles that can be served best at each level. Services agreed to be provided best at the state level have been left to the states. Those determined to be best served by national or local programs have been assumed by the local association or the NEA. A source of conflict has been eliminated. He has also endeavored with comparable effectiveness to maintain a close working relationship among the three elected NEA officers—the president, vice president, and treasurer—and the staff of the executive office.

Problems could develop as changes occur in the personnel occupying the offices. The apparent freedom from conflict may be but a testimonial to the personalities and characters of the incumbents. Experience reveals that the best possible definition of roles does not necessarily assure freedom from conflict. It helps, but in the final analysis it is the quality of the personnel that has the greatest influence on the quality and effectiveness of the relationships.

Herndon does not hesitate to take stands on issues. But one associate said, "He always has a well reasoned logical basis for his position." His relations are frank and open and he relies on logic and reason to make a point rather than personal feelings and rhetoric. He has a keen intellect, good judgment, an instant grasp of complex problems, and the ability to remain cool under pressure.

His reorganization of staff responsibilities is motivated by a desire to place staff members in positions where their talents will be most useful, and then only after full discussion with those involved.

Herndon believes collective bargaining is an effective, orderly process for reaching agreement on conditions of employment in the public schools. He told the 1979 meeting of the National School Boards Association:

> "I must tell you that I understand our differences. I manage a large organization of 600 employees; I balance a tough budget; I demand productivity; and as an employer, I bargain with three unions. But I am a teacher representative and nowhere in this land is there a more ardent advocate of collective bargaining. I believe it is right, fair, and necessary. None present is more determined to oppose it than I am determined to achieve it. And so there will be times, places, and circumstances that find some of us in acrimonious contest. However, to allow this reality of such incidents to distract us from the larger reality of our mutual commitment to the fundamental necessity for vigorous, effective, universal, free public schools is a type of . . . frivolous distraction."[24]

The Herndon administration in its first seven years has followed a consistent course adhering to the programs and offensive strategies outlined in Terry Herndon's maiden address to the 1973 Representative Assembly. It has been a period of unity and significant achievement.

CHAPTER TEN

Looking Ahead

The seventies was a decade of turmoil and conflict, a period in which Americans felt powerless to change conditions that affected their daily lives. The crisis in energy, foreign competition, and the rising expectations of third world countries created problems that neither individual nor national decisions could control. Inflation reduced the value of incomes. Confidence in private and public leadership was eroded as a result of oil profits and shortages, Watergate, and congressional improprieties. Criticisms of the schools escalated as Scholastic Aptitude Test scores declined and school discipline became the chief concern of both parents and teachers.

What are the prospects for the 1980s? The NEA is better equipped to deal with whatever problems the eighties bring as a result of its reorganization and renewal efforts achieved in the 1970s. It enters the eighties a more confident, efficient, unified, self-directed, and adaptable organization than it was ten or twenty years ago.

Social change is likely to continue at a rapid pace. There are trends that will influence schools, teachers, and pupils. And there are areas of unfinished business to be reckoned with.

Collective bargaining for teachers and other public employees spread rapidly in the 1960s and early 1970s. But in the late seventies the pace lagged. The chief unfinished business in employer-employee relations is the passage of a federal collective-bargaining statute assuring public employees of the right to bargain with their employers in all states. In January 1980, the right to bargain for teachers was limited to those states with state laws. A federal statute would establish the right nationwide, promote uniformity of procedural provisions, and simplify the administration of the process. In addition, existing laws should be strengthened in a majority of the states having such laws.

A combination of developments is causing university and college faculties to take an active interest in collective bargaining as a means of influencing institutional policies. Among those developments are declining enrollments, an oversupply of qualified candidates with Ph.D.'s seeking faculty positions, unfair tenure regulations, authoritarian administration, inadequate budgets, and too few opportunities for faculty members to influence institutional policies. Unless university and college administrators provide more effective mechanisms for faculty members to participate in policy decisions affecting them, the trend to collective bargaining in higher education will likely accelerate in the next decade.

Only recently, the court ruled that the NEA, because it represents some employees in private institutions, is subject to the provisions of the Landrum-Griffin Act. This act forbids the use of ethnic quotas and provides that all members, including secretaries and associate members, be extended the right to be delegates to the Representative Assembly and to seek and hold offices in the Association. This is a departure from past Association practice and an issue with which the NEA must deal. If it enrolls such members, they must be granted the same rights as classroom teachers. The alternative course would be to discontinue enrolling employees in private schools and institutions and paraprofessionals now classified as associate members.

The court has ruled that the NEA must comply with the provisions of the Landrum-Griffin Act because of its activities to improve working conditions for its members through collective bargaining. The Association remains a professional organization, however, committed to the dual mission—to improve the conditions of work for teachers and to improve education for American school children. These two goals are not mutually exclusive; they are mutually reinforcing. As the NEA works to improve standards for teachers, to strengthen the quality of teacher education and engage in research into the complex process of teaching, it strengthens the ability of the Association to improve conditions of work for teachers. A good argument can also be made that good working conditions for teachers can produce better education for the students.

Civil rights problems in education will continue to be with us in the 1980s. The NEA has given effective leadership for the desegregation of schools and the protection of teachers' rights. Much more needs to be done. Polls taken on the twenty-fifth anniversary of the Supreme Court's 1954 *Brown* v. *Topeka Board of Education* desegregation decision show a mixed picture. On the positive side, a poll of 500 adults in ten southern states taken on May 16, 1979, by the Darden Research Corporation for the *Atlanta Constitution* showed that 57 percent of southerners said the 1954 decision of the Supreme Court was a good decision.

The same question asked in a Gallup poll in July 1954 had shown that only 24 percent of southerners approved of the Court decision—a marked change in attitude.

The Darden poll also revealed that age and level of education correlate with attitudes on race relations. Among southerners eighteen to twenty-four years of age, 73 percent said the Supreme Court's 1954 decision was a good one. Of those sixty-five and over, only about half approved of the Court's decision. Fifty-two percent of southerners with no college education said the decision was good, while 66 percent of those with some college education supported it.

Asked if in the long run they felt the country would be better or worse off with racially integrated public schools, 61 percent of the total sample said the country would be better off with integrated schools.

These data, while revealing positive change, also indicate that a substantial segment of the population still does not approve of integrated schools. "It reminds Americans," said the *Atlanta Constitution*, "of 'How Far We Have Come—and of How Far We Have to Go.' "

The changing American family has had and will continue to have an impact on education. Divorce rates, the increase in one-parent families, the trend toward two-income families, and family attitudes and values all have implications for preschool education, day-care centers, and regular school services.

Population trends, such as the prospective sharp rise in the elderly population, have implications for continuing education programs for the younger old and day-care and institutional care for the older old.

The sharply rising immigration of Hispanic people from Mexico, Puerto Rico, Cuba, and the Caribbean countries, plus the higher-than-average birth rate of the resident Hispanic population, indicates the need for special programs such as bilingual education.

Inflation appears to be a continuing phenomenon, at least for the fore-seeable future, which indicates a need for continuing pressure for state and federal appropriations for school operations.

Economic Services

Economic services for members were provided by a number of the NEA's state affiliates in 1957, but the NEA had not entered that field. By 1980, however, the NEA offered a variety of insurance plans at favorable group rates, including term life insurance for members, spouse, and dependent children; homeowners insurance; accidental death and dismemberment insurance; hospital insurance; and tax-deferred annuities. In addition, the payment of the annual membership dues automatically covered all members under a group liability policy providing protection against legal actions resulting from the performance of their professional duties.

The Association operated travel plans for members including plans tailored to the interests of members, ranging from those desiring to travel purely for pleasure to those seeking intensive study programs abroad.

A mail order prescription drug service, a book club membership, various discount cards, and a consumer guide service to assist members in planning their purchase wisely and prudently were offered by the NEA. To avoid duplication with the services of affiliates, the NEA negotiated contracts with each state group in which it has been agreed what services would be provided by the NEA and what would be left to the state affiliate.

The NEA believes there are two ways the Association can help members cope with inflation: by increasing school revenues through legislation and collective bargaining and by helping members buy services and merchandise they need at group rates below the market prices.

These services can be expected to continue and expand.

A serious problem for the 1980s is that of adjusting pension funds to compensate for the effects of inflation. At 1979–80 rates of inflation, prices could double in less than a decade, rendering retirement allowances seriously inadequate.

School financing will be a continuing problem in the future. A number of legal cases, beginning in 1971 with *Serrano* v. *Priest*, have had great impact on the financing of schools and will continue to do so. These cases resulted in decisions holding that school districts relying on property tax revenues to support schools may violate the equal protection clause in the Fourteenth Amendment, which declares that "no state will . . . deny to any person within its jurisdiction the equal protection of the laws."

A recent decision in this series of cases occurred in January 1980 when the Wyoming Supreme Court struck down the state's system of financing schools.

The Wyoming decision directed the legislature to design a system that offered equal educational opportunity to each child. The court stated the decision was based on the system's reliance on local property taxes, which varied widely among the state's school districts.

These cases, which seek a highly desirable result—the equalization of school opportunities for the children of all school districts in the states—may require changes in Association methods. Some feel the locus of bargaining will move from the local school board to the governor's office and legislative chambers. In any event, larger state appropriations will be required from nonproperty tax sources.

Property, sales, and income taxes are the chief sources of school revenue in most states.

State income tax revenues are limited due to the virtual preemption of that source by the federal government. The elimination of further use of the property tax would place heavy reliance on the sales tax. And the regressive nature of the sales tax limits a major increase in that source. The logical result of this movement is a much greater acceptance of responsibility for financing the schools by the federal government. Increased federal appropriations for schools must continue to command a high priority in the NEA program for the future.

Another problem of school financing with which the Association must continue to grapple is that posed by the trend toward imposing arbitrary spending limits. James Farmer, executive director of the Coalition of American Public Employees (CAPE) told a conference on spending limits held in Washington on March 26, 1980, that only one state imposed a spending limit in 1976 and 1977. Five states imposed such limits in 1979. In 1980, Mr. Farmer stated, twenty-six states are considering tax and spending limitation proposals on state and local governments.[1]

The growing power of the right wing poses a threat to the public schools that must not be underestimated. Their promises to scuttle federal programs of financial aid to the schools, eliminate the newly established cabinet level Department of Education, and support voucher plans that undermine support for the public schools, unless countered effectively, could have serious consequences for the nation. While their proposals have been defeated in the past, the growing number of citizens unemployed or unable to make ends meet as a result of inflation, may be more receptive to the appeals of the Far Right in the 1980s.

No matter how strong the NEA becomes, teachers alone will not win victories for education without allies; continual efforts must be made to keep old alliances in repair and to form new, broad-based relationships. The schools should be of concern to a large majority of the population. Yet too many citizens exercise only a passive concern for their welfare. Ways must be found to engage the active interest of more community leaders with a deep appreciation for the social values of education to the community and nation.

Executive Director Herndon has proposed the mobilization of public school alumni from every field of endeavor—academia, politics, religion, athletics, labor, industry, commerce, art, and the professions—with a membership in the millions including all who feel that the public school contributed to their lives.[2]

Such broad-based support could conceivably be developed. It might do for the public schools what the military-industrial alliance has done to create the public will to make the sacrifices necessary for an adequate national defense.

The foregoing trends are now with us and will likely continue. There are many others on the horizon, and the NEA must be alert to recognize them early, anticipate their impact on the schools and teachers, and be prepared to deal with them.

There are many agencies and organizations in the nation with a sincere desire to strengthen the American schools. The officers of official agencies are often inhibited by bipartisan boards and politically motivated superiors from giving the bold leadership needed. The NEA, on the other hand, has freedom of action, within the limits set only by its members and the general welfare.

The Association has a progressive, young leadership team, a concerned and active membership of almost two million unified members with a presence in virtually every congressional district in the nation, a long tradition of leadership for the improvement of education, and a proven adaptability in meeting new social demands. The NEA is the logical power base for American education to continue to pursue the goal "to elevate the character and advance the interests of the profession of teaching and to promote the cause of popular education in the United States."

Appendix

LIST OF NEA STATE AFFILIATES
AND YEAR OF ADOPTION OF UNIFIED MEMBERSHIP

State	Year
Oregon	1944–45
Hawaii	1945–46
Montana	1945–46
Arizona	1947–48
Idaho	1947–48
Nevada	1949–50
West Virginia	1959–60
Washington	1963–64
Michigan	1967–68
Alaska	1968–69
Kentucky	1968–69
New Mexico	1968–69
Wyoming	1968–69
Delaware	1969–70
District of Columbia	1969–70
Florida	1969–70
Kansas	1969–70
Minnesota	1969–70
Overseas	1969–70
Pennsylvania	1969–70

Illinois	1970–71
Iowa	1970–71
Maine	1970–71
Mississippi	1970–71
New Hampshire	1970–71
Utah	1970–71
Colorado	1971–72
Connecticut	1971–72
Louisiana	1971–72
New Jersey	1971–72
Rhode Island	1971–72
South Carolina	1971–72
Indiana	1972–73
North Dakota	1972–73
Vermont	1972–73
Wisconsin	1972–73
Alabama	1973–74
Maryland	1973–74
Missouri	1973–74
New York	1973–74
South Dakota	1973–74
Georgia	1974–75
Massachusetts	1974–75
Nebraska	1974–75
North Carolina	1974–75
Ohio	1974–75
Virginia	1974–75
Arkansas	1975–76
California	1975–76
Oklahoma	1975–76
Puerto Rico	1975–76
Tennessee	1975–76
Texas	1975–76

STATES WITH COLLECTIVE BARGAINING STATUTES COVERING TEACHERS AND YEAR OF ENACTMENT

State	Year
1. Wisconsin	1959
2. Connecticut	1965
3. Massachusetts	1965
4. Michigan	1965
5. Rhode Island	1966
6. New York	1967
7. New Jersey	1968
8. Delaware	1969

9.	Maine	1969
10.	Maryland	1969
11.	Nebraska	1969
12.	Nevada	1969
13.	North Dakota	1969
14.	South Dakota	1969
15.	Vermont	1969
16.	Hawaii	1970
17.	Kansas	1970
18.	Pennsylvania	1970
19.	Idaho	1971
20.	Minnesota	1971
21.	Oklahoma	1971
22.	Alaska	1972
23.	Indiana	1973
24.	Montana	1973
25.	Oregon	1973
26.	Florida	1974
27.	Iowa	1974
28.	California	1975
29.	New Hampshire	1975
30.	Washington	1975
31.	Tennessee	1978

NATIONAL EDUCATION ASSOCIATION
1201 SIXTEENTH STREET, N.W.
WASHINGTON D.C. 20036

CRITERIA FOR EVALUATING MERGER PLANS AND COMPLIANCE WITH RESOLUTION 12

October 10, 1968

The purpose of this statement of criteria is to assist NEA affiliates to form fair and workable organizations for the achievement of a strong united teaching profession. They are written in the belief that all state affiliates concerned desire to effect a single, viable and effective merged organization capable of serving the needs and protecting the interests of all of their members. The criteria have been developed with the conviction that the achievement of merger is feasible in the six remaining states within the time limits set forth in the respective plans.

These principles are not intended to become a blueprint for merger but shall form a basis for the evaluation of merger plans as to compliance with Resolution 12.

In developing these criteria the Compliance Committee recognizes that the problems of racial representation, staffing and related problems are not confined to any one region. Therefore, the Compliance Committee, lacking authority to deal with such questions, will recommend to the Executive Committee that it require compliance with the concepts set forth in Resolution 12 which will apply to all fifty states.

Merger plans shall include conditions which will:

1. Recognize that the spirit of Resolution 12 requires that the merged association mark the termination of both previous associations and the creation of a completely new one.

   COMMENT:

   (If the name of one of the existing organizations is selected as the name for the merged association, suitable public recognition should be made that the merged association is not a continuation of the old association, but a completely different organization which is beginning a new life. The action program of the new organization should incorporate features of the programs and appropriate traditional activities of both associations. Parallel committees and commissions of the two merging associations should begin meeting together immediately to establish the habit of working together.)

2. Provide for a grievance procedure for resolving disputes which may arise as a result of alleged failure of the merged association to comply with the provisions of Resolution 12.

   COMMENT:

   (A procedure should be established by the joint committee which would make it possible for a member of the merged association to file a grievance if he feels that the association has:

   (a) failed to comply with the provisions of Resolution 12, or
   (b) not properly interpreted the provisions of Resolution 12, the merger agreement, or other documents related to the application of Resolution 12, and
   (c) failed to fulfill in practice the requirements of Resolution 12 or the merger agreement.

   Any individual member or affiliate who is not satisfied with the decision of the state association may appeal to the NEA Executive Committee for resolution of a dispute relating to the application or interpretation of the provisions of Resolution 12.)

3. Provide assurance that the association structure gives protection to the rights of minority group members to enable them to influence policy decisions in the merged association, participate in all association activities, and hold office. In areas involving race or other question of special interest or sensitivity there shall be afforded determinative power.

   COMMENT:

   (At some point, or points, in the decision-making process of the merged association, provision must be made for a balance of power to enable members of the minority group to exert their influence on matters of their special interest and to protect them from actions which may be contrary to their interest or welfare. Examples of practices which would balance power are: A requirement for a two-thirds vote on certain kinds of decisions; equal representation at points at which critical decisions are made; and, provision for initiating actions by petition.)

4. Provide that merger agreements for the state associations must include procedures for the orderly merger of local affiliates to be consummated within one year of the effective date of the merger of the state associations. Proselytizing of members of each association must be avoided during the completion of the mergers. Local affiliates should be reminded of this requirement by each state association.

COMMENT:

(State associations shall be responsible to secure written plans for all local affiliates with merger dates effective no later than one year following the effective date of merger of the state associations. Such plans must include:

- Name of new association
- Representation and officers
- Committees and commissions
- Staff (if any)
- Assets and liabilities
- Schedule of joint meetings
- Target date for action by official bodies and effective date of merger

The merging state affiliates shall encourage membership in the current associations until such time as merger plans are agreed to.)

5. Provide for a representative staff of black and white personnel at both professional and nonprofessional levels with the assurance that employees occupying professional positions will be given latitude for the exercise of independent judgment.

COMMENT:

(All staff members of both associations shall be continued in employment in the merged association with no reduction in salary and in comparable job categories. In the recruitment of new staff members the racial composition of the staff shall be maintained as nearly as possible, proportionate to the racial composition of the membership. A set of written personnel policies should be developed jointly by the two merging associations and adopted by the governing bodies prior to the effective date of the merger.)

6. Provide that there shall be no assumption that either Executive Secretary shall become the executive secretary of the merged association. The selection of the Executive Secretary of the merged association shall be on the basis of an objective procedure based on professional qualifications. Both Executive Secretaries of the present associations shall comprise the nominees for the position. The

Executive Secretary not appointed to head the merged association shall be assigned an appropriate position acceptable to the governing boards, reporting directly to the Executive Secretary, with a salary which is at least equal to the person who is second in command.

7. Provide that, if no agreement is reached by December 1, 1968, associations may elect to engage the services of a neutral third party to assist them in their efforts to reach agreement. Such third party may be any person agreeable to the two associations. If the two associations cannot agree upon a neutral third party the dispute settlement machinery provided by NEA must be used.

   In the event that the neutral third party chosen either by the disputants or the NEA is unsuccessful in resolving all of the disputed issues by December 15, 1968, the NEA will require that the remaining issues be submitted to binding arbitration under the rules and procedures of the Center for Dispute Settlement of the American Arbitration Association.

8. Provide that a merger plan once agreed to shall be submitted to the NEA Executive Committee before being presented to the governing bodies of the state associations for final approval.

COMMENT:

(The plans will be reviewed by the Executive Committee to determine whether they meet the requirements of the criteria herein set forth. The Executive Committee's review and ratification by the official bodies will provide the basis for determining the continued affiliation of an association.)

9. Provide for the completion of an approved merger plan to be presented to the delegate assemblies of both merging organizations in the 1968–69 school year. Completed plans must be in the hands of the Compliance Committee by January 1, 1969.

> IRVAMAE APPLEGATE, *Chairman*
> HELEN BAIN
> GEORGE FISCHER
> HELEN KRAUSE
> MABEL MCKELVEY
> DAVID SCHULZ

STATEMENT OF PROCEDURE FOR NEA FACTFINDING HEARING TO SECURE MERGER IN ACCORDANCE WITH RESOLUTION 12.

1. *Purpose*

The purpose of this proceeding is to ascertain the unresolved issues relating to merger of the affiliates, the position of the parties with respect to each issue and the arguments in support of each party's proposals on appropriate merger terms.

Since the proceeding is for the purpose of formulating fair and workable merger terms based upon the proposals of the parties it will be an informal and not an adversary proceeding.

2. *Selection of Fact-Finder*

The fact-finder for each state shall be designated by the NEA Executive Committee after consultation with the state affiliates involved. Such consultation shall be held as soon as practicable, and the Executive Committee shall announce its selection of a fact-finder no later than March 12, 1969.

The expenses and fees, if any, of the fact-finder shall be borne by the NEA. The fact-finder may be aided by assistants provided by the Executive Committee.

3. *Hearing Arrangements.*

The hearing shall be scheduled by the fact-finder as soon as practicable after his designation, ordinarily no later than March 19. The hearing shall be open only to those persons specifically designated by the officers of each affiliate to assist in the presentation of its position or by the NEA Executive Committee. The hearing shall not be open to the public.

The proceedings shall be recorded by a qualified reporter solely for the use of the fact-finder and the NEA Executive Committee. The costs of such service shall be borne by the NEA.

4. *Form of Presentation*

The parties shall determine the order of presentation by lot. Each party shall be given three hours to make its initial presentation, but the fact-finder may extend such period at his discretion.

Each party should state the issues that in its judgment stand in the way of merger, its position with respect to resolution of each issue, and any supporting data or arguments. The fact-finder may ask questions to assist his inquiry. Each party shall be given an additional hour and one half for further presentation at the conclusion of the initial presentations of both parties. Since the hearing is an informal proceeding for the purpose of ascertaining the positions of the parties, the presentations should be more in the nature of exposition and supporting argument than the formal presentation of evidence. Spokesmen will not be sworn, nor is the fact-finder empowered to issue subpoenas or compel testimony. The published criteria of the Compliance Committee shall be made available to assist the fact-finder.

If at the completion of the hearing the fact-finder determines that further inquiry is necessary he shall so notify the parties.

The parties are encouraged to agree in advance of the hearing upon an agenda of unresolved items and to follow that agenda in their presentation. In addition, the parties are encouraged to stipulate in advance of the hearing as to those issues that may be or have been resolved by mutual agreement and to submit language embodying such agreements. The fact-finder may encourage such agreement in order to expedite the hearing.

Briefs shall not be submitted by the parties, but the fact-finder may in his discretion call for written memoranda, the submission of which shall not delay the rendering of his report.

5. *Report and Recommendations of Fact-Finder*

The fact-finder shall issue a report setting forth the issues separating the parties and his recommendations for resolving them. The report shall be issued by April 5, with copies sent to the Executive Secretaries of each of the affiliates involved and to the Executive Committee of the NEA. The report and recommendations shall not be made available to the public unless authorized by the NEA Executive Committee.

6. *Procedures Following Issuance of Report and Recommendations*

Upon receipt of the fact-finder's report and recommendations the Board of Directors of the affiliates involved shall determine whether to recommend to their delegate assemblies acceptance in its entirety of the recommended terms of merger. If both affiliates determine to recommend acceptance, or if agreement on merger terms results from the fact-finder's recommendations, immediate steps should be taken by each affiliate to secure final approval by the close of the 1968–69 school year. The NEA Executive Committee shall be notified of all steps taken in this regard by each affiliate.

If the fact-finder's recommendation is not accepted by the Board of Directors of both affiliates by April 15, the NEA Executive Committee shall formulate and submit to each affiliate by May 1 a proposed plan of merger based upon the report and recommendations of the hearing officer, together with written comments of the parties on the recommendations, on terms which in its judgment will be equitable to all concerned. It is expected that such plan shall be submitted by the Board of Directors of each affiliate to its Delegate Assembly for ratification by June 1.

If the parties fail to accept the plan recommended by the Executive Committee, the Executive Committee will take such further steps as are judged necessary to achieve a single organization for all educators in the state in conformity with Resolution 12. In so doing it will consider the viewpoints of the affiliates involved.

Notes

Throughout, the abbreviation "NEA" indicates a publication of the National Education Association, Washington, D.C. "NEA *Proceedings*" stands for *Addresses and Proceedings of the Representative Assembly* of the National Education Association. For other works, shortened forms of citation are used after the first full citation within each chapter.

Preface (pp. vii-viii)

1. John W. Gardner, *No Easy Victories* (New York: Harper & Row, 1968), p. 169.

Chapter 1 IN THE BEGINNING (pp. 1-20)

1. Edgar B. Wesley, *NEA: The First Hundred Years* (New York: Harper, 1957), p. 24.
2. Mildred S. Fenner, *NEA History* (NEA, 1945), p. 15.
3. Calvin D. Linton, ed., *The American Almanac* (Nashville: Thomas Nelson, 1977), p. 155.
4. Ibid., p. 192.
5. Wesley, *NEA*, pp. 46-47.
6. Ibid., pp. 48-49.
7. Ibid., p. 258.
8. Ibid., p. 210.

9. Ibid., p. 330.

10. Fenner, *NEA History*, p. 32.

11. The Department of Higher Education was reinstated in 1942. It changed its name to the Association for Higher Education and continued as an NEA department until 1969, at which time it withdrew as a result of its disagreement with the NEA's policy on collective bargaining. A new higher-education unit was established in 1969 with policies compatible with those of the NEA.

12. Wesley, *NEA*, pp. 298–299.

13. NEA *Proceedings*, 1918, pp. 45–49.

14. Fenner, *NEA History*, p. 37.

15. *NEA Handbook, 1957–58* (NEA), p. 95.

16. Fenner, *NEA History*, p. 37.

Chapter 2 CHANGE (pp. 21–27)

1. *Congressional Record*, June 27, 1969, p. 17638.

2. Robert A. Dobkin, "NEA: Once Sleeping Giant Awakes to Position of Power," *Roanoke Times*, December 26, 1976.

3. NEA *Proceedings*, 1957, p. 33.

4. Ibid., p. 272.

5. *NEA Handbook, 1978–79* (NEA), Resolution H-5 and New Business Items D, 10, and 32; pp. 237, 247, 255.

Chapter 3 CAUSES OF CHANGE (pp. 28–38)

1. *Washington Insight* by Joseph Kraft, October 6, 1978, © 1978 Field Enterprises, Inc. Courtesy of Field Newspaper Syndicate.

2. John K. Norton, "Report of the NEA Special Project on Urban Services," February 1962, p. 9.

3. James B. Conant, *Slums and Suburbs* (New York: McGraw-Hill, 1961), pp. 10, 16, 24.

4. Michael Harrington, *The Other America* (New York: Macmillan, 1962), pp. 17, 166.

5. U.S. Department of Labor, *Monthly Labor Review*, February 1962, p. iv.

6. Mildred S. Fenner, *NEA History* (NEA, 1945), p. 13.

7. Edgar B. Wesley, *NEA: The First Hundred Years* (New York: Harper, 1957), p. 44.

8. For a list of unified states and the year of unification, see Appendix.

Chapter 4 THE RIGHT TO BARGAIN (pp. 39–87)

1. T. M. Stinnett, Jack H. Kleinmann, and Martha L. Ware, *Professional Negotiation in Public Education* (New York: Macmillan, 1966), p. 7.

2. Donald A. Erickson, "Rebel Principals and Teacher Power" (Address to the National Seminar on Professional Negotiation in Public Education, sponsored

by the NEA and the University of Chicago Center for Continuing Education, August 18, 1967).

3. NEA *Proceedings*, 1961, pp. 216–217.

4. Ibid., pp. 217–218.

5. Robert W. Bogen, "Organizational Change: Emergence of the Urban Movement within the National Education Association" (Ph.D. dissertation, George Peabody College for Teachers, 1970), pp. 69–70.

6. NEA *Proceedings*, 1961, p. 222.

7. Ibid., pp. 223–224.

8. T. M. Stinnett, *Turmoil in Teaching* (New York: Macmillan, 1968), p. 43.

9. Myron Lieberman and Michael H. Moscow, *Collective Negotiation for Teachers* (Chicago: Rand McNally, 1966), p. 35.

10. NEA *Proceedings*, 1961, p. 263.

11. Lieberman and Moscow, *Collective Negotiation*, pp. 36–37.

12. Robert Braun, *Teachers and Power* (New York: Simon & Schuster, 1972), p. 60.

13. Ibid., pp. 61–62.

14. Victor G. Reuther, *The Brothers Reuther* (Boston: Houghton Mifflin, 1976), p. 367.

15. Stinnett, *Turmoil in Teaching*, pp. 49–50.

16. Lieberman and Moscow, *Collective Negotiation*, pp. 38–39.

17. William G. Carr, *The Continuing Education of William G. Carr* (NEA, 1978), p. 377.

18. Reuther, *The Brothers Reuther*, p. 367.

19. John K. Norton, "Report of the NEA Special Project on Urban Services," February 1962, pp. 47–48.

20. Bogen, "Organizational Change," p. 174.

21. NEA *Proceedings*, 1962, p. 28.

22. Ibid., p. 52.

23. Ibid., p. 26.

24. Ibid., pp. 175–176.

25. Ibid., pp. 142–146.

26. Ibid., pp. 182–184.

27. For a complete list of state statutes relating to negotiation for teachers and the year of enactment, see Appendix.

28. *The Nation*, June 29, 1964, pp. 651–653.

29. Robert H. Chanin, address to Twenty-ninth Annual Conference on Labor, New York University, 1976, p. 239.

30. Ibid., p. 240.

31. Ibid., pp. 240, 241.

32. Jonathan P. West, "The Scope and Impact of Collective Negotiations in Selected Urban and Suburban School Systems: Implications for Public Policy" (Ph.D. dissertation, Northwestern University, 1969), pp. 329–331.

33. John F. Burton, Jr., and Charles Krider, "The Role and Consequences of Strikes by Public Employees," in *Readings in Labor Economics and Labor Relations*, 2d ed., ed. Lloyd G. Reynolds, Stanley H. Masters, and Collette H. Moser (Englewood Cliffs, N.J.: Prentice-Hall, 1978), p. 367.

34. Chanin, address, 1976, pp. 251, 252.

35. Ibid., pp. 246, 247, 248.

36. Ibid., pp. 254, 255.

37. NEA *Proceedings*, 1969, p. 24.

38. Robert H. Chanin, "NEA and the Landrum-Griffin Act" (Paper delivered to the NEA Council of the Southeast, May 18, 1979), p. 12.

39. Ibid.

Chapter 5 EQUALITY (pp. 88–161)

1. *Public Papers of President John F. Kennedy, 1963*, (Washington, D.C.: Government Printing Office, 1964), p. 469.

2. Albert P. Blaustein and Robert L. Zangrando, eds., *Civil Rights and the American Negro* (New York: Washington Square Press, 1968), pp. 524–525.

3. NEA *Proceedings*, 1957, pp. 193–194.

4. Ibid., p. 195.

5. NEA *Proceedings*, 1959, pp. 185, 186.

6. The NEA has never had racial restrictions on membership. One of the founders of the NEA in 1857 was a black immigrant from Jamaica, Robert Campbell. Conforming to both state law and custom, black teachers organized separately in local communities and at the state level. They could join the NEA, but they had no basis for representation in the Representative Assembly, since only the larger white associations held charters. To correct this unfair condition, the officers of the seventeen black state associations requested that the NEA recognize both groups. This was done, and since 1952, and until completion of the mergers, the NEA had two affiliates in some states, one white and one black.

7. NEA *Proceedings*, 1959, pp. 197–198.

8. Ibid., pp. 199–200.

9. Ibid., p. 200.

10. NEA *Proceedings*, 1960, pp. 170.

11. NEA *Proceedings*, 1963, pp. 105–106.

12. Seventeen states and the District of Columbia had originally maintained dual associations. However, by 1963, six states and the District of Columbia had acted to remove racial restrictions: Missouri (1948), Maryland (1951), West Virginia (1954), Kentucky (1954), District of Columbia (1955), Oklahoma (1956), Delaware (1958).

13. NEA *Proceedings*, 1963, p. 173.

14. The NEA Representative Assembly meeting in Indianapolis on June 29, 1943, adopted a New Business item: "Be it resolved that in choosing the city for its conventions, The National Education Association shall see to it that only

those cities shall be selected where it is possible to make provisions without discrimination for the housing, feeding, seating at the convention, and general welfare of all delegates and teachers, regardless of race, color, or creed." NEA *Proceedings*, 1943, p. 194.

15. NEA *Proceedings*, 1970, p. 585.

16. NEA *Proceedings*, 1943, p. 186.

17. Thelma D. Perry, *History of the American Teachers' Association* (NEA, 1975), p. 176.

18. Ibid., p. 176.

19. The chairman of the Sub-Committee to Study Health Education for Negroes reported to the full committee in Atlantic City in 1932 that the death rate of black children was six times that of whites of the same age.

20. Mildred S. Fenner, *NEA History* (NEA, 1945), pp. 21–22.

21. NEA *Proceedings*, 1966, p. 15.

22. R. J. Martin (president), Hudson Barksdale (president-elect), Joseph Brooks (executive secretary), C. B. Robinson, I. E. Washington, Mrs. Eliza McDaniel, Vernon McDaniel, Norman Dickson, Mrs. Bessie Estelle, C. J. Duckworth, Walter Ridley, E. J. Oliver, Mr. Fred McNiel, Joseph C. Duncan, William Lehr, Mrs. Katherine McGormick, Edward Brice, and Rupert Picott.

23. For a list of activities carried on by the NEA since the merger, see Perry, *History of the American Teachers' Association*, pp. 357–373.

24. Perry, *History of the American Teachers' Association*, p. 329.

25. The years in which the formation of a single state association was accomplished in each state were as follows: 1948, Missouri and Maryland; 1954, West Virginia and Kentucky; 1955, District of Columbia; 1956, Oklahoma; 1958, Delaware.

26. Perry, *History of the American Teachers' Association*, p. 337.

27. From an address by H.C. Tate to NCOSTA, 1966.

28. The cost of the building as reported by Porter exceeded $50,000, but ultimately the assessed valuation of the land, equipment, and building was more than $100,000. See Gilbert L. Porter and L. W. Neyland, *History of the Florida State Teachers' Association* (NEA, 1977), p. 145.

29. Vernon McDaniel, *History of the Teachers' State Association of Texas* (NEA, 1977), p. 81.

30. For a complete list of the criteria for evaluating merger plans as approved by the Executive Committee on October 10, 1968, see Appendix.

31. See Frederick H. Bullen, "Mediation Efforts to Resolve Merger Disputes between Dual Affiliates in Southern States" (Paper delivered to the Conference of the National Association of Teacher Attorneys, Denver, October 15, 1969).

32. The name of the NEA Committee on Professional Rights and Responsibilities has been changed since consummation of the Georgia merger. The Standing Committee on Teacher Rights is now responsible for those activities heretofore provided by the PR&R Committee.

33. Roger Williams, "The Delicate Compromise," *Atlanta Magazine*, April 19, 1970, pp. 55–70.

34. Bullen, "Mediation Efforts."

35. Taped interview with James H. Williams, Atlanta, September 29, 1978.

36. Personal interview with Henry D. M. Woods, Detroit, July 1979.

37. Personal interview with Helen Moore, Detroit, July 1979.

38. Personal interview with John Ashley, Detroit, Michigan, July 1979.

39. Taped response from Arvid Anderson to a series of questions posed by Allan M. West.

Chapter 6 LEGISLATION (pp. 162–186)

1. Edgar B. Wesley, *NEA: The First Hundred Years* (New York: Harper, 1957), p. 21.

2. NEA *Proceedings*, 1918, p. 40.

3. *Congressional Record*, October 20, 1943, p. 8558.

4. Ibid., pp. 8565–8566.

5. From a transcript of the original Discussion Program.

6. NEA *Proceedings*, 1960, p. 29.

7. Ibid., p. 61.

8. Ibid., pp. 150–151.

9. NEA *Proceedings*, 1961, p. 27.

10. John F. Kennedy, message to the Congress of the United States, February 6, 1962, printed in full in the *NEA News Supplement*, February 18, 1962.

11. *NEA Reporter*, December 6, 1963, p. 2.

12. NEA *Proceedings*, 1965, p. 7.

13. NEA *Proceedings*, 1965, p. 206.

14. *World Almanac and Book of Facts* (New York: Grosset & Dunlap, 1979), p. 48.

15. See Philip Moranto, *The Politics of Federal Aid to Education in 1965: A Study in Political Innovation* (Syracuse University Press, 1967), p. 89.

16. Ibid., p. 90.

17. William G. Carr, *The Continuing Education of William G. Carr* (NEA, 1978), pp. 331–332.

18. NEA *Proceedings*, 1963, pp. 192–193.

19. From a tape of the president's statement made for the NEA by Telenews, March 1, 1965.

20. Tape from Robert E. McKay, September 1979, to Allan M. West in response to an earlier request for answers to a series of questions relating to the Elementary and Secondary Education Act.

21. *Congressional Record*, July 17, 1979, p. H6074.

22. Ibid., p. H6075.

23. See Samuel Halperin, testimony before the U.S. Senate Committee on Governmental Affairs, October 12, 1977, p. 17.

24. Albert Shanker, "Where We Stand," *American Teacher*, April 1979, p. 8.
25. Quoted by Faye Ford, "NEA Gets Plum, AFT Munches Sour Grapes," *NEA Reporter*, March 1978, p. 3.

Chapter 7 POLITICAL ACTION (pp. 187–201)

1. Eugene H. Methvin, "The NEA: A Washington Lobby Run Rampant," *Reader's Digest*, November 1978, p. 97.
2. William L. Chaze, "When Educators Put the Arm on Congress," *U.S. News and World Report*, June 11, 1979, p. 71.
3. Terry Herndon, *Phi Delta Kappan*, February 1979, p. 423.
4. Ibid., p. 420.
5. Minutes of the Board of Directors, February 15, 1969, p. 366.
6. Minutes of the Board of Directors, June 28, 1970, p. 353.
7. Ibid., p. 355.
8. Ibid., p. 363.
9. Minutes of the Executive Committee, November 4, 1969, pp. 529–530.
10. Minutes of the Executive Committee, Feburary 14, 1970, p. 578.
11. Minutes of the Executive Committee, September 11, 1972, pp. 291–292.
12. Ibid., p. 292.
13. NEA *Proceedings*, 1973, p. 8.
14. Ibid., p. 17.
15. Ibid., p. 20.
16. Ibid., pp. 8, 9.
17. "Leading PACs in 1978 Elections," *Congressional Quarterly*, June 2, 1979, p. 1045, with permission of Congressional Quarterly, Inc., Washington, D.C.
18. Robert W. Merry, "Teacher Group's Clout on Carter's Behalf is New Brand of Special-Interest Politics," *Wall Street Journal*, August 13, 1980.
19. Ibid.

Chapter 8 INSTRUCTION (pp. 202–213)

1. John Ryor, "Teacher Centers," *Today's Education*, April–May 1979, p. 5.
2. Taped interview with Willard McGuire, Washington, D.C., May 24, 1979.
3. Taped interview with Terry Herndon, Washington, D.C., May 25, 1979.
4. NEA *Proceedings*, 1960, p. 56.
5. NEA *Proceedings*, 1964, p. 380.
6. NEA *Proceedings*, 1971, p. 18.

Chapter 9 FROM STRESS TO UNITY (pp. 214–255)

1. William G. Carr, *The Continuing Education of William G. Carr* (NEA, 1978), p. 409.
2. NEA *Proceedings*, 1967, p. 331.

3. Ibid., p. 89.

4. Carr, *Continuing Education*, pp. 343, 344.

5. NEA *Proceedings*, 1960, p. 255.

6. NEA *Proceedings*, 1964, p. 20.

7. Ibid., p. 219.

8. Ibid., p. 305.

9. Sam M. Lambert, "Angry Young Men in Teaching," *NEA Journal*, February 1963, p. 20.

10. Douglas Looney, "Boss Teacher: I Am the Smartest—the Most—the Best," *Omaha World Herald*, January 23, 1969.

11. NEA *Proceedings*, 1969, p. 354.

12. Sixteen months later, on June 30, 1970, a motion was made and carried unanimously "that the motion to give the president a vote of confidence made at the February 1969 meeting in Atlanta, Georgia, be removed from the table and that the Board of Directors express its confidence in President George D. Fischer." (See *Proceedings*, 1971, p. 404.)

13. NEA *Proceedings*, 1972, p. 8.

14. NEA *Proceedings*, 1969, pp. 99–106, 153–173.

15. NEA *Proceedings*, 1971, p. 20.

16. NEA *Proceedings*, 1974, p. 525.

17. NEA *Proceedings*, 1972, p. 14; NEA *Proceedings*, 1968, p. 16.

18. Ibid., p. 15.

19. Ibid., pp. 15, 16, 17.

20. Ibid., pp. 17, 18, 19.

21. Taped interview with Terry Herndon, Washington, D.C., May 25, 1979.

22. Philip Shabecoff, "Carter and Kennedy Step up Fight for Labor Backing," *New York Times*, Feb. 3, 1980.

23. David S. Broder and Kathy Sawyer, "Teachers Union Becomes Powerful Force in Party Politics," *Washington Post*, Jan. 20, 1980, p. A-7.

24. Terry Herndon, "Teachers, School Boards, and the Destiny of Public Schools," Address to the National School Boards Association Annual Convention, Miami Beach, Florida, April 21, 1979.

Chapter 10 LOOKING AHEAD (pp. 256–261)

1. James Farmer, Address to Conference on Spending Limits, Washington, D.C., March 26, 1980, from *Today* at the National Education Association, p. 1.

2. Terry Herndon, "Teachers, School Boards, and the Destiny of Public Schools," Address to the National School Boards Association Annual Convention, Miami Beach, Florida, April 21, 1979.

Bibliography

Adler, Mortimer J., and Mayer, Milton. *The Revolution in Education*. Chicago: University of Chicago Press, 1958.

Allen, Roy B., and Schmid, John. *Collective Negotiations and Educational Administration*. College of Education, University of Arkansas and The University Council for Educational Administration, 1966.

American Association of School Administrators. *Public Relations for America's Schools*, Twenty-eighth Yearbook. Washington, D.C.: The Association, 1950.

_____. *Staff Relations in School Administration*, 1955.

_____. *Imperatives in Education*, 1966.

_____. *The School Administrator and Negotiation*. Washington, D.C.: The Association.

The American Almanac. Calvin D. Linton, ed. Nashville, Tenn.: Thomas Nelson, Inc., 1977, pp. 155, 192.

Anderson, Arvid. Taped response to a series of questions furnished by the author.

Armstrong, Gregory. *Protest: Man Against Society*. New York: Bantam Books, 1969.

Bendiner, Robert. *The Politics of Schools*. New York: Mentor Books, an authorized reprint of a hardcover edition published by Harper and Row, 1970.

Bickley, Ancella R. *History of the West Virginia State Teachers Association*. Washington, D.C.: National Education Association, 1979.

Bishop, Leslee J. *Collective Negotiations in Curriculum and Instruction: Questions and Concerns*. Washington, D.C.: Association for Supervision and Curriculum Development, 1967.

Blaustein, Albert P., and Zangrando, Robert L. *Civil Rights and the American Negro*. New York: Washington Square Press, 1968.

Bogen, Robert W. *Organizational Change: Emergence of the Urban Movement Within the National Education Association*. Unpublished Ph.D. dissertation, George Peabody College for Teachers, Nashville, Tenn., 1970.

Bowers, C. A.; Housego, Ian; and Dyke, Doris. *Education and Social Policy*. New York: Random House, 1970.

Braun, Robert J. *Teachers and Power*. New York: Simon and Schuster, 1972.

Brenton, Myron. *What's Happened to Teacher?* New York: Avon Books, 1970.

Brinkmeier, Oria A.; Ubben, Gerald C.; and Williams, Richard C. *Inside the Organized Teacher*. Danville, Ill.: Interstate Printers and Publishers, 1967.

Brooks, George W. *History of the Tennessee Education Congress*. Washington, D.C.: National Education Association, 1975.

Bullen, Frederick H. "Mediation Efforts to Resolve Merger Disputes Between Dual State Affiliates in Southern States, 1968–69." Paper delivered to the Conference of the National Association of Teacher Attorneys, October 15, 1969, Denver, Colorado.

Burton, John F., Jr., and Krider, Charles. "The Role and Consequences of Strikes by Public Employees." In *Readings in Labor Economics and Labor Relations*, 2d ed., edited by Lloyd G. Reynolds, Stanley H. Masters, and Collette H. Moser. Englewood Cliffs, N.J.: Prentice-Hall, 1978.

Campbell, Roald F.; Cunningham, Luvern L.; and McPhee, Roderick F. *The Organization and Control of American Schools*. Columbus, Ohio: Charles E. Merrill, 1965.

Carr, William G. *The Continuing Education of William Carr*. Washington, D.C.: National Education Association, 1978.

Cartwright, Darwin. *Studies in Social Power*. Ann Arbor: University of Michigan, 1959.

Chanin, Robert H. Address to Collective Bargaining Seminar, January 21, 1979, Salt Lake City, Utah.

———. Address to Twenty-ninth Annual Conference on Labor, New York University, 1976, pp. 239, 240, 241.

———. "NEA and the Landrum-Griffin Act." Address to a Meeting of the NEA Council of the Southeast, May 19, 1979.

Chaze, William L. *U.S. News and World Report*, June 11, 1979, p. 71.

Conant, James B. *The American High School Today*. New York: McGraw-Hill, 1959.

———. *Slums and Suburbs*. New York: McGraw-Hill, 1961.

Conant, James Bryant. *The Child, the Parent and the State*. Cambridge, Mass.: Harvard University Press, 1959.

Congressional Record, October 20, 1943, p. 8558.

———, October 20, 1943, pp. 8565, 8566.

———, U.S. House of Representatives, June 27, 1969, p. 17638.

———, July 17, 1979, p. H6074.

Corey, Arthur F. *The Responsibility of the Organized Profession for the Improvement of Instruction*. Washington, D.C.: National Education Association, 1966.

Cox Commission Report, *Crisis at Columbia*. New York: Vintage Books, a division of Random House, 1968.

Dobkin, Robert. "NEA: Once Sleeping Giant Awakes to Position of Power." *Roanoke Virginia Times*, December 26, 1976.

Doherty, Robert E., and Oberer, Walter E. *Teachers, School Boards and Collective Bargaining: A Changing of the Guard*. Ithaca, N.Y.: New York State School of Industrial and Labor Relations, Cornell University, 1967.

Douglas, William O. *Points of Rebellion*. New York: Vintage Books, a divison of Random House, 1970.

Elam, Stanley. *The Nation*, June 29, 1964, pp. 651–653.

Employer-Employee Relations in Public Schools. Ithaca, N.Y.: New York State School of Industrial and Labor Relations, Cornell University, 1967.

Erickson, Donald A. "Rebel Principals and Teacher Power." Address to National Seminar on Professional Negotiations in Public Education, University of Chicago, August 18, 1967.

Featherstone, Joseph. *Schools Where Children Learn*. New York: Liveright, 1971.

Fenner, Mildred S. *NEA History*. Washington, D.C.: National Education Association, 1945.

Flexner, Eleanor. *Century of Struggle*. New York: Atheneum, reprinted by arrangement with Harvard University Press, 1974.

Flynn, Ralph J. *Public Work, Public Workers*. Washington, D.C.: New Republic, 1975.

French, Wendell L., and Bell, Cecil H., Jr. *Organization Development, Behavioral Science Interventions for Organization Improvement*. Englewood Cliffs, N.J.: Prentice-Hall, 1978.

Froman, Lewis A., Jr. *People and Politics*. Englewood Cliffs, N.J.: Prentice-Hall, 1962.

Gardner, John W. *Self Renewal*. New York: Harper & Row, 1963.

———. *No Easy Victories*. New York: Harper & Row, 1968.

Gilroy, Thomas P.; Sinicropt, Anthony Z.; Stone, Franklin D.; and Urich, Theodore R. *Educator's Guide to Collective Negotiations*. Columbus, Ohio: Merrill, 1969.

Gittell, Marilyn, and Hevesi, Alan G. *The Politics of Urban Education*. New York: Praeger, 1969.

Givens, Willard E., and Schlagle, F. L. Letter to NEA State Affiliates, 1944.

Golembiewski, Robert T.; Gibson, Frank; and Cornog, Geoffrey Y. *Public Administration*. Chicago: Rand McNally, College Publishing, 1976.

Green, Mark J.; Fallows, James M.; and Zwick, David R. *Who Runs Congress? The President, Big Business, or You?* New York: Bantam Books jointly with Grossman Publishers, 1972.

Halperin, Samuel. Testimony before the U.S. Senate Committee on Government Affairs, October 12, 1977.

Harrington, Michael. *The Other America—Poverty in the United States*. Baltimore: Penguin Books, 1963. Published by arrangement with Macmillan, New York.

———. *The Vast Majority*. New York: Simon and Schuster, 1977.

Havighurst, Robert J., and Richey, Herman G. *Metropolitanism—Its Challenge to Education*, Sixty-seventh Yearbook of the National Society for the Study of Education. Chicago: University of Chicago Press, 1968.

282 **The National Education Association**

Herndon, Terry. Annotating a *Reader's Digest* article: "The NEA: A Washington Lobby Run Rampant." *Phi Delta Kappan*, The Phi Delta Kappa Fraternity, Bloomington, Indiana, February 1979, pp. 420, 423.
————. Taped interview with the author in Washington, D.C., on May 25, 1979.
Hurwitz, Emanuel, Jr., and Tesconi, Charles A., Jr. *Challenges to Education*. New York: Dodd Mead, 1972.
Iannaccone, Laurence. *Politics in Education*. New York: The Center for Applied Research in Education, 1967.
Institute for the Study of Educational Policy. *Equal Educational Opportunity for Blacks in U.S. Higher Education—An Assessment*. Washington, D.C.: Howard University Press, 1976.
Johnson, President Lyndon B. Statement to a group of NEA leaders in the White House, Washington, D.C., March 1, 1965, taped for NEA by Telenews.
Keach, Everett T., Jr.; Fulton, Robert; and Gardner, William E. *Education and Social Crisis*. New York: Wiley, 1967.
Kerber, August, and Bommarito, Barbara. *The Schools and the Urban Crisis*. New York: Holt, Rinehart and Winston, 1966.
Kraft, Joseph. Column, *Philadelphia Bulletin*, October 6, 1978.
Leinwand, Gerald. *Problems of American Society—Poverty and the Poor*. New York: Washington Square Press, 1968.
Levine, Marvin J., and Hagburg, Eugene C. *Labor Relations in the Public Sector*. Salt Lake City, Utah: Brighton Publishing Co., 1979.
Lieberman, Myron, and Moskow, Michael H. *Collective Negotiation for Teachers*. New York: Rand McNally, 1966.
Likert, Rensis. *New Patterns of Management*. New York: McGraw-Hill, 1961.
Lipset, Seymour Martin. *Revolution and Counter Revolution*. Garden City, N.Y.: Doubleday, 1970.
Looney, Douglas. "Boss Teacher: I am the Smartest—the Most—the Best." *Omaha World Herald*, January 23, 1969.
Maccoby, Michael. *The Gamesman*. New York: Bantam Books, published by arrangement with Simon and Schuster, 1976.
McDaniel, Vernon. *History of the Teachers State Association of Texas*. Washington, D.C.: National Education Association, 1977.
McDonnell, Lorraine, and Pascal, Anthony. *Organized Teachers in American Schools*. Santa Monica, Calif.: The Rand Corporation, 1979.
McGuire, Willard. Taped interview with the author on May 24, 1979, in Washington, D.C.
McKay, Robert E. Taped response to a series of questions posed by the author.
Meranto, Philip. *The Politics of Federal Aid to Education in 1965: A Study in Political Innovation*. Syracuse, N.Y.: Syracuse University Press, 1967.
Methvin, Eugene H. "The NEA: A Washington Lobby Run Rampant." *The Reader's Digest*, November 1978.
Miles, Rufus E., Jr. *A Cabinet Department of Education*. Washington, D.C.: American Council on Education, 1976.
Miller, Harry L., and Smiley, Marjorie B. *Education in the Metropolis*. New York: The Free Press, 1967.
Morse, Arthur D. *Schools of Tomorrow—Today*. Garden City, N.Y.: Doubleday, 1960.

Morphet, Edgar L., and Ryan, Charles O. *Prospective Changes in Society by 1980*. Designing Education for the Future, an eight-state project, Denver, Colo., 1966.

Morphet, Edgar L., and Jesser, David L. *Emerging State Responsibilities for Education*. Improving State Leadership in Education, Denver, Colo., 1970.

_____. *Designing Education for the Future: Rationale, Procedures and Appraisal*. Designing Education for the Future, an eight-state project, Denver, Colo., 1969.

Morphet, Edgar L.; Jesser, David L.; and Ludka, Arthur P. *Planning and Providing for Excellence in Education*. Improving State Leadership in Education, Denver, Colo., 1971.

National Commission on the Causes and Prevention of Violence. *To Establish Justice, To Insure Domestic Tranquility*. New York: Award Books, 1969.

National Education Association, Official Publications:

Addresses and Proceedings of the Representative Assembly, 1918, 1943, 1957, 1959, 1960, 1961, 1962, 1963, 1964, 1965, 1966, 1967, 1969, 1970, 1971, 1972, 1973, 1974. Washington, D.C.: National Education Association.

American Association for Higher Education. *Faculty Participation in Academic Governance*. Washington, D.C.: The Association, 1967.

Change and Renewal. Report of the NEA Development Project. Washington, D.C.: The Association, 1967.

Kennedy, John F. Message to the Congress of the United States, February 6, 1962. Printed in full in the *NEA News Supplement* of February 18, 1962.

The National Education Association. *The NEA Journal*. Washington, D.C., February 1963, p. 17.

National Education Association Research Bulletin, 1946, *School Finance Goals*.

NEA Handbook. The National Education Association, 1957–58. Washington, D.C., p. 95.

NEA Handbook. The National Education Association, 1978–79. Washington, D.C., pp. 237, 247, 255.

NEA Reporter, December 6, 1963, p. 2.

NEA Reporter, March 1978. Kaye Ford, "NEA Gets Plum, AFT Munches Sour Grapes," p. 3.

Norton, John K. *Report of the NEA Special Project on Urban Services*. February 1962.

Perry, Thelma D. *History of the American Teachers Association*. Washington, D.C.: National Education Association, 1975.

Picott, J. Rupert. *History of the Virginia Teachers Association*. Washington, D.C.: National Education Association, 1975.

Porter, Gilbert L., and Neyland, Leedell W. *History of the Florida State Teachers Association*. Washington, D.C.: National Education Association, 1977.

Potts, John F., Sr. *A History of the Palmetto Education Association*. Washington, D.C.: National Education Association, 1978.

Public Papers of President John F. Kennedy, 1963. Washington, D.C.: U.S. Government Printing Office, 1964.

Quattlebaum, Charles A. *Federal Aid to Elementary and Secondary Education*. Chicago: Public Administration Service, 1948.

Rehmus, Charles M., and Wilner, Evan. *The Economic Results of Teacher Bar-*

gaining: Michigan's First Two Years. Institute of Labor and Industrial Relations, the University of Michigan, Wayne State University, Ann Arbor-Detroit, 1968.

Reuther, Victor G. The Brothers Reuther. Boston, Mass.: Houghton Mifflin, 1976.

Reynolds, Lloyd G.; Masters, Stanley, H.; and Moser, Collete H. Readings in Labor Economics and Labor Relations, 2d. ed. Englewood Cliffs, N.J.: Prentice-Hall, 1978.

Rosenthal, Alan. Governing Education. Garden City, N.Y.: Doubleday, 1969.

_____. Pedagogues and Power: Teacher Groups in School Politics. Syracuse, N.Y.: Syracuse University Press, 1969.

Rubin, David. The Rights of Teachers. New York: Avon Books, 1972.

Rubin, Lillian B. Busing and Backlash. Berkeley, Calif.: University of California Press, 1972.

Ryor, John. "Teacher Centers." Today's Education, April-May 1979, p. 5.

Schelling, Thomas C. The Strategy of Conflict. New York: Oxford University Press, 1960.

Schlesinger, Arthur M., Jr. A Thousand Days. Boston, Mass.: Houghton Mifflin, 1965.

Schmidt, Charles T., Jr.; Parker, Hyman; and Repas, Bob. A Guide to Collective Negotiations in Education, the School of Labor and Industrial Relations, Michigan State University in cooperation with the Michigan State Board of Education, Social Science Research Bureau, Michigan State University, East Lansing, 1967.

Shanker, Albert. "Where We Stand." American Teacher, American Federation of Teachers, Washington, D.C., April 1979, p. 8.

Shotts, Constance Trisler. The Origin and Development of the National Education Association Political Action Committee. Unpublished Ph.D. Dissertation, Indiana University, 1976.

Somers, Gerald G. Collective Bargaining in the Public Service. Industrial Relations Research Association, 1966.

Steffensen, James P. Teachers Negotiate with Their School Boards. U.S. Department of Health, Education and Welfare, Office of Education, Washington, D.C., 1964.

Stinnett, T. M.; Kleinmann, Jack H.; and Ware, Martha L. Professional Negotiation in Public Education. New York: Macmillan, 1966.

Stinnett, T. M. Turmoil in Teaching. New York: Macmillan, 1968.

Tesconi, Charles A., Jr., and Hurwitz, Emanuel, Jr. Education for Whom? New York: Dodd Mead, 1974.

Thomas, Norman C. Education in National Politics? New York: David McKay, 1975.

Thompson, Cleopatra D. The History of the Mississippi Teachers Association. Washington, D.C.: N.E.A. Teacher Rights and Jackson Miss.: Mississippi Teachers Association, 1973.

U.S. Commission on Civil Rights. Civil Rights U.S.A.! Public Schools North and West, 1962. Washington, D.C.: U.S. Government Printing Office, 1962.

U.S. Department of Labor. Monthly Labor Review. Washington, D.C., February 1962, p. iv.

Usdan, Michael D.; Minar, David W.; Hurwitz, Emanuel, Jr. *Education and State Politics*. New York: Teachers College Press, Columbia University, 1969.

Wade, Richard C. *Slavery in the Cities, The South 1820–1860*. New York: Oxford University Press, 1964.

Wesley, Edgar B. *The First Hundred Years*. New York: Harper, 1957.

West, Jonathan P. *The Scope and Impact of Collective Negotiations in Selected Urban and Suburban School Systems: Implications for Public Policy*. Unpublished Ph.D. Dissertation, Northwestern University, Evanston, Ill., 1969.

Williams, James H. Taped interview with the author in Atlanta, Georgia, on September 29, 1978.

Williams, Roger. "The Delicate Compromise." *Atlanta Magazine*, April 19, 1970, pp. 55–70.

Wirt, Frederick M., and Kirst, Michael W. *The Political Web of American Schools*. Boston, Mass.: Little Brown, 1972.

Wirtz, W. Willard. *Labor and the Public Interest*. New York: Harper and Row, 1967.

World Almanac, and Book of Facts, 1979. New York: Grosset and Dunlap.

Zeigler, Harmon. *The Political World of the High School Teacher*. Eugene, Ore.: University of Oregon Press, 1966.

_____. *The Political Life of American Teachers*. Englewood Cliffs, N.J.: Prentice Hall, 1967.

Index